LIFE CALLING

To my wife Anita, who has patiently traveled the Life Calling exploration road with me for many years; and to my mother Dorothy, who inspired me to believe I had a calling, and who too early left this earth to pursue a higher calling.

LIFE CALLING

Living Your Life with the Power of Purpose

BILL MILLARD

 Life Discovery

Marion, Indiana

Life Discovery

Life Discovery LLC
1406 N. Marlin Drive
Marion, Indiana 46952
ldi@ldinteractive.com
www.ldinteractive.com

Layout and Production Editor
Kristy Eske-Ballard

Copy Editor
Susanna Spencer

Photographer
Stephen Millard

Printed in the United States of America

ISBN 978-0-9965934-1-0
PDF

Brief Contents

Detailed Contents

List of Figures

Acknowledgments

When a book like this is printed, an author's name goes on the cover as if he or she was the only person involved with producing the book. That is far from the truth. Many people go into the production process, and *Life Calling: Living Your Life with the Power of Purpose* is no exception.

First, I want to acknowledge and thank Kristy Eske-Ballard at Life Discovery who nobly took on the dual role of Production Editor and Layout Editor. A great deal of the quality of this book is the result of her work. I also want to thank Susanna Spencer, copy editor, for her excellent work and her unique strengths that make her actually enjoy it. Hunting down wrongly italicized commas drives me crazy, but it makes her excited, and she can actually see them!

I want to thank Megan Gilmore who contributed activities to many of the chapters in this book. She truly believes in people and has a great way of bringing out creative thought in them. I also want to thank Stephen Milllard, who is not only a great son, but a talented photographic artist who helped with many of the images in this book.

The pathway to this book has been a long one, and many faithful colleagues and friends have walked with me during some portion of the journey.

Mike, Jim, Charles and Chris have walked the longest with me as not only philosophical and conceptual colleagues, but good friends.

Evrett has been a true supporter, friend and fellow explorer for Life Calling.

Phil has taken on research of Life Calling alongside me, and has worked to infuse it into schools all across the US and the world. In the process we have become good friends.

Megan caught the vision of Life Calling and is now taking on the mantle to continue with me and beyond and accelerate the concept and implementation of Life Calling to a new level.

Bud, Todd, By, Judy, Kay, Dan, Burt, Connie, Rick and Jill worked with me in the oversight of research and projects that added valuable insight to my investigations.

Latrese, Cindy, Ellen, Kay, Dan, Amy, Nancy, Megan, Heather, Nicole, Jill, Stephanie, Karen, Petros, Caitlin, and Jackie are all faithful life coaches working with Life Calling who have served alongside me at one time or another during this journey. They all helped me see how this plays out in real life.

Finally, I would like to thank all of my students, from the earliest days teaching high school to these last years I am spending at the college and graduate level. They have all inspired me and kept me honest!

INTRODUCTION

Figure 1.1 // Life Calling Model

CHAPTER 1

INTRODUCTION

My wife and I have a little house on a barrier island in North Carolina along the Atlantic Coast, and that's where we live nearly every summer and any other vacation time in our schedule. It is about a five-minute walk from our place to the beach, and every summer on that beach something remarkable happens. Leatherback and green turtles return to the beach in the spring and build nests in the sand where they lay over a hundred eggs in each nest. In about sixty days the eggs hatch and the little turtles dig their way to the surface and then make a mad dash down the beach to the ocean where they will grow and live. It is one of the more remarkable and inspiring spectacles in nature to witness. But here is something more remarkable. During their lives, these turtles may travel incredible distances of more than 19,000 kilometers (12,000 miles), but when they reach a point in their adulthood where they are ready to lay eggs on their own, they will navigate their way back to the exact beach where they were born, and the process will start all over again.

This ability of animals to migrate large distances is fascinating. A group of dragonflies, insects about 5-10 centimeters (2-4 inches) in length, provide an intriguing example of this. They travel from the Maldives, an island nation in the Indian Ocean, to the African continent and then back to the Maldives. This route can cover over 18,000 kilometers (11,250 miles). One fascinating aspect of this migration is that no single dragonfly can live through the entire journey. The epic migration spans four generations, with each generation playing an important role in the journey. Think of it like a relay race in the track-and-field competition at the Olympics.

The longest migration belongs to the Arctic tern, a small bird that travels back and forth between the Arctic and the Antarctic each year. When the zigs and the zags are added into this journey, it can end up covering over 70,000 kilometers (or 44,000 miles).

Life on our planet seems to be characterized by an underlying sense of direction and guidance. Yet we as humans, who we presume to be the most intelligent of the species, have so much difficulty finding it in our own lives. As part of my work I have had the opportunity to dialogue with thousands of people in all fifty of the United States and in nearly thirty countries on five different continents of the world. I have discovered an amazing insight through these conversations. In every location and culture I have encountered, I find people have a strong desire for meaning, significance and hope in their lives–no matter how rich or how poor their circumstances are. But the second, and more disturbing, insight I have discovered is that in spite of their desires, most people end up living their lives without any compelling feelings of that meaning, significance, or hope. And as these people reach the last stages of their lives, feelings of despair often overwhelm them. Ironically, as I have been engaged in conversation with these people, I have been able to detect in their words and lives that there actually was a purpose in their lives that could have given them meaning, significance, and hope had they only recognized it.

Just like whatever force it is that guides the animals on those amazing migrations, direction is right there in the hands of humans if they can only learn how to recognize it and follow it. This is the Life Calling we will explore in this book.

You might be wondering why animals with brains much smaller than humans can detect and follow guidance in their lives, yet so few people recognize this purpose, and as a result end up living their lives without following any real guidance and not realizing their true calling. One major reason people are not able to recognize a purpose in their lives is that society has often pressured them to chase after jobs and money by pursuing a typical career development model. But the problem is that this model tends to put too much emphasis at the beginning on careers and income instead of focusing first on a higher purpose——a *Life Calling*.

This career-development process plays out in what I call the Tale of Two Kingdoms. In the philosophy and teachings of Jesus, he identified those two kingdoms. The first one he called the kingdom of this world. He characterized it as a kingdom where people strive to save their lives, but in the end they lose their lives. It's a kingdom where the goal is to gain the whole world, but people in this kingdom of the world achieve that kind of success at the cost of forfeiting their souls. The second kingdom

Jesus called the kingdom of heaven. In this kingdom Jesus said people are willing to lose their lives for his sake, but in the end they find life. It's a kingdom where people deny themselves and, instead, take up their cross and follow Jesus. This kingdom of heaven is not a "pie-in-the sky" approach. Jesus pointed out very emphatically that this kingdom is at hand (meaning it is here right now), and that it is in you (in other words, you don't have to look all over to find it).

Unfortunately, typical career development pursues the kingdom of this world approach. In this model you are urged to chase after the so-called "best" jobs with the belief that your sense of meaning, significance, and hope will be found in those jobs. Here's the path you are encouraged to follow: (1) you are encouraged to determine your interests and then follow an educational or training plan based on these interests; (2) you are then directed to find a career that goes along with your education or training, based on the potential that it will also give you success and security; (3) you are finally left to make some sense of meaning in your life from what you experience in your job–a struggle that is usually futile. The problem with this approach based on self-interests is that the initial interests have often been aroused, for the most part, by the amount of pay, job availability, and job growth. Although these concerns have some value, if you look at them closely, they very easily lead to a self-centered approach. An entire self-help industry has emerged out of this, with claims to help you pursue this approach successfully and quickly. But these self-centered, quick-fix approaches are not from the kingdom of heaven and never bring long-lasting meaning, significance, and hope.

The self-centered approach that comes out of the kingdom of this world is totally backward. You need to move, instead, to the kingdom of heaven to find the better approach. In this kingdom you begin by looking for deeper meaning in your life. You ask, "What is the higher purpose of my life?" While this purpose will be somewhat unique for each person, the fundamental core will be the same: the focus will not be on striving to better yourself, but, in contrast, it focuses on what God is doing and what you can do to join him in his efforts. Once this purpose has been discovered or recognized, then you can decide on a career that will help fulfill this purpose. Finally, a decision on an educational or training plan that will help you prepare for that career can be effectively determined. Then, when you graduate from school or complete your training and go on to life beyond that point, you realize that your Life Calling is to experience all of life, not just a job. And that is where you will begin to find long-lasting meaning, significance, and hope.

So there they are—two kingdoms with two opposite patterns for life. You need to choose wisely which kingdom you will follow. The kingdom we will explore in this book will be the kingdom of heaven. Our theme throughout will be: Living your life with a sense of purpose.

So what do we mean by "a sense of purpose"? Almost every one of us has a GPS navigational system on our cell phone. We have become very reliant on these systems. We enter a desired destination, and then as we move in that direction, a voice informs us of distances we must go and turns we must take. The accuracy is amazing. Most of us have probably experienced a secret desire to have a similar device give us specific instructions that would guide us on our personal mission in life. Wouldn't it be great to have a voice saying, "Turn right in 700 feet?"

According to Jewish history recorded in the Old Testament, Moses saw the burning bush. Gideon put out a fleece—two actually. Elijah heard a still, small voice. A donkey instructed Balaam. A whale redirected Jonah. The prophets, like Isaiah, Jeremiah and Ezekiel, saw explicit visions. Those all seem alluring when so many of us get up and face each day with little or no sense of deep purpose or direction. However, when we go out and look at the bush, there is no fire. Our fleeces don't work, our donkeys don't talk, and our visions are dim. There is no Life GPS navigational system that we can plug in.

So is there anything we can do? Is there any hope of finding direction for our lives? The answer is yes! It can be found in our Life Calling. Is it discernable? Yes. Is it logical? Yes. Is it mystical? Yes. Is it simple? Yes. Is it complex? Yes. That seems contradictory and confusing, but it really isn't. What it indicates is that the concept of a Life Calling has a great breadth and at the same time a great depth. The bottom line is this: can a Life Calling be discovered? Yes! And that should give us great hope.

The goal of this book is to help prepare each of us to make that discovery of a Life Calling. To accomplish this, we will be looking at concepts, at the lives of other people and at scriptural insights. We will also be completing exercises that can help us learn how to explore our Life Calling.

Life Calling Model

Throughout this book, we will have the opportunity to explore our Life Calling using a specific conceptual model. What is the purpose for a conceptual model? Think of it like looking at earth from different levels. The first view we will identify is from the moon. From this vantage, earth is an orb in the sky with just a few parts visible. That is similar to what we might call a subject model. In our study, that would be the overall concept of Life Calling. At the other extreme would be the view of earth from the ground. Here we see all the parts of earth. There are thousands of them interacting all around us and it is hard to stay focused on one of them. This is what we might call a detail model. In our study that would be the various parts that make up who we are. In between these two views of earth would be a satellite orbiting the earth. Whole continents and oceans are visible, as is their relationship to each other. This is similar to what we might call a conceptual model. And in our study we will be looking at such a conceptual model—the Life Calling Model depicted in Figure 1.1. We don't focus on all of the parts, but we see enough of them working together to form an understanding of what a Life Calling

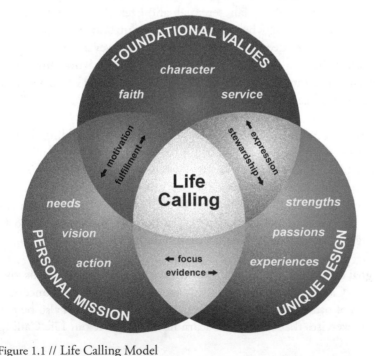

Figure 1.1 // Life Calling Model

is and how it works. The conceptual model lays out each component of the model in enough detail for us to grasp what it means and the basic relationships that join the components together.

The model is comprised of three main components—*Foundational Values*, *Unique Design*, and *Personal Mission*. Each of these components has three distinct elements, resulting in nine total elements in the overall model. Each of the components and elements could be studied independently of the other components and elements. But a sense of an overriding purpose for your life is only found when the components and elements are explored in a manner that in the end brings them all together as indicated by the central light zone in the model. The impact of each main component on the other two components is indicated by the terms and arrows in the smaller shield-shaped areas where two components overlap.

Seven Sources to Explore for a Life Calling

Not only will we use a conceptual model to understand Life Calling, but we will have the opportunity to develop tools that will continue to help us discover our Life Calling throughout our lifetime. Geology is one of the several areas of study and work I have pursued. I have traveled all over the earth in exploring its geologic features and processes. This has often involved one adventure after another, some even at the risk of my life, in search of rare items or hidden answers. Discovering your Life Calling requires a similar adventurous search. I often followed a set of clues or a map to guide me to my destination. We also will need sources of information to guide our discovery of a Life Calling. Here are seven of the most effective ones.

Theory

Many people have already traveled the path before us in search of a Life Calling. As a result, they have been able to leave behind ideas and propositions that they believe explain how to be effective in the search for a life calling. We need to seek out these ideas and study them. This will greatly accelerate our own discovery process. These explanations fall into three broad theories:

Scientific Theories. The study of human characteristics and dynamics and how this can help us understand what kind of person we are. Psychology, sociology, anthropology, and biology are rich sources of information about what it means to be human.

Philosophical Theories. The study of ultimate meaning in the human experience and how this can help us understand the deeper meaning of our life. These theories are often tied directly into biblical and theological studies.

Strategic Theories. The study of how to create effective plans for our life and how this can provide us with a road map to follow as we pursue our Life Calling. Leadership and management studies often look at this in relationship to groups of people and organizations. Self-help and career development studies look at this with an individual focus.

Examples

One of the most common sources that can help us discover our Life Calling can be found in observing the examples of other people. Here are three good groups to watch:

Family. Most people are around their family members more than any other group. If we follow this pattern, we will have the chance to closely observe them in relationship to Life Calling dynamics. We need to be careful, however, that we don't make the mistake of automatically assuming that our Life Calling will be the same as other members of our family.

Modelers. As we think of areas of work, family, or service that seem to be drawing our attention as possibly part of our Life Calling, look at people around us who model success in these areas.

Mentors. One of the real blessings that can come into our life is a trusted counselor or teacher who is willing to walk alongside us as we explore our Life Calling. No matter how old we are, we can learn much from such a person.

Assessments

Social scientists have created numerous assessments that can help us discover the unique characteristics we possess as an individual. These should be used as one set of tools in the discovery process, not the only set of tools. When using assessments, we need to keep in mind three important guidelines. First, seek information from multiple assessments that measure many aspects of your life rather than those that focus on one area only. Second, use assessments that are truly valid social science instruments. Third, when we receive results from assessments, we should not accept them at face value. We need to ask ourselves if they make sense. If they don't, we should question them. We can also ask other people who know us well if the assessment results seem valid. The assessments that will be of the most use in our discovery of a Life Calling fall into three main areas of focus:

Strengths-focus. These assessments emphasize the measurement of strengths rather than highlighting weaknesses.

Temperament-focus. These assessments explore personalities by primarily examining attitudes, preferences, emotions, and predispositions.

Interests-focus. These assessments, while not totally separate from the characteristics of the other two areas, focus primarily on specific activities, jobs, careers, etc. that have a sustaining attraction to individuals based on their uniqueness.

Counsel

We can learn much about ourselves and our sense of calling by working with counselors who are committed to helping us. We can find such counselors in three groupings:

Professional Life Coaches. These are individuals who are trained to help in the exploration process as we search for a Life Calling.

Paraprofessionals. These are individuals such as pastors, youth ministers, and teachers. Though they may not be trained specifically in the area of life coaching, they have training in working with people in life development.

Nonprofessionals. Family members and friends often have good advice that can help us understand our life better. Their counsel should not be ignored.

History

Discovering what lies ahead of us can many times be found in understanding what has already happened behind us.

Life Mapping. This process can provide a very effective approach to collecting the events of our lives and trying to make sense of what we collect. We will look at how to do this later on in this book.

Classic Works. The writings of others throughout history can provide valuable lessons to be learned. These authors often provide insights that we would overlook on our own.

Analyzing Trends. This can be an interesting way to approach history when applying it to our lives. What patterns can be seen in the past and are happening right now? And what do these indicate about the future? Though these trends do not lock the future in place, they do help us be prepared for what might happen.

Experience

One of the most useful sources of information concerning our Life Calling can be gathered from experience. As we evaluate these experiences, we can learn a lot about ourselves and what really connects with us and draws us to a calling.

Circumstantial Experiences. These are experiences that are not necessarily planned, but as they happen to us, we can evaluate them to gain information about our Life Calling.

Experimental Experiences. These are activities that we engage in specifically for the purpose of trying to gain information about our Life Calling. We use these experiences like a laboratory.

Job-related Experiences. These experiences provide us direct information from the world of work. Here we can learn a lot about the career aspects of our Life Calling.

Reflection

As we explore our Life Calling, it is very important that we take time to reflect on what we are learning. However, reflection is one of the hardest things for people in our fast-paced culture to do because it requires us to stop and be quiet for a period of time. Here are three valuable habits you should develop to be more effective at reflection.

Listening. The habit of listening is almost more an art than a habit. Most of us don't really know how to do it. Even when we think we are listening, we aren't. Instead, we are judging what the other person is saying and jumping to conclusions about what is being said long before the person has finished the idea, or even worse, we are planning what we are going to say as soon as the other person is finished though the person is still talking. Patiently listening to another person in a nonjudgmental manner is a difficult skill—one we need to work hard to develop.

Praying and Meditating. As we search for our Life Calling through the other sources listed earlier in this section, we need to find time when we can deliberately and thoughtfully study what we have learned and contemplate deeply on its meaning. This type of thoughtful prayer and meditation requires quiet time, and like listening, this is a difficult habit to develop because of the hectic pace at which most of us live our lives.

Journaling. Finally, a very effective way to make reflection a lasting experience and force in our lives is to journal what we are reflecting on in a written form. This usually is done as a daily routine that chronicles occurrences, experiences, observations, or insights encountered during each day. This activity has the added benefit of providing us a source to which we can return when trying to remember reflections we have had earlier in our lives.

Figure 1.2 shows an easy way to remember these seven sources of information. When we combine the first letter of each of the seven, they combine to spell the word "TEACHER." These sources truly can work together to be a teacher imparting knowledge, skills, wisdom, and understanding that can lead to confidence in an overriding purpose for our life.

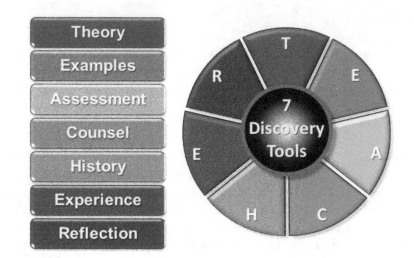

Figure 1.2 // TEACHER Acronym

SCRIPTURAL INSIGHT ————————————————

Scripture provides insight related to each of the seven guiding sources that will help us discover an overriding purpose for our life.

Insight 1 // Using Theory to Discover Life Calling

Teach me knowledge and good judgment, for I trust your commands. Before I was afflicted I went astray, but now I obey your word. PSALM 119:66-67

Here is a good question to explore as we search for direction in our life— Is it better to begin with mystical and transcendental experiences or with solid theoretical information that will allow us to evaluate mystical and transcendental experiences to test their validity? As appealing as the first choice might be, the second choice appears to be the better answer. We will ultimately be led astray in our search for a Life Calling if we ignore the information God has already given us concerning our lives.

How many of us say, "I'm just waiting to hear from God," when in reality we already have! Maybe the problem is not so much that we haven't heard from God but that we weren't listening in the right place. Our discovery of a Life Calling will be greatly enhanced by careful study of good theory, especially theory that God has provided us in the Bible.

The theme of Psalm 119 focuses on the concept that God has already communicated with us in scripture. At the time this Psalm was written, the scriptures were restricted to the Torah—what would be the first five books in our Bible today. Two concepts can be seen in the passage quoted for today. First, by starting with a study of God's commands, we can learn knowledge and good judgment. It is not the other way around. Second, when we don't heed God's word, we tend to end up going astray.

So as we approach our search for Life Calling and God's direction, the first Discovery Tool we should employ is the study of theory, and the study of theory should begin with what God has already revealed to us in the Bible. This can then become the standard by which we evaluate other information, including information that might come in mystical and transcendental experiences.

PERSONAL REFLECTION

God calls us each day. A Life Calling is the collection of all these daily callings. What have I heard today from God in his word that has already told me about my life so that I can evaluate the rest of the day by that message?

Insight 2 // Using Examples to Discover Life Calling

Join together in following my example, brothers and sisters, and just as you have us as a model, keep your eyes on those who live as we do.
PHILIPPIANS 3:17

I have had the opportunity to explore Life Calling with literally tens of thousands of individuals. If I had to identify one area that has had a greater impact on more people than any other, it would have to be the examples they have seen portrayed in their lives by other people. This might be a parent, another relative, a favorite teacher, a pastor, someone working in the community or another country, a sports figure, a government leader, and the list could go on. One of the major reasons this occurs is that the majority of people learn by observation. Even if they are book learners, they often learn a lot by reading the story about someone else's life.

And so it is not surprising that in helping the Christians of Philippi to journey down the right path, Paul encouraged them to follow his example. That was a serious exhortation by Paul because it put the pressure on him to set a good example for the Philippians.

Observing the example of others has, throughout history, been a good source of guidance in discovering a Life Calling. Joshua looked to Moses as his example. Elijah served as an example and mentor for Elisha. Socrates mentored Plato, who, in turn, mentored Aristotle. The philosophical thoughts from that line have had tremendous impact on the thinking of the Western world. They had an impact on the Apostle Paul as well. Jesus instructed his disciples to reproduce his example in their lives after he washed their feet at the Last Supper.

Not all of those we observe always set a good example, so we have to choose wisely when we pick someone as a pattern for our lives. The book of Proverbs provides this admonition: "Walk with the wise and become wise, for a companion of fools suffers harm" (Proverbs 13:26). Take time right now to list in your mind people who are having a significant impact on you, especially if that impact is related to what you want to do with your life. You will find several important factors with those who are having a strong positive impact. First of all, they are following a strong positive pattern themselves. No matter how old they are, they always seem to have someone else they look up to. Second, they live consistently, which is why they can provide a good example. Finally, they have a good understanding of themselves. If you haven't found a person like this to observe in your own life, start looking for one.

PERSONAL REFLECTION

Everybody has other people who are influencing them. The key to making this a valuable dynamic is taking time to evaluate what kind of influence it is and the kind of impact it is having. Who is God using right now in your life to help guide you in your search for a Life Calling?

Insight 3 // Using Assessments to Discover Life Calling

Each of you should test your own actions. Then you can take pride in yourself, without comparing yourself to somebody else, for each of you should carry your own load. GALATIANS 6:4-5

When you are getting ready in the morning and you look in the mirror, how much do you know about the person you see? You might be surprised to know that many people don't know that much about the person they see. The problem for those who might fall into that category is that they end up defining themselves by comparing themselves with others. The Apostle Paul warned the Christians of Galatia about relying on such comparisons. He instead advised them to assess themselves. Implied in that advice is the need to accept who we are; that's what Paul meant when he said we should carry our own load. That does not mean we should not grow and improve. But we need to accept our uniqueness as an important part of our Life Calling.

One way to test our own actions is to complete formal assessments that have been designed specifically to help us conduct such a test of actions and individual uniqueness. When correctly taken and understood, these can provide valuable information about how God has created us and made us unique. We need to be careful, however, that we do not allow assessments to imprison us. How can we detect if this is happening? The Bible tells us that when Jesus sets us free, we are free indeed (John 8:36). Anything that starts to take away that freedom and causes us to begin conforming to some blueprint that primarily compares us to someone else and ignores God's design in our life, is likely not something God is using to speak into our life.

PERSONAL REFLECTION

Everybody has unique characteristics that are strengths and assets. What characteristic have you learned about your uniqueness that you believe God wired into you as part of your Life Calling? Have you ever thanked God for these?

Insight 4 // Using Counsel to Discover Life Calling

Plans fail for lack of counsel, but with many advisers they succeed.
PROVERBS 15:22

It is very rare, if not impossible, that a person can pursue the search for a Life Calling alone and then live it out successfully in the same solitary approach. It is easy, then, to understand why it makes good sense to listen to the counsel and advice of others as we search for our Life Calling. The admonition from the Proverbs puts it in clear focus.

A great example of this occurred in the life of Moses. Moses was leading the people of Israel out of Egypt across the desert on their way to the Promised Land in Canaan. So far so good. The problem was that Moses did all the work of leading by himself. He evidently had a hard time delegating the responsibility of judging disputes that arose among the Israelites, and the heavy load was weighing him down. Then Jethro entered the scene. He was Moses' father-in-law. He gave Moses some good counsel: if you keep doing all the judging yourself, it is going to wear you out; train up others who can help you carry the load. Moses listened to the counsel and developed an effective structure to help him.

There are blind spots in our lives right now that we will discover only with the help of someone else. There are gifts that we have, yet we are unaware of them. Without the counsel of another person, the chances are good that we will never discover these assets. There are choices we have to make, and we are unsure what we should do. The counsel of another wise person can help give us a clearer perspective.

Some people are afraid to seek counsel because they have the mistaken belief that this is a sign of weakness. Actually the opposite is the truth. People who seek counsel are strong because they know that a Life Calling was never meant to be lived in isolation from others.

PERSONAL REFLECTION

Who is offering counsel into your life right now? How is God using this counsel to help you understand your Life Calling?

Insight 5 // Using History to Discover Life Calling

Therefore, since we are surrounded by such a great cloud of witnesses, let us throw off everything that hinders and the sin that so easily entangles. And let us run with perseverance the race marked out for us, fixing our eyes on Jesus, the pioneer and perfecter of faith. For the joy set before him he endured the cross, scorning its shame, and sat down at the right hand of the throne of God. Consider him who endured such opposition from sinners, so that you will not grow weary and lose heart. HEBREWS 12:1-3

Hebrews 11, sometimes referred to as the "Hall of Faith," records the lives of several prominent figures in biblical history. In the first three verses of the chapter that follows, the readers are encouraged to use such examples from history to inspire the way they live their lives.

The old saying, "There is no need to reinvent the wheel," comes to mind. As we search for our Life Calling and ways to live it out as we find it, why not look at the people who have lived before us and discover the secrets from their lives that made them successful in pursuing their Life Calling?

What was it that enabled Abel, Enoch, Noah, Abraham, Isaac, Jacob, Joseph, Moses, Rahab, Gideon, Barak, Samson, Jephthah, David, Samuel and the prophets for lives of spiritual strength and God-given purpose? In discovering that answer, we might find important secrets for our own lives. But it is not just the history of Bible characters. We can learn much from other historical figures like Augustine, Martin Luther, Abraham Lincoln, Mother Teresa, Martin Luther King, Jr., and many others. We can also learn from the history of our own parents and grandparents.

Our own history also provides a very important source that can help reveal our path to us. Have you ever noticed that you really can't tell if you are going the wrong way by looking at what is coming ahead? It is more likely detected by looking at where you have already traveled.

PERSONAL REFLECTION

What person in history has been an inspiration to you as you look at what you want to do in life? What events in your own life have given you direction in what your Life Calling might be?

Insight 6 // Using Experience to Discover Life Calling

Test everything. Hold on to the good. 1 THESSALONIANS 5:21

Some of the most useful advice that comes from the Bible can be found in statements that are short and to the point. The Apostle Paul was a great source of such statements. His statement above is one of his best.

While this counsel was primarily aimed at ideas and philosophy, it can be expanded to many aspects of our lives. As we search for a Life Calling through many different activities, one good approach is to try out different things in our lives. In other words, test them. Then if they work, hold on to the good. If not, set them aside and look for something else.

Have you ever tried to ride a bicycle uphill without pedaling? It doesn't work. You just keep falling over. It is only while you are moving forward that you can actually steer your bike. The same thing holds true in life. Steering your life—finding your Life Calling—will best be revealed as you are moving forward in life. In other words, try different things. Some of them will work out really well, and you will discover that these are paths you will want to continue to follow. Others won't turn out so well. But those aren't wasted experiences either, because you learned that those paths were ones you would be better off not traveling.

The Apostle Paul found direction in such experiences. In the city of Athens he tried a sophisticated and clever approach with philosophers based on an altar to an Unknown God that they had as one of many altars to various gods. He used that for a starting point to talk about Jesus. But in the end this approach resulted in only a few people deciding to follow Jesus. Paul went from Athens to the city of Corinth. He learned something from that Athens experience. In Corinth he followed a different path. He chose not to rely on eloquence or superior wisdom; instead, his message and preaching "were not with wise and persuasive words, but with a demonstration of the Spirit's power, so that your faith might not rest on human wisdom, but on God's power" (1 Corinthians 2:1-5). While no significant Christian church resulted from Paul's work in Athens, a very strong church arose from his work in Corinth. He had learned by experience.

Are we moving forward in our lives and trying different ways of doing things as we move? Suppose a person would never go to see a movie unless the person had seen that movie at least one time before. Stop and think about that for a moment. If we followed that pattern, we would never see a movie. That is very similar to what will happen in our life if we only pursue things when you know they will work. In other words, we're afraid to experiment with them by trying them out. We will probably end up not doing anything if that's our approach to life, and we will never discover a Life Calling.

> **PERSONAL REFLECTION**
>
> What are you learning from your life experiences? What is working? What isn't working? Remember, answers to both of those questions are equally important.

Insight 7 // Using Reflection to Discover Life Calling

I will remember the deeds of the LORD; yes, I will remember your miracles of long ago. I will meditate on all your works and consider all your mighty deeds. Your ways, O God, are holy. What god is so great as our God? You are the God who performs miracles; you display your power among the peoples.
PSALM 77:11-14

Reflection is one of the hardest things for people in our fast-paced culture to do because it requires us to stop and be quiet for a period of time. Think about the way we eat dessert. Let's be honest—none of us eats desserts in order to advance our nutrition or health; we eat dessert for enjoyment. But there's the oddity. Once a spoonful or forkful of the dessert is in our mouth, what do we do with the spoon or fork? Most of us do not set it down while we take time to savor the taste of the dessert. No, instead we sink the spoon or fork into the next portion that we will be moving toward our mouth. Crazy, isn't it? We eat dessert for enjoyment and yet we don't even take time to actually enjoy it.

That pretty much describes our overall approach to life. We don't take time to consider it or enjoy it. Yet it is very important for us to take time to do this if we are going to make sense of what we are learning about a Life Calling. Think about those words from the Psalms.

Reflection accomplishes several things. First, it helps us remember what we have learned. Second, it helps us put what we have learned in perspective. Finally, reflection can inspire us with a sense of God's power to help us live out what we have learned.

Mary, likely a teenage girl living in the small village of Nazareth, was visited by the angel Gabriel. He tells her that she will give birth to a son, and that she should name the son Jesus. This greatly surprised Mary because she was a virgin, and she had no idea how this could come about. Gabriel told her that this would be made possible by a miracle of the Holy Spirit.

When the baby was born in Bethlehem, shepherds came and told her that a host of angles had appeared to them in the fields while they were watching their sheep. The angels had announced to them that the Savior had been born in Bethlehem.

It is Mary's response that can be an inspiration to us as to how we should respond to meaningful events in our lives. The story is recorded in the second chapter of Luke, and in the nineteenth verse it describes Mary's response: "But Mary treasured up all these things and pondered them in her heart." We need to treasure the things that happen in our lives and ponder them. Ponder means to reflect or consider with thoroughness and care. When we do this we will start to see our Life Calling unfold just as Mary began to understand her Life Calling.

> **PERSONAL REFLECTION**
>
> Do you take time to think about what is happening in your life right now and then try to make meaning of it? Or are you already reaching for the next "spoonful" of life by putting your thoughts into tomorrow? What has happened in your life today? What does this reveal to you about your Life Calling?

INTERACTING WITH YOUR LIFE CALLING ————

An interactive feature of this book will come at the end of each chapter entitled, "INTERACTING WITH YOUR LIFE CALLING." In this interaction you will have the change to complete practical activities that will help you explore the Life Calling concepts introduced in each chapter and develop habits that will help you implement the concepts into your life. Because many of these activities involve writing on a piece of paper or typing in a computer document (your choice), they do not fit well into a book of this size. To make it easier for you, we have created a supplement to this book entitled —*Life Calling Activities Supplement*.

At the end of each chapter in this book, you will be given a list of the activities related to the chapter you will find in the supplement. You should then access the supplement and find that activities listed. So let's start right now. Here are the activities related to this chapter.

1. **Activity 1.1** *End of Life Ceremony and Epitaph.* Rather than forging ahead in pursuit of a Life Calling with no idea of where you are headed, this activity will help you to start viewing your purpose in life with the end in mind.

2. **Activity 1.2** *Cultivating Creativity in Your Life Gallery.* This activity will guide you in beginning to view your life as a gallery of experiential works of art to pull from as you begin to create skillfully masterful pieces of intention and beauty that will serve both yourself and your world. You will continue to build on this throughout the rest of this book, so keep that in mind as you begin.

3. **Activity 1.3** *Imagining Life Calling through Metaphor and Impact.* This activity will guide you through a series of "imaginings" that will provide you with new, creative, personal material to generate an initial draft of a Life Purpose Statement at the beginning of this book. You will likely be revising this often throughout the discovery process in this book.

Make sure you save all of these activities in a safe place that is easily accessed as you continue through the rest of this book, because you will want to revisit them as you look at other concepts and activities.

REFERENCES

The following resources have been used in this chapter.

Guiness, O. (1998). *The call: Finding and fulfilling the central purpose of your life*. Nashville, TN: Word Publishing.

Patterson, B. (1994) *Serving God: The grand essentials of work and worship*. Downers Grove, IL: InterVarsity Press.

SECTION I
FOUNDATIONAL VALUES

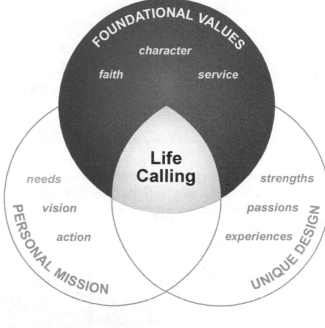

FOUNDATIONAL VALUES

character

faith   service

Life Calling

needs   strengths

vision   passions

action   experiences

PERSONAL MISSION   UNIQUE DESIGN

Faith   *Character*   *Service*

FOUNDATIONAL VALUES

Section I deals with the first main component of the Life Calling Model—*Foundational Values*.

At the core of each person's life, there exists a set of foundational values that we hold about reality, ourselves, and others. Everybody has these values. It doesn't matter whether people think of themselves as atheists or devout fundamentalists. They have developed a personal creed that attempts to explain the reality of the universe and their own existence. From this explanation we develop attitudes of self-worth and worth of others and the world.

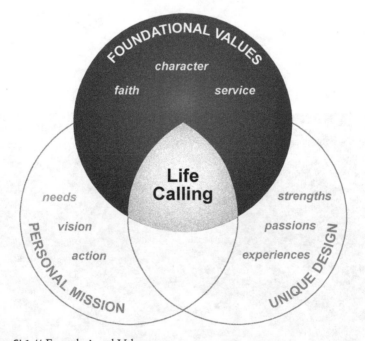

Figure SI.1 // Foundational Values

As people search to discover their Life Calling, these foundational values play a major role. In many ways these foundational values really are where the search for the power of purpose begins because they form the paradigm that creates the "ground rules" for conducting this search.

A good place to explore for these values is in what has been called in educational circles the liberal arts. Good liberal learning empowers individuals with broad knowledge and skills, and a strong sense of values, ethics, civic engagement and social responsibility. Through challenging encounters with important issues, people come to grips with what they really accept as foundational values. One big mistake that many students make is to dismiss this part of their education as a meaningless waste of time. They have been misled to believe that the courses specifically training them for a selected career are the most important. In reality the opposite is the truth. Incidentally, liberal learning is not restricted to educational institutions. It is something everyone can pursue no matter where they are at in life.

In this section we will examine each of these foundational values—reality, self, and others—and discover how these values guide the way in which we discover a Life Calling. We will look at three elements. Our exploration of existential reality will be done in the context of faith. We will then use the context of character to examine how our faith relates to our personal self-worth. Finally, we will consider how this all takes place in the context of service to others and the world around us.

The Life Calling Model in Figure SI.1 is a Venn diagram depicting the three circles of the model overlapping rather than being totally separate from each other. This signifies that the three main components, rather than operating totally distinct from each other, instead interact. Each component (and the elements that make up the component) has a significant influence on the other two components, while at the same time it is influenced itself strongly by the other two.

When we have completed this section, we will see how this interactive model works in relationship to *Foundational Values*. We will have a clearer understanding of how these *Foundational Values* are a dynamic that permeates all other aspects of our lives. We will see how they impart an attitude of stewardship on the various elements that make us unique. Without this attitude, we would end up pursing a narcissistic calling in which we view ourselves as both caller and the called. We will also see how *Foundational Values* motivate us to carry out a personal mission that lives out these values as a calling. Without this motivation, we would tend to go through life just reacting to whatever comes along at the time. In the end we will see how our *Foundational Values* are what really give us the meaning in our lives that is part of the universal need experienced by all humans.

INTERACTING WITH YOUR LIFE CALLING ————

This is your opportunity to interact with the Life Calling concepts introduced in this chapter and develop habits that will help you implement the concepts into your life.

The activity below is related to Section I. You will find it in the *Life Calling Activities Supplement*. Access the supplement and find this activity. Then follow the instructions that will be given there.

1. **Activity SI.1** *Mining for Values.* This activity will help you identify characteristics connected to your beliefs that you hold most dear. In the activity you will explore and identify your five core values.

Make sure you save all of these activities in a safe place that is easily accessed as you continue through the rest of this book, because you will want to revisit them as you look at other concepts and activities.

FAITH

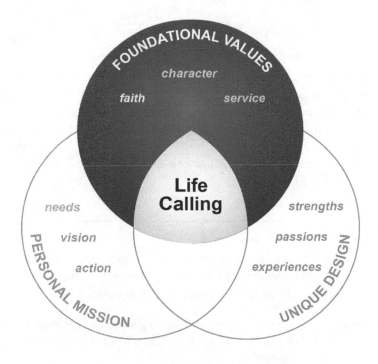

Figure 2.1 // Life Calling Model Focusing on Faith

The first main component of the Life Calling Model is Foundational Values. The first element of this values component focuses on our **faith**.

CHAPTER 2

Faith: Forming our Existential Premises

> *Faith is not simply a set of beliefs that religious people have. It is something that all human beings do.*
>
> Sharon Daloz Parks

Faith forms the first foundational value. We value the reality of a universe that comes from an intelligent design. We see ourselves as an intentional and meaningful part of this universe, placed in it by a power greater than ourselves who gives us our Life Calling. A call presupposes a caller, and this reality is what motivates us to search for our Life Calling. Without that reality, there would be no source of overriding purpose and no reason to search for a Life Calling.

WORDLIST

Words often have multiple meanings. Effective communication requires that we know which meaning of a word we are employing when we use it in our discussion. The following words need that clarification.

Assumption	a statement that is taken for granted or a hypothesis that is assumed to be true and from which a conclusion can be drawn
Belief	mental acceptance of and conviction in the truth, actuality, or validity of something
Chaos	a state of utter confusion or disorder characterized by a total lack of organization

Design	basic plan, scheme, or pattern that guides and controls function or development
Existential	related or belonging to the concept, state or fact of being
Fact	a truth known by actual experience or observation to exist or to have happened
Intentional	something purposely meant to be done or brought about
Mind-set	fundamental, primary mental attitude from which all other aspects of existence are derived, predetermined, and interpreted
Mystical	of, relating to, or stemming from a spiritual reality or import not apparent to the intelligence or external senses
Premise	a basis, stated or assumed, on which reasoning proceeds
Rational	proceeding or derived from conclusions, judgments, or inferences based on observable facts
Reality	the quality or state of being that is actual or true and exists independent of all other things and from which all other things derive
Spiritual	of or pertaining to the aspect of human existence that is apart and distinguished from the physical nature

DESCRIPTION

Nearly everyone wonders at some time in their life where they came from, why they are here, and what happens to them after this life. The answers we find in response to these basic questions become the most fundamental of the *Foundational Values* we hold about reality. Everyone has this fundamental value; for most of us it is hard to define and remains somewhat mysterious. The dimensions of reality seem infinite. The chronology—past to future—seems infinite. And infinity is something that is hard to measure, let alone comprehend. Furthermore, there is the question of whether or not there is some force behind this reality that causes the reality, yet is separate from the reality. By the very nature of that description, the question is impossible to answer with scientific evidence. So in the end, whether we want to admit it or not, the value we hold about reality comes down to an issue of assumptions—what we presume is true. That is what is meant by the word *faith*. For some people a discussion of faith is hard because in their minds faith is associated with specific religious practices. While certainly that is a common use of the word "faith," it arises from a too narrow and distorted understanding of faith. We need to broaden the idea of faith more in the direction of a mind-set that emerges from a combination of facts, assumptions, and beliefs. If we look back at the definitions provided at the beginning of this chapter, we could come up with this definition for faith: confident belief in the truth, value, or trustworthiness of a person, idea, or thing that does not rely purely on logical proof or material evidence to arrive at such a conclusion. These are the premises we adopt about everything around us.

What is an Existential Premise?

When we apply these assumptions to our own lives, they become our existential premises—what we believe about why we exist. This particular focus of faith is what we will explore in this chapter. When we consider reality as being the state, that while including logical proof or material evidence, exists beyond proof or evidence, a philosophical faith is pretty much the mind-set where we all end up—religious fundamentalists through atheists. This is because there is no material evidence from the initial Creation, Big Bang, or whatever paradigm one uses for origins. Nor is there material evidence from the future. In the short span of what we call the present, we collect as much evidence as we can. We then use this to construct as sound a logic as we can. But then we all enter into a world beyond evidence and logic, and from what we encounter there, we make our best guess. This is what the nineteenth-century Danish philosopher Søren Kierkegaard (2009) implied is a leap to faith (verb). And around that process we form our faith (noun)—the existential premises that define what we believe about how and why we are here on earth.

That leaping process is as much an important part in the development of our faith as is the confidence ultimately developed. Sharon Parks (2000), a nationally recognized scholar in faith and leadership, contends that most discussions of faith place too much emphasis on faith as a noun. She advocates the need to include the verb aspects of faith as well in a discussion such as this one related to Life Calling. "Faith is more adequately recognized as the activity of seeking and discovering meaning in the most comprehensive dimensions of our experience."

As we explore the "comprehensive dimensions" related to the Life Calling Model put forth in this book, the process of clarifying the faith for our life will constantly need to combine our beliefs (noun) and the seeking-discovering (verb) process we engage in to continually clarify and update these beliefs. Whether consciously or subconsciously, this faith will become a mind-set that will ultimately shape every other aspect related to the discovery of our Life Calling. Three existential questions in particular within our faith stand out because they address concepts of reality that set the stage for any exploration related to an overriding purpose in life:

1.   How did I come into existence?
2.   Why do I exist?
3.   Where does my existence lead?

Throughout my life, I have encountered a wide variety of answers to these questions. I have also concluded that the Life Calling Model used as the basis for this book can be used by individuals encountering a variety of answers as well. The only persons who will find no help from the Life Calling Model are those who immediately answer all three of those questions with a certainty that there is nothing behind their existence. For them the search for a Life Calling or overriding purpose is over—they have none according to their conclusion! The fact that this book continues beyond this point rests on the rejection of such a conclusion. Instead, the Life Calling Model is based on the assumption that there is a pattern to the universe that includes each person as a part of that pattern in some way.

How Did I Come Into Existence?

The question "How did I come into existence?" starts by examining the larger question of existence related to the universe itself. How did it come into existence?

Exploring the Pattern of Existence

Evidence supports the conclusion that there is a pattern of the universe. And this evidence comes from a variety of vantage points. The study of science searches for patterns that can be observed, measured, and predicted. The study of comparative religions reveals that the multitude of religions around the world all derive their explanations around what they see as some definable pattern of the universe. Even the study of econom- ic, political, and social systems base their rationalization on some pattern. Philosophy explores the implications of all this.

Let's go back to the study of science. Theoretical physicists focus on try- ing to understand this pattern as a framework for the universe. Einstein saw this framework as designed around relativity. Others saw this frame- work as designed around what they called quantum physics. And now many scientists are looking at something they call String Theory as a uni- fied framework and theory of the universe that postulates fundamental ingredients of nature are not zero-dimensional point particles, but tiny one-dimensional filaments called strings (Green, 2003).

One fascinating look at design comes from a study of Chaos Theory. A quick dictionary definition might lead us to believe that chaos is a condi- tion or place of great disorder or confusion. Chaos Theory, however, sug- gests that as we observe apparently random data (the "building blocks" of this disorder or confusion) over time, we will discover an underlying order.

For instance, if we roll a standard die with the numbers 1 through 6 on each face, there is no way to predict which number will come up on each successive roll. However, if we plot these rolls on a graph constructed to transfer the six faces of a three-dimensional die to a two-dimensional hexagon, we will find that these totally random rolls produce a very defi- nite pattern.

I programmed a computer to help me do this over what would be equiva- lent of one year—too long a time for me to roll dice. Figure 2.2 shows the results of that computer program that randomly rolls a die and then plots the resulting number from that roll. The program always plots the point halfway between the last number plotted and the new number rolled. That keeps the plots inside the hexagon. The results shown are from a series of 8,640,000 rolls. This is the number of times we would be able to roll a die in a year if we rolled it one time every six seconds. If we were to accept the dictionary definition of chaos, we would expect a random, chaotic plotting pattern, and after just a few rolls, that is what you think you see. But when we are able to amass a large number of rolls, such as year's worth, a definite pattern begins to emerge. This is a screen shot, so

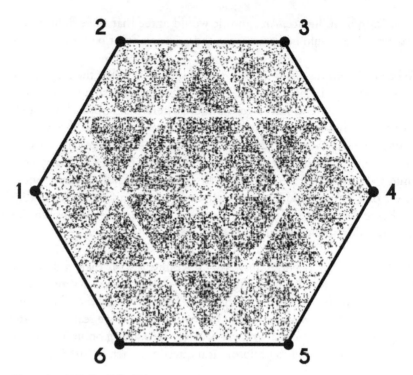

Figure 2.2 // Roll of the Dice

the resolution is low, but we can see that there are zones where few to zero plots occur, and there is a zone where a greater density of plots occurs that takes on the shape of a six-pointed star.

What does this reveal? It reveals that there is some sort of pattern underlying the random rolling of dice. It doesn't really reveal to us why there is a pattern; it just shows us that a pattern exists.

This same kind of pattern can be found in many other areas of exploration in theoretical physics. Much of the pattern comes from the mathematics that underlies all these concepts, and this mathematics may provide the greatest evidence of a pattern to the universe. To a great extent, mathematics is the very language of the universe. Does this presence of a pattern prove there is intelligence or God behind the pattern? It may hint at it, but it does not prove it. It only proves there is a pattern. An atheist might contend that what we have detected is a self-contained pattern inherent in the very nature and fabric of the universe free from any outside imposition or influence. An agnostic would agree that there definitely is a pattern, but would be unsure as to the origins of that pattern.

To be fair in our discussion, however, we must admit that the majority of the world's population would prefer to attribute this design to a mysterious force—God, or at least a god. But even here that approach is widely varied, and that is why we end up with so many religions. The baseline would be what we might call "theistic design"—a definite pattern with a definite separate designer that has initiated the pattern and may continue to do so. That designer may be as impersonal as an amorphous power permeating "godness" throughout all aspects of the universe (like the Force described in Star Wars), to a very personal, superhuman-like God found in many fundamental religions.

So why go to this extent in answering the question, "Is there a design of the universe?" The reason for this extensive answer is that it shows belief in a design to the universe is widespread, even though the philosophy of the one holding that belief may vary widely. Once we realize this and accept it, this *principle of design* will become the starting point for all subsequent explorations into philosophical questions such as Life Calling.

Exploring the Intentionality of the Pattern of the Universe

The discovery of a Life Calling begins with the assumption that there is a pattern of the universe. The intensity and utility of that discovery increases exponentially, however, corresponding to whether or not there is any intention behind that pattern. In other words, the greater the likelihood of an intention underlying the pattern, the greater the likelihood there is for a "purpose" to our lives. Here is the reason this is true. Patterns without intention answers only the question of *how* the universe will occur. Patterns with intention answers not only how it will occur, but also *why* the universe will occur in that manner. Thus, the greater the intention, the greater the *why*, and this greatly increases the likelihood of *purpose*.

The challenge in answering the question of intent, however, is that it requires significantly more speculation than does the question of the pattern by itself. Patterns are far easier to detect than intentions. You may have visited an art museum sometime and during the tour your guide pointed out various paintings. There was no question that the paintings were there and that you could see them. But then you heard your guide try to explain what the artists were attempting to convey through their works. That explanation sounded a whole lot more like opinion. In fact, you may have wondered what would happen if you came back with another guide. Would you hear a different explanation?

The question of whether or not the painting exists is easy to answer. What gave rise to the painting is much more mysterious. The same thing can be said about the relationship between patterns and intention. Patterns can be observed and measured; intention cannot. If we go back to our earlier statement that our faith emerges from a combination of facts, assumptions, and beliefs, we could differentiate patterns and intention in this manner:

- *Faith* related to patterns derives from facts and the assumptions we make about those facts.

- *Faith* related to intention, while incorporating some observable facts, relies much more on assumptions, intuition, and beliefs.

So does belief or faith in an intention underlying a pattern correlate directly to the existence of God? Once again the answer is "not necessarily," although it is moving more strongly in that direction. The range of philosophies and religions based on intentional design of patterns is nearly as broad as our earlier discussion concerning patterns to begin with. On one end would be faith in a self-contained intelligence within the universal matter that imprints an intentional pattern on the evolution of the universe. On the other end would be faith in a human-like God who systematically plans and implements a specific design as he creates the universe.

Where we fall on this philosophical spectrum depends on several factors. In many cases it has a strong basis in what we have been told by the culture and subculture in which we have grown up. Very few of us start off life with a clean slate. A second factor relates to the conclusions we have drawn from our own observations. This combines both an objective and subjective approach to the interpretations that lead to these conclusions. Finally, our conclusions about an intentional pattern will be impacted by personal encounters with mystical experiences that take place beyond the realm of objective observation and explanation.

Earlier we said that we needed to understand that forming the *faith* element of Life Calling contains both a noun and verb component. So what does that mean related to exploring the pattern of the universe? Here are two faith actions we should take in forming our mind-set:

Noun-Action   Describe as clearly as you can what you believe right now concerning the pattern of the universe and whether or not there is an intentional design behind the pattern of the universe. Be careful to describe what is truly your belief rather than someone else's.

Verb-Action   Continually pursue activities of exploration that will expand your understanding of the pattern of the universe and that will help explain why you believe what you believe. Here are some possible sources that can help you:

- Science can help you learn how to explore the pattern of the universe using an objective methodology.
- Philosophy can help you develop critical thinking that will enable you to develop conclusions based on cause-to-effect logic and help you learn how to develop conclusions based on what you encounter in life.
- Religion can help you explore these deeper questions from a more mystical approach. It can also help you explore how others have worked through this subject.
- Read works found in classic literature. Here you can learn how some of the greatest minds in history have struggled with uncertainty about their personal place in the universe.
- Talk to other people about these issues, especially people you respect. Don't be afraid, however, to include people who disagree with you.
- Pursue spirituality on a mystical and personal level, as well as on a rational level.

Why Do I Exist?

Once we come to the conclusion that there is a pattern and intention to existence of the universe, we naturally turn to the question of our place in that universe. Why are we here? The conclusion that there is a pattern to the universe may be the easier discovery. The question of intent is more difficult. The question of our place in the universe, however, produces a greater challenge than the previous questions about patterns or intent. If there is an intentional design to the universe, am I personally a part of it? The true exploration of an individual Life Calling really takes shape as we begin to discover and understand our personal role in the pattern of the universe. Everything prior to this is for the most part general; now it becomes personal. In this whole discussion of pattern, intention, and design, is there a particular place for me? Was I specifically meant to be here? If so, why was I meant to be here? The search for these answers relies much more on a transcendent spiritual level of faith.

Once again, we should avoid placing religious overtones on the word *spiritual*. The definition found at the beginning of this chapter defines *spiritual* as pertaining to the aspect of human existence that is apart and distinguished from the physical nature. This implies that the search for why we exist will rely far more in a realm that is separate from the physical nature so easily studied by science. The "why" answers will be far more mystical and will require a great deal more faith. We enter into the spiritual realm of a cause-and-effect relationship. And there we will encounter the need for an ultimate Source who is the cause of our intentional place in the universe—this is the God of most religions. Because of this, the search for these answers will need to be directed much more toward mystical sources such as the Bible that do not purport to be scientific treatises. These sources clearly claim, rather, to be spiritual in nature and require a significant level of faith to substantiate their claims. The "who" and "what" of God portrayed in these sources, however, will be an ongoing exploration as we continue to develop our personal faith that will become our guiding mind-set.

As these questions find spiritual answers, the sense of purpose and calling starts to emerge. The greater our assumption that we are intentionally meant to be here, the greater will be the potential to discover a purpose for our lives. Richard Leider (1997) calls this the *Power of Purpose*. This assumption that there is an intentional place for us in the universe becomes a spiritual magnet drawing us to something greater than mere existence.

Where Does My Existence Lead?

The third existential question, which moves beyond the question of why we exist, asks, "Where does this lead in the infinite time scale?" The question of whether we have an eternal place in the universe or just a temporary niche is something that humans have pondered over the millennia. The premise we adopt will have a definite impact on our concept of Life Calling. The problem is that the future is definitely something science cannot measure. There are no data sets to examine. This entirely resides within the spiritual realm and relies heavily on the set of other assumptions we have developed. This is often referred to as our *worldview*. James Sire (1997) is a noted scholar who has studied worldviews. He defines a worldview as a set of pre-conceived ideas that we hold about the basic makeup of our world or universe (Sire, 1997). Consider Table 2.1. It contrasts the understanding of Life Calling coming from a worldview based on two different assumptions: one that assumes the presence of God and one that assumes no role of God in the universe. The "godless" worldview assumes that what we view in the visible physical universe contains all there is to know. The "God" worldview is formed around the belief that there is an order of existence, that while including what we observe in science, extends beyond the scientifically visible universe, and there is spiritual or mystical truth from this realm that is just as important and reliable as that derived from the visible or natural realm. Notice the difference that these two different worldviews imprint on the concept of Life Calling.

GOD				GØD
Systematic creation	«	Origins	»	Random emergence
Intentional pattern	«	Blueprint	»	Accidental pattern
Unique purpose	«	Guidance	»	Unpredictable chaos
Permanent place	«	Results	»	Temporary niche
Response to a Life Calling	«	Choices	»	Best guess

Table 2.1 // God vs. Godless Understanding of Life Calling
The contrast between the two worldviews is quite pronounced. This is why our faith, our existential premises, is so foundational in the exploration of our Life Calling.

These contrasting worldviews become even more pronounced as they are played out in the way we view ourselves in relationship to our Life Calling. In this contrast let's assume the presence of God with a view that is primarily informed by the Bible and a godless view that is primarily informed by contemporary pop culture. Table 2.2 looks at such a contrast in five areas. How would you fill in the differing views? We will explore this more in depth in Activity 2.3 later in this chapter.

GOD				GØD
Biblical Point of View				**Pop Culture Point of View**
	«	Beauty	»	
	«	Intelligence	»	
	«	Success	»	
	«	Fun	»	
	«	Dignity	»	

Table 2.2 // Biblical vs. Pop Culture Understanding of Ourselves

The important understanding that comes out of these contrasts is that in a God-permeated exploration of the question as to where our existence leads, there is an eternal place for us, whereas in the godless exploration, we exist only in the present with no discernable future beyond this life. These two diverse paths look at Life Calling very differently.

SCRIPTURAL INSIGHT

The *Description* section discussed existential premises and faith primarily in a philosophical manner. In this *Scriptural Insight* section we want to examine some specific scriptures that supply valuable understanding directly related to the three important questions of faith related to our origin and being.

Insight 1 // Faith is at the Heart of Understanding

Now faith is being sure of what we hope for and certain of what we do not see. This is what the ancients were commended for. By faith we understand that the universe was formed at God's command, so that what is seen was not made out of what was visible. HEBREWS 11:1-3

The words at the beginning of Hebrews 11 clearly describe the role of faith when it comes to the formation of premises about our existence and understanding a Life Calling that emerges from these premises. There is a great deal of evidence concerning the nature of the universe and our place in it, but in the end there will always be an element of things that are not seen that will require a degree of hope and faith.

This passage regarding faith shows three important dimensions. First, faith correlates to what we hope for. That dimension of faith is about the future—we hope something is going to happen. Second, faith correlates to our certainty about what has already happened. That dimension of faith is about the past—we are certain that something happened even though we did not see it. Third, faith is active in what we are trying to understand right now. That dimension of faith is about the present—we engage faith as an active verb to discover meaning in our lives on an on-going basis.

This three-dimensional aspect of faith is a very important dynamic in our search for a Life Calling. Faith about the past is foundational in answering questions related to how we came into existence and why we are here. Neither of these questions can be answered without relying on faith. Ironic, isn't it? The most devoutly religious person and the most dyed-in-the-wool atheist both rely on faith because neither of them can see what happened at the beginning of the universe. The difference between the two is that most religious people openly embrace being persons of faith, while most atheists delude themselves into believing that faith has no place in their thinking.

In Mark 9, when Jesus, Peter, James, and John came down from the mountain where Jesus was transfigured, they encountered a crowd in an uproar. A man had brought his son to be healed; the son was possessed by an evil spirit. The other disciples who did not go up the mountain were unable to heal the son, and a great controversy had erupted. Now Jesus was back and the father came to him and pleaded for help in words prefaced with "if you can." Jesus told him if he could believe, all things would be possible. The father answered with one of the most authentic and open responses in the Bible—"I do believe; help me overcome my unbelief!"

Most of us are right there with the father. We want to have faith, and yet our lives are full of doubt as well. We want to believe that we are intentionally here for some greater purpose that God has. Yet when our path is not clear and things go wrong, it so easy for us to give up and start doubting that there is any real meaning, significance, or hope for our lives. The only solution for that dilemma is to hang on to our faith—sure of what we hope for and certain of what we don't see.

PERSONAL REFLECTION

Do you believe there is a divine design to the universe and that you have an intentional place in that design? What is it that you are hoping for in your life right now? What is keeping you from being certain about things you cannot see?

Insight 2 // Believing is Not Necessarily Seeing

We live by faith, not by sight. 2 CORINTHIANS 5:7

An old saying expresses that "seeing is believing." The words come from the concept that if someone can't show us the evidence or proof, then we will remain skeptical and withhold our belief. On the surface that seems like a good practice that could keep us from being misled and ending up on paths we really did not want to travel. The problem is that if we build our belief about reality on only that which we can see, we will greatly limit our input of information that can help form our faith.

Think about this example. While I am writing this section of the book, I am sitting on my front porch and hear birds singing. However, I do not see them. So do they exist or not? You're probably saying, "Of course they exist! Get up and go look up into the trees." The point is that knowing something exists is not reliant on sight alone. In this example, sound was just as good a source of information.

You might be tempted to counter my example by revising the old saying to "sensory intake is believing." In other words, as long as the senses can take in some measurable input, then you can use that to establish your beliefs; it doesn't have to be just sight. An experience Jesus had during the familiar event we call the Triumphal Entry provides an interesting insight concerning that argument. The story recorded in John 12 describes Jesus coming into Jerusalem riding on a donkey with crowds of people waving palm branches and shouting "Hosanna!" Many people wanted to see Jesus and talk with him; among these were some people of Grecian descent who followed the Jewish faith. A series of conversations went on among these Greeks, Jesus' disciples, and Jesus. At one point Jesus called on God to glorify his name. Immediately a voice called out from heaven, "I have glorified it, and will glorify it again." The interesting thing is that while some people heard the voice, others heard only thunder.

So then, the data we take in through our senses is not necessarily the basis for belief because sometimes it is not interpreted in the same way by different people. As a result of this, it is just as valid to start with faith and let that faith inform our interpretation of data, as it is to gather data and let it inform our faith. That is what Paul meant when he said we live by faith rather than by sight. These words were spoken in the context of a discussion about whether he would rather live in his mortal body in his present situation, or leave this life and live in the life to come in heaven. His conclusion was that he would live by faith in the hope for a better life to come, not by being bound to the hardships that seem so real in the present life.

When we think about the reality of which we are a part and from which we have come, there is evidence within nature itself to provide a rational belief in a divine design to the universe and to our lives. In Romans 1:20 Paul concluded that "since the creation of the world God's invisible qualities—his eternal power and divine nature—have been clearly seen, being understood from what has been made, so that people are without excuse." Our faith, then, is better termed vision-limited rather than totally blind. The data is there if we know how to correctly interpret it.

As Christians we may differ in how we interpret the data regarding the manner or length of time in which our creation took place, but our faith can look beyond our sight and be anchored in the belief that there is a God who created the universe and intends for us to be in that universe. This will guide our discovery of a Life Calling.

PERSONAL REFLECTION

What do you hear in your life right now—the voice of God or thunder? Do you wait to form your faith on what you see, or do you interpret what you see on the basis of your faith? Are you looking for your Life Calling in your faith or in your sight?

PRODUCING THE POWER OF PURPOSE ———————

How does faith help produce the power of purpose in our lives? Just look at the existential questions that probe how we came into existence, why we exist, and where our existence leads. If our answers lead us to believe in a divine Source of life that has infused the universe with an intentional pattern and that pattern includes each one of us as individuals, then that has a strong influence on everything else we believe about our Life Calling. Thus, clarifying our faith really initiates the process of producing the power of purpose is the all-important first step in determining what our purpose and calling are. As we do this, the power that this purpose can bring to our lives will emerge.

CHAPTER SUMMARY ————————————————

The existential questions that probe how we came into existence, why we exist, and where our existence leads are foundational to the search for a Life Calling. The premises we develop and adopt in answering these questions will be just as fundamental in directing the path we take. It's not a matter of whether or not we have these premises—or faith. Everybody has faith…it's just a matter of who or what it is in. As we rely on both noun-actions and verb-actions to clarify our faith, we will begin to develop a better sense of reality and our place in it, and our faith will become a clearer mind-set that can also become a stronger guide to our Life Calling.

INTERACTING WITH YOUR LIFE CALLING ———

This is your opportunity to interact with the Life Calling concepts introduced in this chapter and develop habits that will help you implement the concepts into your life.

The list below outlines the activities related to this chapter you will find in the *Life Calling Activities Supplement*. Access the supplement and find these activities listed. Then follow the instructions that will be given there.

1. **Activity 2.1** *Clarifying Your Faith Using Noun-Actions.* This activity will provide you with an opportunity what your own existential premises are and why you hold these beliefs.

2. **Activity 2.2** *Strengthening Your Mind-Set Using Verb-Actions.* In this activity you will explore how to strengthen your faith, and you will be given a chance to practice it on your life premises identified in Activity 2.1.

3. **Activity 2.3** *What Difference Does Your Worldview Make?* In this activity you examine how a belief in God or a belief that there is no God can make a big difference in the way you view key areas of your life.

As always, make sure you save all of these activities in a safe place that is easily accessed as you continue through the rest of this book, because you will want to revisit them as you look at other concepts and activities.

REFERENCES

The following resources have been used in this chapter.

Green, Brian. (2003). *The elegant universe*. New York: Vintage Books.

Kierkegaard, S. (2009). *Concluding unscientific postscript to the philosophical crumbs*. A. Hannay (Ed. & Trans.). Cambridge, U.K.: Cambridge University Press. (Published within the series Cambridge Texts in the History of Philosophy)

Leider, Richard J. (1997). *The power of purpose: Creating meaning in your life and work*. San Francisco: Berrett-Koehler Publishers.

Parks, Sharon. (2000). B*ig questions, worthy dreams: Mentoring young adults in their search for meaning, purpose, and faith*. San Francisco: Jossey-Bass.

Sire, J. W. (1997). *The universe next door: A basic worldview catalog* (3rd ed.). Downers Grove, Illinois: Intervarsity Press.

The following resources may be useful as you explore the development of faith at the start of your exploration of Life Calling.

Alviar, J. J. (1993) Klesis: *The theology of the Christian vocation according to Origen*. Dublin, Ireland: Four Courts Press.

Bainton, R. H. (1950, 1977). *Here I stand: A life of Martin Luther*. Peabody, Massachusetts: Hendrickson Publishers.

Dykstra, C. R. (1999). *Growing in the life of faith: Education and Christian practices*. Louisville, KY: Geneva Press.

Frankl, F. E. (2006). *Man's search for meaning: An introduction to logotherapy*. Boston, MA: Beacon Press.

Lewis, C. S. (2001). *Mere Christianity* (HarperCollins ed.). New York, New York: HarperCollins Publishers.

Placher, W. C. (Ed.). (2005). *Callings: Twenty centuries of Christian wisdom on vocation*. Grand Rapids, Michigan: Erdmans Publishing Co.

Saint Augustine (2009). *The City of God.* (M. Dods, Trans.) Peabody, Massachusetts: Hendrickson Publishers.

Schuurman, D. J. (2004). *Vocation: Discerning our callings in life.* Grand Rapids, Michigan: Erdmans Publishing Co.

Smith, C. S., & Denton, M. L. (2005). *Soul searching: The religious and spiritual lives of American teenagers.* New York: Oxford University Press.

Smith, C. S., & Snell, P. (2009). *Soul in transition: The religious and spiritual lives of emerging adults.* New York: Oxford University Press.

Tozer, A. W. (1957). *The pursuit of God.* Camp Hill, Pennsylvania: Christian Publications.

Wilkens, S., & Sanford, M. (2009). *Hidden worldviews.* Downers Grove, Illinois: Intervarsity Press.

CHARACTER

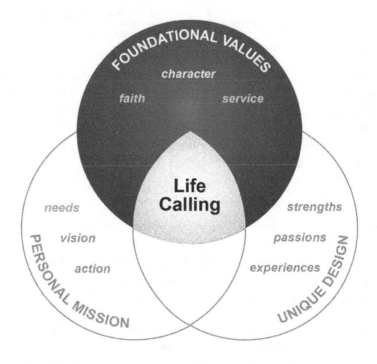

Figure 3.1 // Life Calling Model Focusing on Character

The first main component of the Life Calling Model is Foundational
Values. The second element of this values component focuses on
our **character**.

CHAPTER 3

CHARACTER: INTEGRATING YOUR PREMISES INTO YOUR LIFE

> *A man is but the product of his thoughts . . . what he thinks, he becomes.*
>
> Mohandas Gandhi

Character forms the second foundational value. We value ourselves as individuals within the greater scheme of the universe. Character implies that we do not merely subscribe to the concept of faith in a higher power, but that we take moral and ethical actions in our lives congruent with the faith we have developed. This congruency leads to a clearer understanding of our Life Calling.

WORDLIST

Words often have multiple meanings. Effective communication requires that we know which meaning of a word we are employing when we use it in our discussion. The following words need that clarification.

à la carte	the option to order each dish offered on a menu independently with a separate price
Character	the moral and ethical quality of people demonstrated in the actions taken in life consistent with the mind-set they establish for their lives
Congruence	quality of coinciding exactly when superimposed

Ethical	being in accordance with the accepted principles of right and wrong that govern conduct
Menu	any list or set of items, activities, options, etc., from which to choose
Moral	of, pertaining to, or concerned with the principles or rules of right conduct or the distinction between right and wrong

DESCRIPTION

There is a well-known saying, "Practice what you preach." The thought behind the saying encourages people to act out in their lives what they claim with their words. This concept leads us to the next element of the Life Calling Model. As we establish *Foundational Values* for ourselves, we start by discovering what we hold to be true about reality by exploring three critically important existential questions: 1) How did we come into existence? 2) Why do we exist? and 3) Where does our existence ultimately lead? These existential premises become the mind-set on which our lives are built—our faith. The question that naturally arises out of this process is how then will we live in response to this existential faith? The answer to that question reveals the value we hold about ourselves. In other words, do we value our own lives enough that we live according to what we believe according to our faith? This value of ourselves is observed far more in our actions than in our statements. This is why we look at character to determine this. We define character as Life Congruence— the moral and ethical quality of people demonstrated in the actions taken in life consistent with the faith they establish for their lives.

Let's examine in more detail what we mean by *life congruence*. The morals and ethics identified in the definition come from the standards we have in our lives that arise from what we have discovered as we have established the foundational *mind-set* in our lives that becomes our faith. Character-based logic dictates that we should live our lives consistent with these standards. That is what we mean by life congruence.

Let's go back to the world of science and math to help us clarify this. In geometry, congruent triangles are triangles that coincide exactly when superimposed. They have the same angle and sides. If we take that concept and apply it to our characters, it implies that the way we live our lives should coincide with the beliefs we hold for our lives (Figure 3.2). When we don't live in *life congruence,* we can end up in a condition that psychologists refer to as cognitive dissonance. That's just an elaborate way of saying "disagreement within our mind." What it means is that we will experience life living in two different mind worlds. The one world will be made up of what our mind believes and the other world will be made up of how our mind dictates actions we take in our lives. And when disagreement occurs, our actions are carried out without regard for our beliefs and many times not consistent with our beliefs.

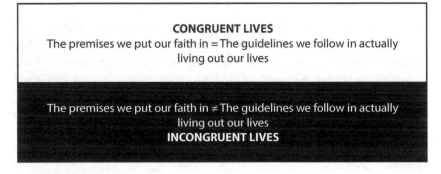

CONGRUENT LIVES
The premises we put our faith in = The guidelines we follow in actually living out our lives

The premises we put our faith in ≠ The guidelines we follow in actually living out our lives
INCONGRUENT LIVES

Figure 3.2 // Life Congruence

This incompatibility or disagreement within our minds often leads to a strange condition. Quite often the two incompatible ways of thinking become a driving force that compels our minds to acquire or invent new thoughts or beliefs to minimize the amount of disagreement between our beliefs and actions.

Sometimes we just modify our existing beliefs to accomplish this. In other words, we allow our actions to determine our beliefs instead of the other way around. The far easier solution would be to live our lives congruent with our beliefs!

Another way people attempt to deal with the disagreements within their minds is to compartmentalize. This phenomenon can be characterized as "morals à la carte."

We've all dined at a restaurant at some time in our life, even if it is just a fast-food restaurant. The menu is usually dominated by meals, and each meal is an integrated package. But many times what comes with the meal is not appealing and so we decide to order à la carte (Figure 3.3).

In this case we just order a whole lot of separate items and put them together into our own idea of a meal. While that may be fine for ordering food, it leads to confusion when we use that pattern to determine the moral values in our lives. What do we mean? If we lived in life congruence, we would have one moral "meal" where we would have a consistent set of life guidelines that enables us to live

Figure 3.3 // Morals à la carte

our lives in harmony with our personal credo (system of principles) based on our faith. In practice, however, we rarely find that the case. Instead, we choose our moral guidelines from the à la carte menu with a different set of guidelines for each moral situation that arises in our lives.

Consider the different approaches that most of us take in relationship to religious situations as compared to driving situations. If we approached both with the "entire mean" approach, we would start by considering the premises that make up our faith and then apply these to both situations. However, while we probably do use that approach in religious situations, we probably do not with driving situations. Very few of us could honestly say that we always drive the speed limit. More likely we would say that when the speed limit on the interstate highway is 65, we drive 70. If asked why, we would likely explain that we're pretty sure we would not be stopped by a state trooper for driving at those five extra miles per hour (and we would probably be right from what many troopers have told me). When we examine the guidelines for driving that we have selected from the à la carte items, we would have to conclude that the main guideline is if we don't get caught, it's okay.

You might feel that is an extreme contrast, and you would be right. Driving 70 in a 65 zone is not a major issue in the moral fabric of the universe. However, it does illustrate how easy it is for us to start selecting different guidelines for the various areas of our lives. It also illustrates how easy it is to exempt various areas of our lives from the faith premises that form the moral fabric that should guide our lives.

With driving this probably doesn't matter. But what happens when we move to the other areas of life that are more serious, e.g. intellectual honesty, financial integrity, sexual purity, or employment truthfulness? Hopefully, we don't resort to the same approach as driving—if we don't get caught, it's okay. The problem is that if we don't start with foundational guidelines that come from our faith, we will likely not find a consistent guideline for these other areas.

Why is this important when it comes to finding a Life Calling? The net effect of the à la carte approach to life tends to lead us away from life congruence and toward a life where we say one thing with our mouths and do something different with our actions. If this disconnect that leads to inconsistency begins to permeate our ideas about Life Calling, it will often become a source of great confusion when it comes to finding direction.

Let's look at this more closely in relationship to our model for discovering a Life Calling. In the last chapter we looked at the faith we establish for our lives. We explained this faith in the context of our model as the foundational value we hold about our existence—existential premises. We further said that there were three important existential questions to be answered in establishing our faith:

1. How did I come into existence?
2. Why do I exist?
3. Where does my existence lead?

How we answer each of these questions and the actions we live out once we've reached those conclusions directly relates to our understanding of the "character" element in this model.

If our answer to Question #1 leads us to believe that there is a pattern to the overall universe and that we have been created to fill an intentional place in that pattern, then in trying to understand our Life Calling, we would want to understand the pattern of the universe, discover our place in that pattern, and then live our lives *congruent* with that pattern and place. That is nothing more than a simple principle of universal *harmony*.

If, on the other hand, we believe there is a pattern to the overall universe and that we have been created to fill an intentional place in that pattern, but we then live our lives totally ignoring this while hoping to find a Life Calling, we are pursuing senseless *disharmony*.

If our answer to Question #2 leads us to believe that there is a personal role for us in the pattern of the universe, then in trying to understand our Life Calling, we would want to search for that personal role with the realization that this role provides a sense of reason for our existence. This would encourage us even more to live our lives *congruent* with that role. That is nothing more than a simple principle of universal *purpose*. If, on the other hand, we believe there is a personal role for us in the pattern of the universe, but we then take actions in our lives that reflect an attitude that there is no personal role for us in the pattern of the universe, our actions lead us down a path of *purposelessness*.

If our answer to Question #3 leads us to believe that we have an eternal place in the universe, then in trying to live out our Life Calling, we would make decisions based on guidelines with eternity in mind. That is nothing more than a simple principle of universal *significance*. If, on the other hand, we believe that we have an eternal place in the universe, but we make all our decisions about life as if there was no eternal place for us in the universe, our lives would seem to be totally *insignificant* as if we didn't matter.

SCRIPTURAL INSIGHT

The *Description* section introduced the need for life congruency. This was defined as living our lives in such a way that they coincide exactly with the faith we hold for our lives. In this section we will look more closely at what the Bible says about life congruency.

Insight 1 // Faith Needs to Be Followed by Action

What good is it, my brothers and sisters, if people claim to have faith but have no deeds? Can such faith save them? JAMES 2:14

Have you ever seen a slab poured to become the foundation for a house, but then for whatever reason, the builder was unable to build any structure on the foundation? It just sits there for months or years with no one able to live on it or to take any advantage of it. That is what our lives are like, according to James, when we develop a faith but it does not have any impact on the way we live our lives.

The people who find great effectiveness in pursuing their Life Calling are those who live in a totally opposite manner from what we just described. These are people whose faith moves directly into a life of character. They live their lives in such a way that actions taken coincide exactly with the faith they hold. We can call that concept life congruency. James' questions clearly reveal the strong belief that faith must be accompanied by corresponding actions if the faith is to serve any useful purpose.

The Apostle Paul called for something similar in Galatians 5:25 with these words: "Since we live by the Spirit, let us keep in step with the Spirit." A person can have faith in something and not be spiritual in any way. But that is not the kind of faith that will lead us to find our Life Calling. Such a purpose results from God's call on our lives, and is powered by a faith that can come only by God's Spirit working on our spirit. Paul likens this to walking in step with the Spirit. What does this mean? It means the spiritual life we claim should be matched by the spiritual walk we take. So then, Galatians 5 introduces the Spirit's power as the key to success in the call to action found in James 2.

Israel's first king, Saul, had a struggle with this concept. He claimed to be a follower of God but really lived his life following his own direction rather than God's. On one occasion Israel was going to war with one of its many enemies and the prophet Samuel delivered a message from God to the king telling him to destroy everything in the battle and not to bring back any spoils. Saul decided he did not need to live according to God's word even though he claimed to be a follower of God, so when he saw livestock of the enemy that was strong, he decided to capture it and take it with him. This was a direct violation of God's instructions. When Samuel scolded Saul for his disobedience, Saul made a lame excuse that he had brought the animals back to sacrifice to God. Samuel did not buy this excuse at all. Instead he rebuked Saul with these well-known words found in 1 Samuel 15:22: "Does the LORD delight in burnt offerings and sacrifices as much as in obeying the LORD? To obey is better than sacrifice, and to heed is better than the fat of rams." As a result of this God rejected Saul as king and turned instead to David.

What is the implication for us as we pursue our Life Calling? It means that when we find out God's direction for our lives, God expects us to live accordingly. For instance, in the last chapter we examined passages that assured us that God was our Creator and that he has plans for our future that are meant to give us hope. If we then go out and live our lives as if there were no plans or hope and make decisions for our lives accordingly, then we are no better off than Saul. The key to keep this from happening is to maintain a steady process, moving our faith directly into the actions of our lives—just as James advised.

PERSONAL REFLECTION

Where are you at right now? Are you walking in step with the Spirit as your Life Calling is being revealed to you, matching the actions in your life with direction being revealed? Or are you talking as if you had a Life Calling but living as if it doesn't exist or doesn't matter?

Insight 2 // Actions Speak Louder Than Words

Jesus told this parable: "There was a man who had two sons. He went to the first and said, 'Son, go and work today in the vineyard.' 'I will not,' he answered, but later he changed his mind and went. Then the father went to the other son and said the same thing. He answered, 'I will, sir,' but he did not go." Jesus then asked: "Which of the two did what his father wanted?"
MATTHEW 21:28-31

This passage ended prior to the answer being given so that you as the reader could have the chance to think in your own mind what answer you would give. The first son seems so defiant. How could he be the correct one? The second son seems so much more respectful. But even the hostile crowd challenging Jesus was able to figure out the best answer.

"The first," they answered.

And Jesus agreed.

So what can we learn about character and life congruency from this story? Looking at all the elements in the faith-character equation, words are the least important. What that means is that saying something is not enough. Saying you will do the right thing and then not doing it is worse than saying you won't do the right thing and then changing your mind and doing it. Of course the best thing would be to say you will do the right thing and then do it!

The bottom line is that actions better reflect the heart than words do, and that is consistent with what we have been reading in the earlier passages. Life congruency begins with what we believe in our heart and then finds fruition in how those beliefs play out in our actions, not just in our words.

When I was a young boy, my father had a saying that he constantly reminded me of in many situations: "Your word is your bond." Here's the explanation of what he meant by that saying. The term "bond" in this saying means a binding security or firm assurance. So if I say something with my words, it should be binding and provide others with an assurance that they can rely on these words. They should have no doubt that I will follow up my word with corresponding action. My father was constantly encouraging me to pursue life congruence (though he never used those words). He wanted me to be a person of character. And even now, so many years later when he has passed on from this earth, I can still hear that advice.

Have you decided to live in such a way that you maintain three-fold congruence—words, faith, and action? If not, your life will be in confusion because you will not know which path to follow. Life congruency is an important key to Life Calling and to living a truly effective life.

PERSONAL REFLECTION

What is more important to you, to sound good or to have good actions? Is your word your bond, where others can always depend on you to do what you say? How can you increase this in your life?

Insight 3 // Nobody Said a Life of Character Would Be Easy

So I find this law at work: Although I want to do good, evil is right there with me. For in my inner being I delight in God's law; but I see another law at work in me, waging war against the law of my mind and making me a prisoner of the law of sin at work within me. What a wretched man I am! Who will rescue me from this body of death? Thanks be to God, who delivers me through Jesus Christ our Lord! ROMANS 7:21-25

Engaging our faith into a life of action and character is not necessarily an easy thing to do. Paul's description in Romans 7 clearly describes the struggle related with the attempt for such life congruency. What compounds this problem even more is the tendency to be living with strong moral actions of character in one area of our lives while wrestling or even failing with morals in another area.

When we live in total life congruence according to our faith, as described in the first insight concerning James 2, we have one set of life guidelines that enables us to live our lives consistently according to our faith no matter what issue we confront. In practice, however, we find some areas of our faith a real struggle and set our standard lower, resulting in a multiple set of faith guidelines for our lives. This was called "moral à la carte" in the *Description* section. The problem with this approach is that it causes confusion in our search for a Life Calling. We begin to see a purpose in some areas of our lives and not in others. The problem is that the lowest level of morals and character begins to tear down all the others as well, and in the end we begin to doubt that we have any purpose for our lives at all.

Is there any hope? Look at Paul's last words in the passage for today. Our hope is in the deliverance that can come only through Jesus.

When David was chosen by God to become king of Israel, the prophet Samuel described him as a man after God's own heart (1 Samuel 13:14). But wait a minute; how can this be true about David? This is the same David who saw Bathsheba taking a bath on her roof, and arranged to have a sexual affair with her even though she was married to one of his trusted military leaders, Uriah. When she became pregnant from this act of moral failure, David compounded the moral breakdown even further by arranging to place Uriah directly in the line of fire during battle where he was killed. David then took Bathsheba to be his own wife. You talk about living a life with a conflicting moral à la carte approach—David was deep into this! Yet he is described as a man after God's own heart. How can that be? It is seen in David's response when confronted by Nathan the prophet about David's failure. Listen to a few of David's contrite words from the powerful Psalm 51:

> Have mercy on me, O God, according to your unfailing love; according to your great compassion blot out my transgressions. Wash away all my iniquity and cleanse me from my sin…Create in me a pure heart, O God, and renew a steadfast spirit within me. Do not cast me from your presence or take your Holy Spirit from me. Restore to me the joy of your salvation and grant me a willing spirit, to sustain me. (Verses 1, 2, 10-12)

When we struggle with living a life of character marked by moral inconsistency, and we will, according to Romans 7, we need to be quick to look to Jesus as our hope of deliverance and confess openly to him and ask for his help as David did in his times of moral failure. That's what it means to be people after God's own heart. John the disciple of Jesus assures us that when we confess like this, God will forgive us and cleanse our failures (1

John 1:9). This is what will continually keep us coming back to a path of Life Calling.

> **PERSONAL REFLECTION**
>
> What are you struggling with right now that is making it difficult to see a Life Calling? What is keeping you from going in prayer to God right now and openly confessing and asking for his help to deliver you?

PRODUCING THE POWER OF PURPOSE ————

How does character help produce the power of purpose in our lives? Faith really initiates the process of producing the power of purpose in our lives. Because character actualizes our faith by living it out in our lives, it follows, then, that character actualizes the power of purpose that faith produces. When we live lives that are congruent with our faith, a harmony is produced that results in living out a Life Calling of great effectiveness. This becomes a true source in determining what our purpose and calling are. As we do this, the power that this purpose can bring to our lives will grow.

CHAPTER SUMMARY ————————————

The answers to the existential questions that probe how we came into existence, why we exist, and where our existence leads govern the way we should live our lives in relationship to our discovery of a Life Calling. We need to live lives congruent with the faith we have developed and are continuing to develop. What happens when we do not pursue life congruence in the search for a Life Calling and end up in a state of disharmony, purposelessness, and insignificance? Almost always we will fall into the "mind disagreement" condition described earlier and illustrated in the discussion of moral à la carte. When we are in this state, we will try to find ways to lessen the distress caused by this unsettled circumstance. The most common way is to invent new patterns of thought or revise current ones in such a way that we can convince ourselves that we are pursuing a Life Calling when in actuality we are not, or we tell ourselves that there is no such thing as a Life Calling or that it isn't important. Many people have fallen into this trap, and at the end of their lives, they often look back with remorse, feeling that they have not achieved what they were meant to accomplish. The way to keep this from happening is to develop a life of character that pursues life congruence—where the premises we believe guide the way we act.

INTERACTING WITH YOUR LIFE CALLING ———

This is your opportunity to interact with the Life Calling concepts introduced in this chapter and develop habits that will help you implement the concepts into your life.

The list below outlines the activities related to this chapter you will find in the *Life Calling Activities Supplement*. Access the supplement and find these activities listed. Then follow the instructions that will be given there.

1. **Activity 3.1** *Character Counts.* This activity will provide you with a case study to consider that looks at the impact of incongruencey in a person's life.

2. **Activity 3.2** *Morals à la carte.* This activity can help you start to see what level of congruency takes place in your life.

As always, make sure you save all of these activities in a safe place that is easily accessed as you continue through the rest of this book, because you will want to revisit them as you look at other concepts and activities.

REFERENCES

The following resources have been used in this chapter.

Gandhi, M. K., & Attenborough, R. (2000). *The words of Gandhi*. New York: Newmarket Press.

Palmer, P. J. (2000). *Let your life speak*. San Francisco: Jossey-Bass.

The following resources may be useful as you explore the development of character at the start of your exploration of Life Calling.

Albion, M. S. (2000). *Making a life, making a living: Reclaiming your purpose and passion in business and in life*. New York: Warner Books.

Belmonte, K. (2002). *Hero for humanity: A biography of William Wilberforce*. Colorado Springs, Colorado: Navpress Publishing Group.

Bennet, W. J., (Ed.). (2008). *The moral compass: Stories for a life's journey*. New York: Touchstone.

Smith, G. T. (2011). *Courage and calling: Embracing your God-given potential*. Downers Grove, Illinois: Intervarsity Press.

Schwen, M. R., & Bass, D. C. (Eds.). (2006). *Leading lives that matter: What we should do and who we should be*. Grand Rapids, Michigan: Erdmans Publishing Co.

SERVICE

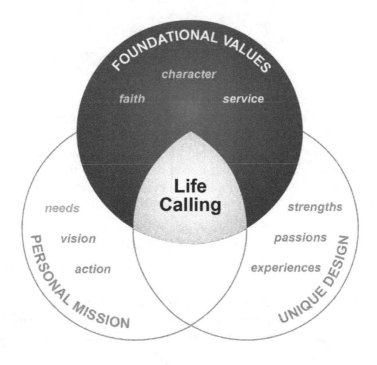

Figure 4.1 // Life Calling Model Focusing on Service

The first main component of the Life Calling Model is Foundational Values. The third of these values is **service**.

CHAPTER 4

SERVICE: THE CONTEXT OF OUR EXISTENCE

> *All men are caught in an inescapable network of mutuality, tied in a single garment of destiny...I can never be what I ought to be until you are what you ought to be, and you can never be what you ought to be until I am what I ought to be. This is the inter-related structure of reality.*
>
> Martin Luther King, Jr.

Service forms the third foundational value. We value others around us in a spirit of community. Service implies that our actions of character are carried out with a sense of responsibility to others. Ultimate meaning is found not in self-centeredness but in community-connectedness with a deep awareness of and for the condition of others characterized by empathy and compassion.

WORDLIST

Words often have multiple meanings. Effective communication requires that we know which meaning of a word we are employing when we use it in our discussion. The following words need that clarification.

Action	an exertion of energy, power, or force to accomplish a desired end
Community	a group sharing common characteristics, interests, and heritage

Concern	a matter that engages a person's close attention, deep interest, or significant care
Connection	linking relationship and association that joins, unites, and binds
Respect	a feeling of appreciative, often deferential, regard and esteem
Responsibility	answerable or accountable for something or someone within our ability, power, or control to care for
Servanthood	the noblest form of love carried out in life's relationships

DESCRIPTION

Faith, in relationship to Life Calling, contains the premises we adopt about our existence. *Character*, in relationship to Life Calling, integrates our premises into the actual living out of our existence. As we explore the foundational nature of faith and character in forming a sense of Life Calling, we will quickly discover that our existence is not in isolation. From the smallest sub-atomic particle to the largest luster of galaxies, each element in the universe exists in some sort of relationship to everything else. In a real sense, the entire universe interacts in a symbiotic dynamic. In other words, the parts are reliant on each other and the result is infinitely more effective than if the individual parts tried to exist on their own (which is actually not even possible).

Our Life Calling exists within this symbiotic nature of the universe. We cannot find purpose in our lives when we try to exist in isolation. As we begin to understand our personal place in the universe, we will quickly realize that our personal place is in a context of everyone else on earth as well. We realize that our life of character is meant to be lived out in a commitment of *service* to others. We define this as *Life Connection*—the mind-set of community where we value others with respect and seek to understand them in a spirit of community. Within this context, we take actions of character that are carried out with a sense of concern and responsibility for others.

How does this play out in the search for a Life Calling? There are five key concepts we just identified in our understanding of service that can help us see this.

The first concept involves our *respect* for others. Within the symbiotic relationship of our Life Calling, not only do we have a personal place with purpose, but we will see that every person on earth has a similar personal place in the universe and must be given the same respect that we hold for ourselves based on the premises established in our faith. Respect also means that we serve others in a way that does not rob them of their dignity. We will seek to honor, rather than demean, those we serve. Let's look at an example to help explain what we mean. Often after a disaster in one part of the world, especially if it is in an area that has economic challenges, people from wealthier situations will travel to the stricken areas to "help" the people who are in need. The "helpers" come believing they have all the money, resources, and expertise to "take care" of the situation. Rather than searching for ways to empower local people to solve their own problems, the outside help takes nearly all the responsibility. This often produces a feeling of inferiority and or resentment in the local people, even though out of desperation they take the "help." If the same situation was encountered with an attitude of respect, service would be carried out by finding ways to develop and empower local people to have the money, resources, and expertise to solve their problems. This takes longer, and in a culture of "quick fixes" in which most of us live, we are not willing to take this time. But one thing about discovering a Life Calling that will become apparent rather early is that it is not a "quick fix." In fact, it takes a lifetime!

The second concept that characterizes service is *community*. The discovery of our Life Calling takes place in the environment of a community. What we mean by community is an interacting body of individuals with common characteristics or interests. A Life Calling cannot be discovered or pursued in isolation from other people. Actually, the less connected a person is from others in society, the less capable that person will be to discover a Life Calling. So we need to be a part of those we serve, rather than staying apart from those we serve. Consider again the words of Dr. Martin Luther King, Jr. used in the chapter heading: "I can never be what I ought to be until you are what you ought to be, and you can never be what you ought to be until I am what I ought to be. This is the interrelated structure of reality." Those who pursue Life Calling (or what would probably be better characterized as "pseudo calling") by focusing almost entirely on self-help and personal development, will never really find a true Life Calling that enables them to live their lives in the power of purpose.

The third concept critical to understanding service is **concern**. Using the definition provided from the *Wordlist* in this chapter, this is a regard for someone else that engages our close attention, deep interest, or significant care. Living within a community may lead us to commingle with each other, but not necessarily to service. It is rather when that regard of concern rises to a level of close attention, deep interest, or significant care that a commitment to service starts to emerge. We need to be careful, however, that the concerns that rise within us are truly fulfilling a need of those we serve rather than just addressing problems that bother us. In other words, are we motivated to serve others or to serve ourselves? Understanding and experiencing concern are very important to the discovery of a Life Calling because every Life Calling includes a significant component of concern; it forms the drawing power that gives Life Calling its *calling* aspect. When people stifle the attitude of concern in their lives, they begin to pursue a pseudo calling, which in reality turns out to be a pursuit of selfishness. Selfishness is the antithesis of Life Calling. When we pursue a selfish path focused only on ourselves, we are almost always traveling in the exact opposite direction of our Life Calling.

The fourth concept that will help us understand true service is **responsibility**. As concerns arise in us for others in our world community, an internal social force will develop that will create in us a sense of obligation, and this social force will demand courses of action. This is what we mean by responsibility. It can be ignored, but it cannot be avoided. It will confront us just as surely as the force of gravity will. How we respond will determine at what level service is realized in our life and whether or not we will truly experience the drawing force of a Life Calling. Everyone's Life Calling involves a call to service. If this call to service is avoided, then our Life Calling will be avoided as well, and we will not experience what it means to live our lives with the power of purpose.

The fifth and final concept that we will consider in understanding service is **action**. Serving communities interact. Again, let's use the definition for action from the *Wordlist*. People who serve each other in a community exert energy, power, or force to accomplish a desired end for each other. Service is not just a state of mind or attitude. Service is never fully realized until action has been taken. Life Calling is far more often found in action than it is in inaction. Some have said it is like a car. It is easier to steer a moving car than a parked car. Hence, action taken in the context of service is important in searching for a Life Calling. When we fail to take action, we tend to stay in one place in our lives, and we are always trying to determine where we are going from the same vantage point. The problem is that when we are frozen in place by inaction, the vantage point is more of a blind spot, and we are not really able to see what lies ahead and in what direction we should be going. The better choice is to take action and begin moving. And the most productive action for discovering a Life Calling is action arising from compassionate service to others in our world community.

In order to better understand how service exhibits the five qualities just discussed, it will be useful to examine three different levels at which people consider serving others (Table 4.1).

3 LEVELS OF SERVING

When we are forced to serve others, we comply with our bodies, but our minds and spirits resist. This is what could be referred to as "servitude." Let's use the Thanksgiving holiday as an example. You return to your parents' home and are surprised when your mother tells you that you will be going with the whole family to serve meals at the local rescue mission. You, on the other hand, were looking forward to a relaxing holiday with a good meal. You go with your family because you respect your parents' authority, but down deep you feel like you are being forced to do this. That is serving coming from "servitude."

Level of Serving	Description	Level of Operation
force	*Serving Another Person Involuntarily*	body
duty	*Serving Another Person Out of a Sense of Duty or Obligation*	mind
heart	*Serving Another Person from an Attitude That is Always Present*	spirit

Table 4.1 // 3 Levels of Serving

It is only when we begin to voluntarily offer service that it is elevated to a nobler level in our lives. This starts with individual acts of service where we make a conscience decision to serve. Let's go back to our example. Your mother comes to you and asks if you think it would be a worthy action for your family to serve meals at the local rescue mission. You think about it and decide that this really is the spirit of Thanksgiving, so you say yes and go with your family. This is serving done truly in the spirit of "service."

However, for serving to reach the highest level where it is an integral part of our character, it must develop to the point where it is an ongoing, continuous attitude within us to serve whenever we detect a legitimate need. This is what is meant by the term "servanthood." If we look in the dictionary for a definition, we won't find it because it is such an unknown quality in our society. Here is the best way to understand servanthood: love acted out continually in life's relationships in a way that places the needs of others before one's own self interests. However, this should be carried out without burning yourself out, otherwise you will have nothing left to offer in service. Let's go to our example one more time. This time you go to your mother and suggest to her that you think it would be worth your family considering to serve meals at the local rescue mission on Thanksgiving because you believe this is the true spirit of the holiday. This is that highest level of serving because it comes from a continuous attitude in your spirit of caring about others and always being on the lookout for their needs.

This concept is illustrated clearly in the Mutual Influence Model developed by Chris Clum, the executive director of Experience Mission, a nonprofit international community service and development organization. This model (Figure 4.2) examines attitudes that exist when we interact with others who are different from us. The model characterizes the natural tendencies of people–to judge and control in an attempt to force change on others.

The better way to bring about change is through an attitude of servanthood that leads to mutual influence. Here you must push beyond your natural tendencies and develop a spirit that loves and accepts others, learning from and about them, and truly partnering with them. As we read carefully the brief description of these attitudes at the bottom of the model, we need to ask ourselves if the mutual influence role comes easily to us, or if it will be something that will take significant effort for us to develop.

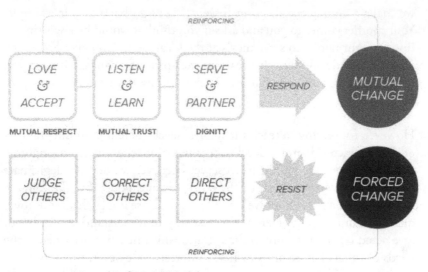

Figure 4.2 // Mutual Influence Model
© Copyright 2005, Experience Mission, Inc. All rights reserved. Used by permission.

Based on the model in Figure 4.2, we could define mutual influence as a set of attitudes and actions that will provide the best approach to the important issues of establishing respect and trust in relationships with others, especially those we serve. Our goal in service should be to reach this state of mutual influence. Only at this level can growth occur that will lead to the "inescapable network of mutuality" and the "inter-related structure of reality" that Martin Luther King, Jr. identified in the opening quote of this chapter. He said we must reach this mutual influence if we are ever going to truly discover who we ought to be and fulfill our Life Calling.

SCRIPTURAL INSIGHT

The *Description* section introduced the need for life connection. This was defined as the mind-set of community where we value others with respect and seek to understand them in a spirit of community, and where within this context, we take actions of service that are carried out with a sense of concern and responsibility for others.

When the Bible is studied as a whole, serving others is seen to be a common theme that is dominate throughout scripture. We will find that as our foundational value concerning others increases, this will greatly enhance our ability to discover our Life Calling.

Insight 1 // A Story Where It All Comes Together

A man was going down from Jerusalem to Jericho, when he fell into the hands of robbers. They stripped him of his clothes, beat him and went away, leaving him half dead…A Samaritan, as he traveled, came where the man was; and when he saw him, he took pity on him. He went to him and bandaged his wounds, pouring on oil and wine. Then he put the man on his own donkey, took him to an inn and took care of him. The next day he took out two silver coins and gave them to the innkeeper. "Look after him," he said, "and when I return, I will reimburse you for any extra expense you may have.
LUKE 10:30-35

The different aspects of service come together in story of the Good Samaritan in Luke 10, one of the greatest stories of compassionate service. The story came about in response to a question asked of Jesus by a man who considered himself very religious—an expert in the law. The man wanted to know what he could do to secure eternal life for himself. When Jesus confirmed that he needed to love God and to love his neighbor, the man asked, "Who is my neighbor?" Jesus answered this question with the well-known story of the Good Samaritan—which, incidentally, he was telling to a man, and the crowd around the man, who didn't like Samaritans at all.

As we consider the persons in this story, everybody involved was a human being. In fact, they were all of an ethnic background that had far more similarities than differences, so their characteristics as humans were much more in common than were the religious or philosophical differences they might have had. Furthermore, they really all should have had the same interests: attendance to physical needs. The conveyor of compassion in this story, the Good Samaritan, understood this nature of common unity—community—and made decisions based on that understanding. The priest and the Levite did not.

An important concept compassionate concern brings to service is the realization that the focus is others-centered rather than self-centered. This was clearly the case with the Good Samaritan. The safest and easiest decision would have been to ignore the man who had been beaten and robbed, and continue on the trip with no responsibilities or liabilities. Instead, the Samaritan had regard for the suffering condition of the man attacked by robbers and put the needs of the man before his own self-interests. When we take that same attitude into our realm of service, we will find that it opens a unique portal to the discovery of Life Calling that can really not be found in any other way.

Service never really becomes a regular practice in our lives until we begin to accept it as a *responsibility*. This was true in the story of the Good Samaritan. The priest and the Levite felt no responsibility for bringing aid to a bad situation and just ignored it. In fact the story points out that they took drastic measures to avoid the situation. How drastic? I have been to the site where this took place. The path runs along a narrow canyon between Jericho and Jerusalem. The path, or more correctly, paths were so tight on the canyon walls that there was a path on each side of the canyon with traffic traveling in opposite directions on the respective sides—sort of like our present day divided highways. So the priest and Levite did not just take a step to the other side of the same path; they left the path, descended clear down the canyon, climbed back up to the other side where a separate path carried the travelers in the opposite direction, and then walked against traffic to avoid the man.

Responsibility means being answerable or accountable for something or someone within our ability, power, or control to care for. This means that service is not really something that is optional. It is, rather, something that we should do when we have the ability, power, or control to give such service.

The Good Samaritan had decided in his heart long before arriving on the scene of the crime that wherever it was in his power, it was his responsibility to bring goodness into a situation where evil was prevailing.

Prior to a football game, it is common for the coach to work with the team during the week ahead of the game developing theory, strategy and plans for how they should play the game. Even the day of the game, there is often a pep talk in the locker room to inspire the players to give their all to the game. While all of this is good and helps prepare the players for the game, the fact of the matter is that the game does not take place until the kick-off. Furthermore, the players can stand around in the huddle and talk about what they hope to do, but until they actually hike the ball and execute the play, it is all talk.

The same is true for service. We can talk about the reason for service and the best way to do it. But until we finally take action, no service will actually be given.

Based on his understanding of respect, community, concern, and responsibility, the Good Samaritan took actions that brought both provision and healing to desperate situations. Again, it is interesting to note in the story of the Good Samaritan that the priest and Levite took action as well, based on their incorrect understanding that led them to shirk any spirit of compassion. This same spirit likely tempted the man of the law who asked Jesus the question that led to the telling of the story of the Good Samaritan. He lacked an understanding of the value of service, and this likely contributed greatly to his inability to determine what led to eternal life (his Life Calling).

And that leads us to an important application in our own lives concerning these reflections regarding service. When we find ourselves following the attitudes of the priest and Levite more than that of the Good Samaritan, we tend to turn away from the community of people around us and avoid taking responsibility for others and showing compassionate actions. If we fall into this trap, we will find it very difficult to discover the true nature of Life Calling because a significant aspect of Life Calling arises from compassionate service that is required in a spirit of community. So here are five important steps we can take to make sure that compassion is part of our experience:

1. Keep your eyes out for the plight of others in your communities just as much as you do for yourself.

2. Always approach situations with others in a positive spirit of respect for them as unique creations of God.

3. Maintain compassionate concern and regard for or interest in their situation rather than a negative, critical attitude about their situation.

4. Determine in your heart before you encounter situations that whenever it is in your power to do it, you will take responsibility to bring goodness into a situation where evil is prevailing.

5. Commit yourself to taking your compassion to the stage of action. Don't be caught in the misconception that an attitude of pity or sympathy is enough to demonstrate compassion. The final test of compassion is found in action.

As we take these five steps in our lives, we will find that our foundational value concerning others increases, and this will greatly enhance our ability to discover our Life Calling.

PERSONAL REFLECTION

When you serve others, is your focus others-centered or self-centered? How can you develop or strengthen the five attitudes outlined in this insight? How can this help you discover your Life Calling?

PRODUCING THE POWER OF PURPOSE ———————

How do strengths help produce the power of purpose in our lives? To answer this we need to go clear back to our beginning discussion of faith where we examined the existential questions that probe how we came into existence, why we exist, and where our existence leads. If our answers lead us to believe in a divine Source of life that has infused the universe with an intentional pattern that includes each one of us as individuals, then we also need to believe that the internal design we are given has intent as well. This takes us to Psalm 139. God created us with an intricate design in a fearful and wonderful manner that was part of his intent before we ever came into being. It follows, then, that this intricate design is directly related to our Life Calling. The greater we can live in harmony with our design, the greater will be the fulfillment of purpose in our lives. Thus, discovering our strengths is a critically important step in determining what our purpose and calling are. As we do this, the power that this purpose can bring to our lives will emerge.

CHAPTER SUMMARY ———————————————

We exist within a universe where everything interacts in a symbiotic relationship. When we apply this to our search for a Life Calling, we discover that we cannot find purpose in our lives when we try to exist in isolation. As our personal place in the universe becomes clearer to us, we find that our personal place is in a context of everyone else on earth as well. Because of this, we learn that our Life Calling requires that it be lived out in a commitment of service to others.

What happens when we do not engage in service as we search for a Life Calling? Earlier we said that service could be thought of as life connection. When we do not engage in service as we search for a Life Calling, the search will be greatly limited because we will fail to connect with other people. Without that connection, a valuable source of information will be lost—information about ourselves, information about the world around us, and information about the universal pattern of which we are a part. Without those elements, it will be impossible to discover a Life Calling.

INTERACTING WITH YOUR LIFE CALLING ———

This is your opportunity to interact with the Life Calling concepts introduced in this chapter and develop habits that will help you implement the concepts into your life.

The list below outlines the activities related to this chapter you will find in the *Life Calling Activities Supplement*. Access the supplement and find these activities listed. Then follow the instructions that will be given there.

1. **Activity 4.1** *Levels of Serving Case Study.* This activity will provide you with a case study to consider how the different levels of service are encountered in a person's life.

2. **Activity 4.2** *Responding to Differences.* This activity will help you apply the lessons of the Good Samaritan story to your life.

As always, make sure you save all of these activities in a safe place that is easily accessed as you continue through the rest of this book, because you will want to revisit them as you look at other concepts and activities.

REFERENCES

The following resources have been used in this chapter.

Buechner, F. (1992). *Listening to your life*. San Francisco: HarperSanFrancisco.

Clum, C. (2005). *Mutual influence model.* Port Townsend, Washington: Experience Mission, Inc.

King, M. L., & Washington, J. M. (1990). *A testament of hope: The essential writings and speeches of Martin Luther King, Jr.* New York: HarperCollins Publishers.

Levine, A., & Cureton, J. S. (1998). *When hope and fear collide.* San Francisco: Jossey-Bass.

The following resources may be useful as you explore the development of an attitude of service at the start of your exploration of Life Calling.

Blaikie, W. G. (1881). *The personal life of David Livingstone.* New York: Harper and Brothers. Reprinted by BiblioLife Reproduction Service.

Bonaventure, Saint, & Manning, Cardinal. (1898). *The Life of St. Francis of Assisi* (4th ed.). London, R. Washbourne; New York, Benziger Bros.

Chawla, N. (1992). *Mother Teresa: The authorized biography.* Darby, Pennsylvania: Diane Pub Co.

Miller, M. R. (Ed.). (2007). *Doing more with life: Connecting Christian higher education to a call to service.* Waco, TX: Baylor University Press.

Nouwen, H. J. M. (1989). *In the name of Jesus: Reflections on Christian leadership.* New York: Crossroad.

Placher, W. C. (Ed.). (2005). *Callings: Twenty centuries of Christian wisdom on vocation.* Grand Rapids, Michigan: Erdmans Publishing Co.

Schwen, M. R., & Bass, D. C. (Eds.). (2006). *Leading lives that matter: What we should do and who we should be.* Grand Rapids, Michigan: Erdmans Publishing Co.

SECTION I

FOUNDATIONAL VALUES: SUMMARY INTEGRATION

Element Integration

The elements of our *Foundational Values* do not operate independently in isolation from each other. Rather they are synergistically connected, each having an enhancing influence on the others (Figure SIS.1).

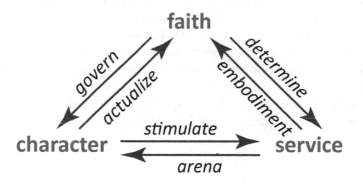

Figure SIS.1 // Foundational Values Integration

Faith, the premises for our existence, sets the rules and governs the way we live out our Life Calling as revealed in our *character*. The premises of our *faith* that we develop concerning others determines whether or not we live in the proper context of *service* necessary for a Life Calling.

Character actualizes the seriousness of our *faith* by giving action to what we say we believe. We do what we really believe, not what we say we believe. If our faith leads us to value others and believe that serving them is the context of our existence, then *character* will stimulate us to live out that context of *service* as the core of our Life Calling.

Service is an embodiment of our *faith*. It reveals a valuation of others. The absence of service indicates we have a shallow and misguided faith that will not lead us to a Life Calling. *Service* also forms the arena in which we carry out the actions inspired by our *character*. If we truly are following a God-inspired Life Calling, then our actions will be dominated by the mind-set of service.

Component Integration

The *Foundational Values* component does not operate totally distinct from the *Unique Design* and *Personal Mission* components. The more thoroughly we examine our foundational values the clearer our understanding will be of how these foundational values are a dynamic that permeates all other aspects of our lives. They impart an attitude of stewardship on the various elements that make us unique. Without this attitude, we would end up pursing a narcissistic calling in which we view ourselves as both caller and the called. Foundational values also motivate us to carry out a personal mission that lives out these values as a calling. Without this motivation, we would tend to go through life just reacting to whatever comes along at the time. In the end we will see how our foundational values are what really give us the meaning in our lives that is part of the universal need experienced by all humans.

SECTION II
UNIQUE DESIGN

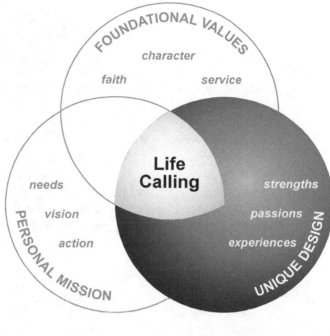

FOUNDATIONAL VALUES

character

faith   service

Life Calling

needs   strengths

vision   passions

action   experiences

PERSONAL MISSION

UNIQUE DESIGN

Strengths   Passions   Experiences

UNIQUE DESIGN

Section II deals with the second main component of the Life Calling Model—*Unique Design*.

Foundational Values may have universal application, but they have individual expression as they are conveyed through our *Unique Design*. People are like the proverbial snowflake—no two are completely alike. This distinctiveness found in each person reflects the design of the universe. In Chapter 1, we explored the concept that there is an intentional place for each of us in the universe. We said this concept is foundational to our *faith*, the mind-set we hold about reality. In Section II, we add to

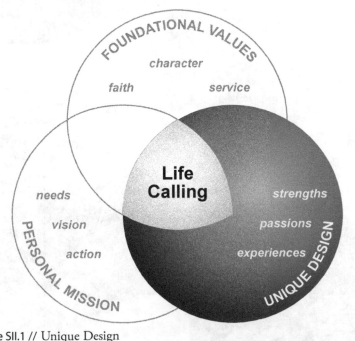

Figure SII.1 // Unique Design

this concept that not only is our place in the universe intentional, but it is also unique. In other words, it is not by accident that we are here and that we are who we are. We are meant to be!

This *Unique Design* can best be observed in the distinct characteristics that combine to make us who we are, the things we deeply care about, and how all of these are shaped by what we encounter throughout life. As we search for our Life Calling, our *Unique Design* is the most fundamental place to look when seeking to discern the unique nature of this calling as it applies to us as individuals.

In this section we will examine the three major elements of our *Unique Design*—strengths, passion, and experiences—and discover their roles in determining our Life Calling. Each person has a unique set of strengths that is the key to success in life. This unique set of strengths is made even more distinct as it interacts with our unique passion. When passion functions at its highest level, it becomes a catalyst that propels us forward to follow our calling. Finally, our strengths and passions undergo intense molding and shaping as we encounter a variety of good and bad experiences in life. The experiences we encounter will be different than anyone else's. And it is this difference, combined with our unique strengths and passions, that gives rise to a unique Life Calling for each of us.

As explained in the introduction to Section I, the Life Calling Model in Figure SII.1 is a Venn diagram depicting the three circles of the model overlapping rather than being totally separate from each other. This signifies that the three main components, rather than operating totally distinct from each other, instead interact. Each component (and the elements that make up the component) has a significant influence on the other two components, while at the same time it is influenced itself strongly by the other two.

When we have completed this section, we will see how this interactive model works in relationship to our *Unique Design*. As we search to discover our Life Calling, the deeper we explore and further analyze all of the elements that make up our *Unique Design*, the greater will be our insight into our Life Calling and we will begin to express in our lives the *Foundational Values* we hold. This really is where the search for a Life Calling begins to separate one person from another. Our *Unique Design* also provides the focus for concentrating our search and keeps us from saying "yes" to everything. When we don't follow this focus, we end up finding ourselves in many situations where we really are a misfit, and we are not truly carrying out our Life Calling. When we do discover our *Unique Design* and live within its focus, what we find will give us the significance to our lives that is part of the universal need experienced by all humans.

INTERACTING WITH YOUR LIFE CALLING

This is your opportunity to interact with the Life Calling concepts introduced in this chapter and develop habits that will help you implement the concepts into your life.

The activity below is related to Section II. You will find it in the *Life Calling Activities Supplement*. Access the supplement and find this activity. Then follow the instructions that will be given there.

1. **Activity SII.1** *Starting Your Life Map.* A very important part of exploring your *Unique Design* will be the creation of your Life Map. This activity will guide you through the process of starting to outline of your map

Make sure you save all of these activities in a safe place that is easily accessed as you continue through the rest of this book, because you will want to revisit them as you look at other concepts and activities.

STRENGTHS

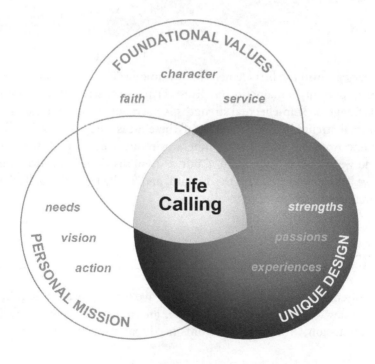

Figure 5.1 // Life Calling Model Focusing on Strengths

The second main component of the Life Calling Model is Unique
Design comprised of three elements. **Strengths** is the first of
these elements.

CHAPTER 5

STRENGTHS: USING THE POWER OF YOUR ASSETS

> *I don't want to come to the end of my life and find that I only impersonated myself.*
>
> Parker Palmer

Our *strengths* form the first element in our unique design. They are found in five important domains in our lives: 1) physical strengths, 2) emotional strengths, 3) intellectual strengths, 4) psychological strengths, and 5) spiritual strengths. Within each of these areas, these strengths take shape first from the gifts that are inherent in our lives, second from the attitude we adopt and maintain about a strengths domain, third from what we learn about the strengths domain, and finally from the skills that we develop through practice.

WORDLIST

Words often have multiple meanings. Effective communication requires that we know which meaning of a word we are employing when we use it in our discussion. The following words need that clarification.

Asset   useful or valuable quality or thing that is an advantage or resource

Attitude   disposition or feeling a person adopts or has with regard to a person or thing

Decline   to deteriorate, dwindle, fail in strength, vigor, character, power, value, etc.

Design   combination of plans, organization, details, features, and structure of an entity

Domain   an area or range of personal distinctness characterized by specific qualities

Feelings   sensations experienced when one is stirred internally from non-physical sources

Gift   a special ability or capacity, natural endowment, talent

Holistic   of or relating to holism (a theory that the universe and especially living nature is correctly seen in terms of interacting wholes)

Mediocrity   condition of being only ordinary or of moderate quality; neither good nor bad; barely adequate

Sensibility   capacity to respond to or be susceptible to sensory stimuli

Skill   excellence in performing in an area in which a person has training, competence, expertise, and experience

Strengths   qualities or features that bring power, force, vigor, or sustenance

Success   achievement of something desired, planned, or attempted

Survive   to endure, live through, get by, or merely subsist

Synergistic   the interaction of elements in such a way that when they combine, they produce a total effect that is greater than the sum of the contributions made by the individual elements

Talent   a special natural ability or aptitude that produces a capacity for achievement or success

Thrive   to flourish, grow or develop vigorously, achieve something desired, planned, or attempted

Uniqueness   state of being the only one or the sole example; single; solitary in type; having no like or equal

Weakness   quality or feature that is inadequate or defective

Will   the power of control that the mind has over choosing one's own actions

DESCRIPTION

About one-third of the Earth receives snowfall sometime each year, but because of the distribution of landmass, 98 percent of this occurs in Earth's northern hemisphere. Even if you live in the two-thirds of the Earth where snow does not fall, you likely have visited areas with snow or at least seen pictures of snow. According to estimates made by the National Snow & Ice Data Center (2015), on the average snow covers about 46 million square kilometers (17.8 million square miles) of Earth's surface each year. That's an area larger than the area of all the countries of North, Central, and South America combined. It's larger than the area of Asia, the largest continent on Earth. So it's a lot of snow! All that snow is created each year by over six octillion snowflakes (that's six billion billion billion, or six followed by 27 zeroes). Yet with all those snowflakes, no two are exactly alike! Amazing, isn't it, that there can be so much uniqueness in something simple as the world of snow. It should not surprise us, then, that uniqueness dominates the human realm as well. Each human being is unique. However, that seems to be a concept that is easy to forget.

One of the more difficult things for people to do is to discover their own uniqueness and to accept it. We live in a society that gives a lot more emphasis to conformity than to uniqueness. You don't have to see very many advertisements to realize conformity is the main goal. Education is no different. The loftiest goals of education should be to help people discover their uniqueness and then develop that uniqueness to its fullest potential in whatever direction it goes. Instead, our educational systems are more like assembly lines turning out plastic widgets, trying to make each widget like the others. Businesses and organizations exhibit the same pattern. They fit people to their plans, requiring them to conform, rather than adapting their plans to their people by making full use of the talents and skills the people have to offer. Unfortunately, churches tend to follow this same pattern. A certain type of person in the church is identified as "good," and everybody else is encouraged, if not expected, to conform to this "good" type.

The frustrating thing about these situations is that this is not

the way we are created. We are each very unique individuals,
and each of us has distinct characteristics that combine to make
us who we are. (Millard, 2004, p. 17)

In the Life Calling Model, we have labeled the second component as
our Unique Design, suggesting that we will examine elements that make
us unique. Our *strengths* will be the first element we will explore. In the
Wordlist we defined *strengths* as qualities or features that bring power,
force, vigor, or sustenance to our lives. Clearly these form the capacities
in our lives that are (or have the potential to be) the most fruitful—
definitely considered our top resources and should be the primary focus
when exploring our uniqueness rather than our liabilities or even our
middle-of-the-road features. Strengths need to be examined from two
perspectives: first, from an assets-based perspective and second, from a
holistic perspective.

Assets-Based Perspective

Understanding strengths as assets in the Life Calling Model produces
far greater effectiveness in our lives. The quote at the beginning of this
section states that organizations of all types tend to concentrate on conformity more than uniqueness in individuals. Unfortunately, they do the
same thing with strengths.

In many cases the focus is more on the remediation of weaknesses than
it is on the leveraging of strengths. That doesn't mean there is no value in
shoring up our weaknesses to a level where they will not be detrimental to
our lives. We all want to do that. But beyond that, focusing on the areas
of our weaknesses will never make us effective or successful. This is a lia-
bilities-based perspective that really does not lead to effective outcomes.

Let's illustrate this in Figure 5.2. Let's consider the plain in front of the
mountains to represent life in general, with the road running across the
plain as our particular life path. Above the mountains two arrows extend
in opposite directions. The arrow pointing to the left we will use to indicate "weaknesses" in our lives. The arrow pointing to the right we will
use to indicate "strengths" in our lives.

At the left-hand extreme of the illustration we will put "declining," on the
right-hand extreme we will put "thriving," and in the middle we will put

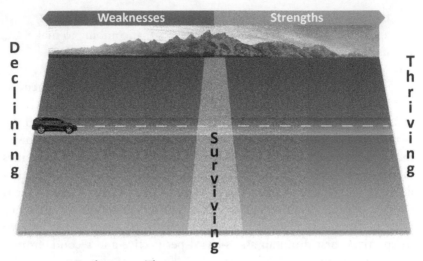

Figure 5.2 // Declining vs. Thriving

"surviving." Now let's put a car to the left end of the road representing us on our life path. The position of the car illustrates us as individuals dealing with weaknesses and strengths in an attempt to drive away from declining toward thriving.

Many organizations and institutions follow a mistaken belief that eliminating weaknesses in people will produce movement clear across the plain from declining to thriving. What happens in reality, however, is

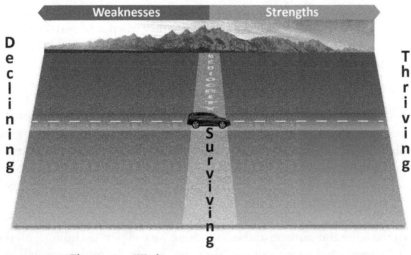

Figure 5.3 // Eliminating Weaknesses

depicted in Figure 5.3.

People who do nothing more than eliminate weaknesses in their lives, while certainly "driving" away from declining, never go beyond a middle zone of merely surviving—a zone best understood as a "zone of mediocrity." This is certainly better than remaining stuck in life on the left-hand side of the picture—declining. However, it is not great. Have you ever met anyone whose primary goal in life was to be mediocre? Probably not. Earlier in this book we pointed out that a common desire among almost all people is for meaning, significance, and hope. Mediocrity is definitely not going to satisfy these needs. We need to get clear across to "thriving" if we want to find meaning, significance, and hope. So how do we get there? How can we accomplish those things in life we desire, plan for, and attempt? The arrow pointing to the right in Figure 5.4 shows the answer—by developing our strengths. In other words, as we focus on identifying, building on, and utilizing our strengths, we will greatly increase our ability to thrive in life.

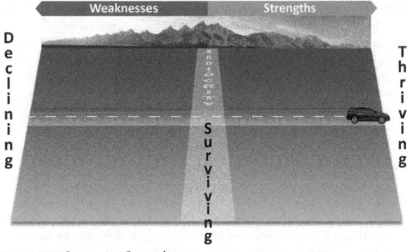

Figure 5.4 // Leveraging Strengths

In many ways what we accomplish when we do this is leveraging our strengths. Leveraging is a term borrowed from the financial world. In that world it refers to the use of various financial instruments or borrowed capital to increase the potential return on an investment. If we apply this concept to our discussion, we are employing our strengths to increase the potential to thrive in life. In fact, this is the best way to deal with weaknesses as well. We can leverage our strengths to make up for areas of weakness in our lives.

Let's look at a simple example to illustrate how this works. When I was in elementary school, students were evaluated in handwriting. I didn't have good handwriting. This was in part due to the fact that I was not born with excellence in working precisely with my hands. But it was probably impacted more by the fact that I was not born with patience to work diligently on developing handwriting. And so I always received a bad grade in handwriting and handwritten assignments. My mind, however, is good at picking up patterns and learning procedures, so I found that learning to type on a keyboard came very easily to me. I quickly learned to leverage this strength to produce my written assignments in school, and my grades went up because the teachers could easily read my assignments. This had not been the case when I turned them in as handwritten assignments.

It should not surprise us, then, that people who concentrate on strengths like this in all areas of their lives are the most successful. You may hear stories of how they struggle to overcome their weaknesses, but if you listen carefully, you will discover that they did this by finding ways to use their strengths. You will also find that people who concentrate on identifying and developing their strengths find it far easier to discover their Life Calling because our strengths form one of the best pointers toward our Life Calling.

Holistic Perspective

Not only do we need to see strengths as assets in our lives, we need to look at them with a holistic perspective. This will give us a clarity that will ensure that we do not overlook areas of strength that may be less obvious to us. A common problem among many strengths-based approaches to human uniqueness is that they employ a narrow, often singular focus looking at one aspect of uniqueness. A far more effective approach is to include as many areas of strengths as possible in looking at uniqueness. Howard Gardner (1983), a psychologist at Harvard University, proposed a theory he called multiple intelligences. He advocated the idea that human capacities need to be evaluated across a broad spectrum and placed these in seven categories summarized in Table 5-1 (Gardner, 1983).

Linguistic	Words and language
Logical-Mathematical	Logic and numbers
Musical	Music, sound, rhythm
Bodily-Kinesthetic	Body movement control
Spatial-Visual	Images and space
Interpersonal	Other people's feelings
Intrapersonal	Self-awareness

Table 5.1 // Gardner's Seven Intelligences

Though Gardner is not ready to expand his list, he has considered adding four other intelligences (as cited in Smith, 2002). They are shown in Table 5.2.

Naturalist	Environmental concern
Spiritual	Truth and values
Existential	Ultimate issues
Moral	Sanctity of life

Table 5.2 // Four Other Possible Intelligences

The Gallup organization is another strong proponent of a strengths-based approach to individuality. Gallup's *StrengthsQuest™* focuses individuals on strengths rather than weaknesses, believing that top achievers understand their talents and strengths and build their lives on them. *StrengthsQuest™* leads each person in an exploration of natural talents in 34 different themes.

Achiever	Deliberative	Learner
Activator	Developer	Maximizer
Adaptability	Discipline	Positivity
Analytical	Empathy	Relator
Arranger	Focus	Responsibility
Belief	Futuristic	Restorative
Command	Harmony	Self-Assurance
Communication	Ideation	Significance
Competition	Includer	Strategic
Connectedness	Individualization	Woo
Consistency	Input	
Context		

Table 5.3 // 34 Strengths

The results identify the top five themes for the individual completing the assessment. Each person is then given unique and valuable insights into developing those talents into strengths (Clifton & Anderson, 2001).

The 34 themes identified in *StrengthsQuest*™ combine attributes from a broad variety of aspects that go into a person's makeup. This provides a synergistic approach to looking at strengths that is valuable and is recommended in the *Activities* section at the end of this chapter. But it is also useful in understanding our unique design, to explore specific domains that contribute to our uniqueness. Accordingly, in our exploration we will take a differentiated approach to the concept of strengths. We will search for the pattern of strengths that we have across five comprehensive domains (Figure 5.5).

Physical Strengths are the capacity of our lives that gives our body distinct features and enables us to perform actions with our body.

Emotional Strengths are the capacity of our lives that enables us to correctly experience and use feelings and sensibility.

Intellectual Strengths are the capacity of our lives that enables us to acquire knowledge and develop an ever-expanding understanding of this knowledge in a manner that produces wisdom.

Psychological Strengths are the capacity of our lives that enables us to exercise our will in deciding on courses of action.

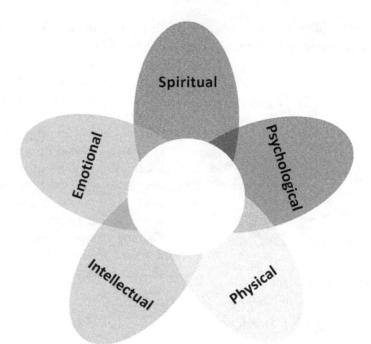

Figure 5.5 // Strengths Domains

Spiritual Strengths are the capacity of our lives that enables us to discern and respond in service to the mysterious inner leading of God.

Figure 5.6 illustrates the different emphases of *StrengthsQuest*™ and the five strengths domains. One focuses on the mix of all areas while the other focuses on the differentiated attributes of the separate domains.

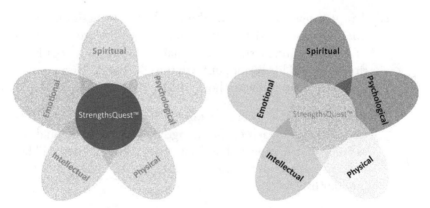

Figure 5.6 // *StrengthsQuest*™ Compared with Five Domains

A major problem with our society is that it tends to place its focus only on the physical and intellectual strengths (Figure 5.7).

Table 5.7 // Society's Focus

As a result of society's focus, many people tend to restrict their search to these areas when looking for a sense of purpose or calling and end up with an incomplete or inadequate understanding of their uniqueness. If we are to be truly effective in our search for a Life Calling, we need to explore all five strengths domains and find the strengths we have in each one.

Developing Our Strengths

In the definitions for each of the five strengths domains, the first part of the definition states, "the capacity of our lives." It is important to understand the difference between this capacity and a gift or talent. Gifts and talents are capabilities and features in a strengths domain that came into our lives without our own doing. We were basically born with these. Whether or not these gifts and talents become strengths in our lives, however, depends on what we do with them. Three critical actions will help develop gifts and talents into strengths.

1. **Adopt a positive attitude about all five strengths domains.** The frame of mind that we adopt will reflect our beliefs and values concerning a strengths domain. If we have a negative attitude, we will likely not put forth the effort to develop ourselves in this domain no matter how gifted we are.

2. **Learn about the gifts and talents we have.** As we discover gifts we have in each of the strengths domains, we should seek as much information and understanding as we can that will help us learn more about those gifts and how to incorporate them into our lives.

3. **Practice the skills associated with a gift and talent.** No matter which of the five domains we look at, we will find that simply having a gift is not enough for it to be a strength in our lives. For this to happen we will need to repeatedly practice the disciplines and actions associated with the strength.

The search for a Life Calling needs to not only explore all five strengths domains, but it also needs to pursue all three of these actions. This is why we have described this as a holistic approach to strengths.

Blended Perspective

One final point is important in understanding our strengths, and it can be seen in the arrangement of the five domains in Figure 5.5. A problem can arise when we try to view each of the strengths domains as completely separate from the others. There is a great deal of interaction and interdependence from one domain to another. That is why Figure 5.5 shows them overlapping each other and, in fact, intersecting with all the others at the center of the diagram.

Some of the most productive areas of our lives will be in that central zone where all the domains overlap. To a great extent, this overlap is what is being measured in *StrengthsQuest*™.

SCRIPTURAL INSIGHT

The Bible contains numerous passages about the gifts God gives us to make us strong in his power. These can become a great source of guidance concerning our Life Calling.

Insight 1 // You are Fearfully and Wonderfully Made

For you created my inmost being; you knit me together in my mother's womb. I praise you because I am fearfully and wonderfully made; your works are wonderful, I know that full well. My frame was not hidden from you when I was made in the secret place. When I was woven together in the depths of the earth, your eyes saw my unformed body. All the days ordained for me were written in your book before one of them came to be. PSALMS 139:13-16

This is one of the most encouraging passages in scripture related to who we are as individuals and the purpose and calling we have for our lives. Three ideas stand out in particular.

First, God was and continues to be intensely involved in our creation as people. Then analogy of being knit or woven together suggests that this involvement is on an intricate level. It is tempting to wonder at times if anyone cares about the particulars of our lives. Psalm 139 gives us the answer that "yes," God does.

Second, God made us to be awesome creatures. David praised God because he was "fearfully and wonderfully made." When is the last time you looked in the mirror and said, "Praise God; I am fearfully and wonderfully made"? That really is how we should start off each day because it is true. We tend to avoid such statements because we think it will display pride. Our false conceptions of humility lead us to instead put ourselves down. When we do that, in reality we are not truly displaying humility. Instead, we are criticizing God for what he made. And that is the key to this passage. We are not bragging about our fearfulness or wonderfulness. David did not praise God because "I am fearful and wonderful." He instead praised God because he was "fearfully and wonderfully made." The praise went to God for God's work, not David's work.

Third, God's involvement in our lives began before we showed up and it continues on throughout all of our days. Have you ever heard parents talk about their son or daughter as being "their accident?" Psalm 139 directly challenges that idea. There are no accidents with God. We can have confidence that God knew we were coming before we got here and worked to put us together just as we are. Furthermore, he knows about all the days of our life that will continue coming and is at work in those days as well. God's got us "covered" from start to finish.

It is no wonder that David praised God for all of this. It gave him tremendous hope that he truly did have a Life Calling.

PERSONAL REFLECTION

When is the last time (if ever) that you praised God for how fearfully and wonderfully he made you? What keeps you from doing that right now?

Insight 2 // God Has a Sizeable Investment in You and Expects You to Use It

Again, it will be like a man going on a journey, who called his servants and entrusted his wealth to them. To one he gave five bags of gold, to another two bags, and to another one bag, each according to his ability. Then he went on his journey. The man who had received five bags of gold went at once and put his money to work and gained five bags more. So also, the one with two bags of gold gained two more. But the man who had received one bag went off, dug a hole in the ground and hid his master's money.

After a long time the master of those servants returned and settled accounts with them. The man who had received five bags of gold brought the other five. "Master," he said, "you entrusted me with five bags of gold. See, I have gained five more."

His master replied, "Well done, good and faithful servant! You have been faithful with a few things; I will put you in charge of many things. Come and share your master's happiness!"

The man with two bags of gold also came. "Master," he said, "you entrusted me with two bags of gold; see, I have gained two more."

His master replied, "Well done, good and faithful servant! You have been faithful with a few things; I will put you in charge of many things. Come and share your master's happiness!"

Then the man who had received one bag of gold came. "Master," he said, "I knew that you are a hard man, harvesting where you have not sown and gathering where you have not scattered seed. So I was afraid and went out and hid your gold in the ground. See, here is what belongs to you."

His master replied, "You wicked, lazy servant! So you knew that I harvest where I have not sown and gather where I have not scattered seed? Well then, you should have put my money on deposit with the bankers, so that when I returned I would have received it back with interest.

"Take the bag of gold from him and give it to the one who has ten bags. For those who have will be given more, and they will have an abundance. As for those who do not have, even what they have will be taken from them. And throw that worthless servant outside, into the darkness, where there will be weeping and gnashing of teeth." MATTHEW 25:14-30

This parable can help us understand strengths by beginning to see how God distributes strengths, and what he expects us to do with these gifts. A master gets ready to leave on a long trip and puts his wealth in the hands of servants with the intent that they do something with it to increase its value. He left quite a bit of wealth. Each of these bags weighed 1,200 ounces. On the day this chapter was written, gold was valued at $1,188 (US dollars) per ounce and headed higher. If we use that rate, each bag would be worth $1,425,600. The master was happy with the servants who did what he intended; he was not happy with the one who did nothing.

Let's list some observations from this powerful story.

The first observation is that the master put something very valuable into the hands of all three servants. From this we can safely conclude that everyone has been entrusted with strengths from God. Think about it— the servant given just one bag of gold still was entrusted with nearly two million dollars of wealth. That's a lot, and that's what makes this story so powerful. God entrusts every one of us with a great deal of strengths even at a bare minimum. Our problem is not that we don't have strengths; it is, instead, that we don't take time or have the ability to identify them. I was speaking about this once to a group of young women who were in troubled situations. One of them confronted me right in front of the others claiming that she had no strengths. In response, I challenged her to give me twenty minutes with her, and in that time I would identify at least five strengths in her life. She wanted it done right there in front of the others, so I obliged and told her to start talking. Within five minutes we had identified six strengths. I have yet to find anyone who does not have some strength.

The second observation that we can find in these first two verses of this story is that each of the servants received his bags of gold from the master. We learn from this that all of our strengths are gifts ultimately from God. In fact, the Apostle James concludes in James 1:17 that every good and perfect gift comes from God. The importance of this concept is that our strengths should be dealt with in our lives with a sense of stewardship. They are not ours, but rather they are investments placed in us by God. And he expects us to put them to good use.

A third observation we can make is that the three servants did not re-ceive equal numbers of bags of gold. The master determined their abil-ity to handle this wealth and distributed the wealth accordingly. From this we can learn that God determines what our capacity is and then gives us strengths as he deems appropriate. One person may seem to have strengths in all five dimensions while another seems to have them in just two. Now, we can spend the rest of our lives resentful if we have fewer than another person, but that is not going to accomplish good in our lives and will deter our search for our Life Calling.

This is one of those places where the interactive nature of all three com-ponents in the Life Calling Model comes into play. Our *Foundational Values* start with faith that there is a God who created the universe with an intentional plan that includes each one of us. We have to exercise this same faith that God knows what he is doing and knows our capacity for strengths better than we know ourselves.

The Apostle Paul reminds us in 1 Corinthians 6:19&29 "that your bodies are temples of the Holy Spirit, who is in you, whom you have received from God? You are not your own; you were bought at a price. Therefore honor God with your bodies." It is very easy to start viewing that what we have in our lives belongs to us or is our own doing. When we take this view, it becomes easier to start looking at others and wondering why some of them have more than we do. When we see our strengths as investments in us from God according to his wisdom and plan, then we can concentrate more on being good stewards of what he has placed in us and our Life Calling will be much clearer.

A fourth observation, and one of the most important observations that can be made from this story, is that the master's reward of the servants was based on what each of them did with what each had been given. No servant was challenged to do something with bags of gold not given to him. Too many people worry more about working on what they don't have rather than expanding what they do have. We can learn from the Parable of the Talents that God's blessing of our Life Calling comes based on what we do with the strengths we have, not the ones we do not have!

As we conclude our look at the Parable of the Talents, let's look at the master's words to the first two servants who invested their gold; the commendation is exactly the same. He did not say "Great job!" to the servant with five bags and "Pretty good job" to the one with two. He said "Well done!" to both of them because they had both doubled their gold. We can learn from this that God expects us to work with what we have been given, and when we do, he is pleased.

Our final observation comes from the ending of this story. Nobody who reads the story of the talents comes away liking the end of the story. The punishment that was meted out to the servant who did nothing with the one bag of gold seems so severe. What he had was taken from him, and he was banished to a place that sounds pretty bad. As harsh as it sounds in the story, the important truth that we can glean from this is that ignoring and doing nothing with the strengths that God has given us makes it a serious failure in God's eyes. And when it comes to the discovery of our Life Calling, failure to use our strengths will make it difficult—if not impossible—to discern our Life Calling or to be blessed by God in our pursuit of it. The moral of the story: take God's gifts seriously and do something with them!

PERSONAL REFLECTION

Do you recognize the strengths God has placed in your life as investments and comprehend the great value he has invested in your life? Do you express gratitude and care for what God has given you, or do you look at what others have with envy? How can you increase your gratitude for what God has given you on a regular basis? What are you doing right now in your life with what God has given you? How will this help reveal more clearly your purpose and calling?

PRODUCING THE POWER OF PURPOSE ─────

How do strengths help produce the power of purpose in our lives? To answer this we need to go clear back to our beginning discussion of faith where we examined the existential questions that probe how we came into existence, why we exist, and where our existence leads. If our answers lead us to believe in a divine Source of life that has infused the universe with an intentional pattern that includes each one of us as individuals, then we also need to believe that the internal design we are given has intent as well. This takes us to Psalm 139. God created us with an intricate design in a fearful and wonderful manner that was part of his intent before we ever came into being. It follows, then, that this intricate design is directly related to our Life Calling. The greater we can live in harmony with our design, the greater will be the fulfillment of purpose in our lives. Thus, discovering our strengths is a critically important step in determining what our purpose and calling are. As we do this, the power that this purpose can bring to our lives will emerge.

CHAPTER SUMMARY ─────────────

A major problem with our society is that it tends to place too much focus on conformity and to remediating weakness and not enough focus on identifying and developing areas of strengths in our lives. Another problem arises by society's tendency to search for strengths in only the physical and intellectual domains. As a result, many people tend to restrict their search to these areas when looking for a sense of purpose or calling. In reality, the search for a Life Calling needs to explore five strengths domains—physical, emotional, intellectual, psychological, and spiritual. Understanding all these strengths domains is so important that the next five chapters will examine each domain. Finally, it is important for us to not only identify giftedness that we may have in a strengths domain, but we need to also adopt a positive attitude about each domain, learn as much as we can about our gifts and talents, and then practice the skills associated with these gifts and talents to grow them into productive assets in our lives.

INTERACTING WITH YOUR LIFE CALLING ———

This is your opportunity to interact with the Life Calling concepts introduced in this chapter and develop habits that will help you implement the concepts into your life.

The list below outlines the activities related to this chapter you will find in the *Life Calling Activities Supplement.* Access the supplement and find these activities listed. Then follow the instructions that will be given there.

1. **Activity 5.1** *Understanding Your Strengths through StrenthgsFinder®.* If you are able to engage in this activity, you will have the opportunity to discover your top five strengths themes out of the thirty-four identified by this tool.

2. **Activity 5.2** *Expanding Your Understanding of Your Strengths Using the Strengths 360.* This activity will enable you to engage people all around you who know you well and have them give input into your understanding of your unique strengths.

As always, make sure you save all of these activities in a safe place that is easily accessed as you continue through the rest of this book, because you will want to revisit them as you look at other concepts and activities.

REFERENCES

The following resources have been used in this chapter.

Boulder, Colorado USA: National Snow and Ice Data Center. (2015). *All about snow*. Retrieved from https://nsidc.org/cryosphere/snow/climate.html

Gardner, H. (1983). *Frames of mind: The theory of multiple intelligences*. New York: Basic Books.

Millard, B. (2004). *Discover your uniqueness and value!* Marion, Indiana: Life Discovery Publications.

Palmer, P. J. (2008, February). *Creating "circles of trust" in academic life*. Preconference Workshop. 27th Annual Conference on the First-Year Experience, San Francisco, California.

Smith, M. K. (2002). Howard Gardner and multiple intelligences. *The Encyclopedia of Informal Education*. Retrieved from http://www.infed. org/thinkers/gardner.htm

The following resources may be useful as you explore the development of your strengths at the start of your exploration of Life Calling.

Buckingham, M., & Clifton, D. O. (2001). *Now, discover your strengths*. New York: The Free Press.

Clifton, D. O., & Anderson, E. (2001). *StrengthsQuest: Discover and develop your strengths in academics, career, and beyond*. Washington, DC: Gallup.

Schwen, M. R., & Bass, D. C. (Eds.). (2006). *Leading lives that matter: What we should do and who we should be*. Grand Rapids, Michigan: Erdmans Publishing Co.

STRENGTHS
PHYSICAL

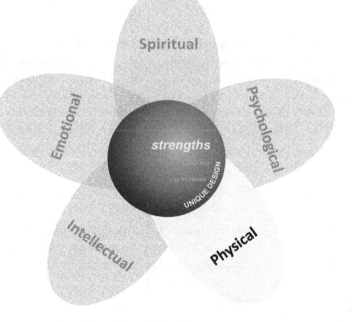

Figure 6.1 // Physical Domain of the Strengths

In looking at strengths, we will consider five domains. In this chapter
we will explore **physical strengths**.

PHYSICAL STRENGTHS: EXPLORING THE ASSETS OF YOUR BODY

One who gains strength by overcoming obstacles possesses the only strength which can overcome adversity.

Albert Schweitzer

Physical strengths are those assets in our lives that we perform with bodily actions. When we discuss strengths in our lives, we often mistakenly limit our thinking to these strengths. Even in the domain of physical strengths we tend to take too narrow of a view, thinking that this primarily involves our ability to exert brute force. Physical strengths, however, encompass a much broader array of bodily actions than just brute force.

WORDLIST

Words often have multiple meanings. Effective communication requires that we know which meaning of a word we are employing when we use it in our discussion. The following words need that clarification.

Brute	entirely physical
Culture	predominating attitudes, values, and behavior that characterize the functioning of a group of people
Domain	an area or range of personal distinctness characterized by specific qualities

Elusive	difficult to detect, grasp by the mind, analyze, define, or describe
Physical	features or actions pertaining to the body
Physical Strengths	the capacity of our lives that gives our body distinct features and enables us to perform actions with our body
Potential	possibility formed by the capability of being or becoming
Society	structured system of human organization for large-scale community living at the national or multi-national level that furnishes continuity, norms, and a sense of identity for its members
Strengths	qualities or features that bring power, force, vigor, or sustenance

DESCRIPTION

If we mention the term strengths to most people, their immediate response will be to think we are talking about physical strength. It is not surprising, then, that when we start looking at a strengths approach to our individual uniqueness, we often think mainly about physical strengths. As we discussed in Chapter 4, this is too narrow a view. Ironically, though, even when we talk about physical strengths, we often have too narrow a view concerning what constitutes our physical strengths. Part of the problem is that our discussion of physical strength in our society is so dominated by athletics. As a result, if people are not particularly gifted athletes, it is easy for them to think they have no physical strengths. If we want to fully understand physical strengths, however, we must look in a far more comprehensive manner. This is why we have defined the physical strengths domain with a broad brush stroke as the capacity of our lives that gives our body distinct features and enables us to perform actions with our body. By keeping our understanding wide, we will likely find that each person has some area of physical strength.

Let's look at a wide-ranging perspective that classifies these into eight broad categories.

1. **Brute Force:** the muscular ability that enables people to excel at
lifting great weights or exerting
great pressure. This is often what
people think of when they hear the
term physical strengths; of course,
there is much more to physical
strengths than brute force. Interest-
ingly, even brute force rarely falls

under the element of pure giftedness. Although some people are born
with the tendency to develop such strength, it primarily comes from re-
peated practice. Bodybuilders, wrestlers, warriors, and football players
are good examples of people who possess brute force. But each of them
have usually worked hard to develop this.

2. **Artistry:** bodily dexterity that
enables a person to arrange colors,
forms, materials, or other elements
in a manner that affects the sense
of beauty, specifically the production of the beautiful in some sort of
manifestation. The hand-eye coordination of these people enables them
to produce works of art that others

of us just cannot do. Good artists rarely result from just having this physical strength. They usually possess emotional strengths as well. Painters,
sculptors, photographers, and filmmakers are good examples of people
who possess artistic strengths. Once again, they have usually worked
hard to develop these strengths.

3. **Music:** the use of the body to
produce or manipulate sounds and
or rhythms. This ability can be ex-
erted by the voice or the hands or
even by the feet. Many times these
individuals are born with voice capabilities or special hearing that
makes them adept at musical endeavors. We often say they have an

ear for music. However, if they do not gain knowledge of music and pursue skills practice, they usually do not progress very far in the musical world. Singers and instrumentalists are good examples of people who possess musical strengths.

4. **Mechanics:** the use of the body to manipulate physical objects and machinery to accomplish tasks. This is usually done, with a great deal of practice, in a synergistic manner that combines the energy of the human with the efficiency of the machine to exceed the capability of either when working by itself. Auto mechanics, farmers, office workers, fast-food workers, heavy machinery operators, pilots, and soldiers are good examples of people who possess mechanical strengths.

5. **Craftsmanship:** bodily dexterity that enables a person to work effectively with the hands or other parts of the body to create exquisite objects. In many cases, this is similar to mechanical strengths only on a finer scale. Good eye-hand coordination is essential to this strength. This strength also requires learning and practice. Carpentry, cooking, sewing, landscaping, and hairstyling are all good examples of people who possess craftsmanship.

6. **Oratory:** the use of the spoken voice to produce captivating tones and clear articulation. In other words, to speak clearly and sound good. Like the strength of music, many times individuals with this strength are born with voice capabilities that make them adept at speaking. However, if they do not gain knowledge of speaking and practice the skills of speaking, they usually do not progress very far as public speakers. Obviously oratory is

more effective if a person possesses emotional and intellectual strengths to enhance what is being said. However, people with exceptional physical strengths in this area are often able to captivate others even when what they say doesn't make much sense! Politicians, lawyers, preachers, and teachers are good examples of people who often exhibit oratorical strengths.

7. **Kinesthetics:** the coordination and control of bodily positions, weight, muscles, or movement to achieve desired outcomes. We often refer to people who exhibit this strength as being athletic or graceful. Athletes, acrobats, and dancers are good examples of people with kinesthetic strengths. Each of  these examples takes a great deal of practice to develop it into an effective strength. This strength is also often observed in a wide variety of recreational activities.

8. **Physical Appearance:** the features of a person's body that we often refer to as good looks. For those of us who do not have this strength, we often are envious of those who do possess it. This is an interesting strength in that it varies by culture and by period. This is because society dictates what constitutes "good looks." A misconception

Leonard Zhukovsky / Shutterstock.com

tion with this strength is that it is something a person is born with. While it is true that some people are born with features that make it easier to develop good physical appearance, full development of this strength as an effective asset is achieved by intentional acquisition and growth of skills. In the *Scriptural Insight* section that follows, we will look at how God uses this strength, confirming that it rightfully should be considered a physical strength. Models and actors are good examples of people with strengths in physical appearance.

As we have pointed out with each category in the domain of physical strengths, contrary to popular opinion, few people excel in this domain by pure giftedness alone. For the most part people have to work hard, even when they are gifted, developing their giftedness through knowledge acquisition and skills improvement.

Here is another observation we can make. Most cultures in our modern society place greater value on physical strengths than the other domains. As a result, we end up with a culture obsessed with performance and appearance. This often leads to feelings of inferiority and self-doubt in individuals who do not find their greatest distinction in this strengths domain. Our society has done a poor job in dealing with this problem, and what has resulted is considerable confusion in the discovery of a Life Calling for those who struggle with this problem. This is why we believe it is so important to look at strengths across all five domains without omitting the exploration of any of the strengths or their elements.

How do we identify physical strengths in our lives? Once they have been developed, it is usually not hard to recognize them. The more elusive aspect may be in identifying potential in the physical strengths domain. One effective way this takes place is by listening to what others who know us say about us. Another way is to complete exercises and assessments that test our physical abilities in a variety of areas. We will look closer at some examples of how to do this in the activities associated with this chapter.

SCRIPTURAL INSIGHT ——————————————————

There are definitely endeavors in life that require certain physical strengths. Those who are gifted in this area will find more success than those who are not. It is a fact of life, and as such, should be used in evaluating where to maximize our strengths in pursuit of our Life Calling. No matter what the level of our physical strengths, however, we should use whatever we are given as an entrustment from God and use it to his glory. The following insights from the Bible help to illustrate this.

Insight 1 // It Makes a Difference When You Are Skilled

Then the LORD said to Moses, "See, I have chosen Bezalel son of Uri, the son of Hur, of the tribe of Judah, and I have filled him with the Spirit of God, with wisdom, with understanding, with knowledge and with all kinds of skills—to make artistic designs for work in gold, silver and bronze, to cut and set stones, to work in wood, and to engage in all kinds of crafts. Moreover, I have appointed Oholiab son of Ahisamak, of the tribe of Dan, to help him. Also I have given ability to all the skilled workers to make everything I have commanded you." EXODUS 31:1-6

The first of the strengths listed in the Strengths Matrix is physical strength. God gives to us and appreciates physical strengths. Consider the example given in Exodus 31.

The example is a man named Bezalel. During the long journey of the Israelites from Egypt to Canaan, known as the Exodus, God directed Moses to build a tabernacle. God further directed Moses to employ a person with needed physical strengths to oversee the project and a team of physically gifted people to help him.

Bazalel, along with his colleagues Oholiab and Ahisamak, had physical strengths in the area of craftsmanship. According to the passage, these physical strengths had been developed across the matrix—ability (gifts), knowledge, skill and disposition. In other words, "these guys were good!" A key concept from this conversation between God and Moses is that these physical strengths were a gift of God. We should never see our strengths as anything other than entrustments of God, and we should be diligent stewards over them.

A second concept is that these physical strengths were enhanced by the fact that God also filled Bazalel with the Spirit of God. The danger of physical strengths is that we begin to view them as our own doing and forget whom they came from or that we need God's Spirit to effectively empower them. We need to remember Paul's words in 1 Corinthians 6:19 that our bodies are temples of the Holy Spirit.

Have you ever noticed the difference between an athlete, actor, speaker, or musician who is obviously sold on him- or herself, and the athlete, actor, speaker, or musician who gives the credit to God? The difference is pretty obvious, and those sold on themselves are not very appealing. This is not to say that we do not need to work hard at developing our physical strengths. There are some people who think they can just pray to God and physical skills will develop miraculously. This doesn't work nor has it ever been God's plan. Just like we saw in the Parable of the Talents, God gives us gifts, but he then expects us to put forth effort to develop them to the fullest.

> **PERSONAL REFLECTION**
> Do you view your physical strengths as building blocks in God's temple? How are you using them to pursue your search for a Life Calling?

Insight 2 // Beauty is Better When it is More Than Skin-deep

Then the king's personal attendants proposed, "Let a search be made for beautiful young virgins for the king. Let the king appoint commissioners in every province of his realm to bring all these beautiful young women into the harem at the citadel of Susa. Let them be placed under the care of Hegai, the king's eunuch, who is in charge of the women; and let beauty treatments be given to them. Then let the young woman who pleases the king be queen instead of Vashti." This advice appealed to the king, and he followed it. Now there was in the citadel of Susa a Jew of the tribe of Benjamin, named Mordecai son of Jair, the son of Shimei, the son of Kish, who had been carried into exile from Jerusalem by Nebuchadnezzar king of Babylon, among those taken captive with Jehoiachin king of Judah. Mordecai had a cousin named Hadassah, whom he had brought up because she had neither father nor mother. This young woman, who was also known as Esther, had a lovely figure and was beautiful. Mordecai had taken her as his own daughter when her father and mother died.

When the king's order and edict had been proclaimed, many young women were brought to the citadel of Susa and put under the care of Hegai. Esther also was taken to the king's palace and entrusted to Hegai, who had charge of the harem. She pleased him and won his favor. Immediately he provided her with her beauty treatments and special food. He assigned to her seven female attendants selected from the king's palace and moved her and her attendants into the best place in the harem. ESTHER 2:2-9

This example of physical strength is a familiar character, Esther. Esther lived in the empire formed of the countries of Persia and Media. She was a young woman of Jewish decent living in Susa, the capital. The Jews had been taken as captives by the Persian Empire after the Persian conquest of the Babylonians who had first taken the Jews captive in their conquest of Israel. The king of Persia, Xerxes, had divorced his queen because she would not give in to his senseless, chauvinistic demands, and he was in the market for a new queen. He decided to choose a new queen by staging a beauty contest. Now God decided to use this opportunity to set things up for a later deliverance of the Jews from the sinister plots of a Persian named Haman. To do this, God needed someone who could win the contest. Here is where Esther enters the scene as described in the scripture passage for today.

Several points concerning physical strengths emerge from this story. First of all, Esther "had a lovely figure and was beautiful." Basically that means Esther was well-built and physically attractive. She probably would have been a supermodel if she lived in our time and culture. But Esther did not rely on her good looks alone; instead she did all she could to develop and enhance them. She got on the good side of Hegai, the eunuch in charge of all the young ladies, and they developed a regimen of beauty treatments and diet to make her a winner. She worked across the matrix to develop her knowledge and skills in the area of her physical strength of beauty.

The outcome of this story is well-known. Esther became queen by nature of her beauty. She was then able to use this position to plead with the king to spare the lives of the Jews who had come under an extermination sentence by the trickery of the evil Haman (who, incidentally, lost his life because of his tricks). To this day Jews celebrate Purim as one of the most joyous and fun holidays on the Jewish calendar. It commemorates this story of Esther, made possible in part by her physical strength of beauty.

You might be tempted, like me, to say that's great for Esther and others who have beauty like that. But what about plain old me? That takes us back to the Parable of the Talents. God determines what is best for us according to our capacity. This may not be an area in which we have capacity—I know in my case it is not! God does not expect us to do something like Esther did if we don't have beauty as one of those "bags of gold." If we do, however, he expects us to develop it and use it to his glory according to his plan.

> **PERSONAL REFLECTION**
>
> Do you have a hard time accepting your physical appearance?
> How can you start to see this as part of God's purpose in your
> life? If physical appearance is one of your strengths, how can you
> make sure you use this to God's glory?

Insight 3 // We Can Learn from a Person with the Complete Physical Package

I have seen a son of Jesse of Bethlehem who knows how to play the harp. He is a brave man and a warrior. He speaks well and is a fine-looking man. And the LORD is with him. 1 SAMUEL 16:18

Our third example of physical strengths comes from the life of the most beloved king of Israel, David. We pick up the story in 1 Samuel 16 where we find the current king of Israel, Saul, deserted by the Spirit of the Lord and now fighting what was referred to as an evil spirit. This may have been a serious mental disorder. Whatever it was, it caused rage in Saul and fear in the heart of his attendants, so they wanted to get him some help. In verse 16 they advised Saul, "Let our Lord command his servants here to search for someone who can play the harp. He will play when the evil spirit...comes upon you, and you will feel better."

Saul agrees that this is a good plan and instructs the attendants to find such a person—someone with the physical strength of musical ability. No sooner was it said when, according to verse 18, one of the servants answered, "I have seen a son of Jesse of Bethlehem who knows how to play the harp. He is a brave man and a warrior. He speaks well and is a fine-looking man. And the LORD is with him."

Here was a comprehensive package of physical strengths: musical strengths, athletic strengths (warrior), oratory skills (speaks well), and good looks. Wow! It doesn't seem quite fair, does it? But the best part of that package for David was that the Lord was with him. David's athletic and warrior strengths came into play later in his confrontation with the giant Goliath recorded in 1 Samuel 17:34-50.

David said to Saul, "Your servant has been keeping his father's sheep. When a lion or a bear came and carried off a sheep from the flock, I went after it, struck it and rescued the sheep from its mouth. When it turned on me, I seized it by its hair, struck it and killed it. Your servant has killed both the lion and the bear; this uncircumcised Philistine [Goliath] will be like one of them, because he has defied the armies of the living God. The LORD who delivered me from the paw of the lion and the paw of the bear will deliver me from the hand of this Philistine." Saul said to David, "Go, and the LORD be with you…"

As the Philistine moved closer to attack him, David ran quickly toward the battle line to meet him. Reaching into his bag and taking out a stone, he slung it and struck the Philistine on the forehead. The stone sank into his forehead, and he fell face-down on the ground.

So David triumphed over the Philistine with a sling and a stone; without a sword in his hand he struck down the Philistine and killed him.

This famous victory would not have been possible if it had not been for David's physical strengths honed to perfection by years of practice as a shepherd. When we are willing to let him, God uses physical strengths for his glory.

PERSONAL REFLECTION

If you are physically gifted in all areas like David was, how can you keep from becoming conceited or ignoring the need for or value in the other domains of strengths? How can you make sure you use this to God's glory?

PRODUCING THE POWER OF PURPOSE ————

How do physical strengths help produce the power of purpose in our lives? To a great a great extent, the answer to this question is very similar to the one given in Chapter 5 in relationship to strengths in general. In this case it has a specific focus related to physical attributes.

God created us with an intricate design in a fearful and wonderful manner that was part of his intent before we ever came into being. This includes the physical features of our bodies. As this intricate design unfolds in our lives and our physical features are developed, an important element of our Life Calling is revealed. Working in harmony with our physicals strengths will enhance the power of purpose in our lives. Thus, discovering these physical strengths is a critically important step in determining what our purpose and calling are.

CHAPTER SUMMARY ————————

Physical strengths are much more than brute strength or strong muscles. They also include artistry, music, mechanics, craftsmanship, oratory, kinesthetics, and physical appearance. Taking time to look over this broad spectrum and examine which are stronger in our lives can help us avoid discounting this area of strength in general too quickly.

Each of the strengths domains provides a synergism among the other dimensions. Physical strengths provide the dynamic of implementation among the other strengths. What do we mean by this? It is through our bodily actions that we actually carry out ideas and initiatives that are generated by the other strengths domains.

INTERACTING WITH YOUR LIFE CALLING ─────

This is your opportunity to interact with the Life Calling concepts introduced in this chapter and develop habits that will help you implement the concepts into your life.

The list below outlines the activities related to this chapter you will find in the *Life Calling Activities Supplement*. Access the supplement and find these activities listed. Then follow the instructions that will be given there.

1. **Activity 6.1** *Your Physical Strengths Inventory.* In this activity you will explore the eight categories of spiritual strength and assess each of these in your own life.

2. **Activity 6.2** *Expanding Your Understanding of Your Physical Strengths Using the Physical Strengths 360.* This activity will enable you to engage people all around you who know you well and have them give input into your understanding of your unique physical strengths.

3. **Activity 6.3** *Physical Strengths and Your Life Map.* Over these next few chapters you will have the opportunity to reflect on the various elements that help make you the unique person you are. You will collect these observations to use in constructing your life map in chapter 12.

As always, make sure you save all of these activities in a safe place that is easily accessed as you continue through the rest of this book, because you will want to revisit them as you look at other concepts and activities.

REFERENCES

The following resources may be useful to you in your continuing exploration of Life Calling as you look at your *Unique Design* and your physical strengths.

Millard, B. (1996). *LifeQuest: Planning your life strategically*. Ventura, CA: Life Discovery Publications.

Schwen, M. R., & Bass, D. C. (Eds.). (2006). *Leading lives that matter: What we should do and who we should be*. Grand Rapids, Michigan: Erdmans Publishing Co.

CHAPTER
// 7

STRENGTHS
EMOTIONAL

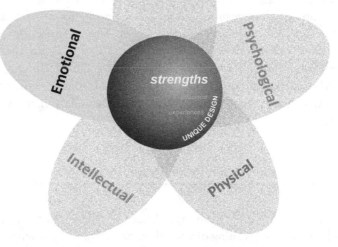

Figure 7.1 // Emotional Domain of the Strengths

In looking at strengths, we will consider five domains. In this chapter
we will explore **emotional strengths**.

EMOTIONAL STRENGTHS: EXPLORING THE ASSETS OF YOUR FEELINGS

> *It is very important to understand that emotional intelligence is not the opposite of intelligence, it is not the triumph of heart over head—it is the unique intersection of both.*
>
> David Caruso

Emotional strengths are those assets in our lives that emerge from an affective state of consciousness that enables us to be aware of and experience feelings like happiness, sadness, anger, fear, surprise, or disgust. In the culture that many of us live, objectivity and logic dominate our decision-making processes, and we mistakenly see these feelings as weaknesses rather than strengths. When we take this restrictive view, we leave ourselves with an incomplete set of data and often end up making wrong decisions.

WORDLIST

Words often have multiple meanings. Effective communication requires that we know which meaning of a word we are employing when we use it in our discussion. The following words need that clarification.

Domain an area or range of personal distinctness characterized by specific qualities

Emotion	that part of the consciousness that involves feeling and the capacity to detect and respond to sensory stimuli
Emotional Strengths	the capacity of our lives that enables us to correctly experience and use feelings and sensibility
Environment	the totality of surrounding things, conditions, or influences
Feeling	non-rational, internal sensation not connected with sight, hearing, taste, smell, or what is classically correlated to touch
Sensibility	responsiveness or susceptibility to sensory stimuli
Strengths	qualities or features that bring power, force, vigor, or sustenance

DESCRIPTION

What are the most important and significant experiences you will have during this year? If you start to list them in your mind, you will find that they will likely be full of emotion. You may start a new job and feel both excitement and apprehension. You may get your first "A" in school and feel pride and satisfaction. You may make a new friend and gain a real sense of belonging. You may give your first speech to a large audience and feel nervous. You may try out for the local theater, and if you don't get the role, you may feel depressed or angry at what you see as rejection. Whether they are positive, negative, or neutral, emotions play an important role in our lives because they alert us to something important in ourselves or our environment.

Successfully navigating the various aspects of our lives will call into play our ability to effectively work with our emotions, and this takes us to the concept of *emotional strengths*. We defined the *emotional strengths* domain as the capacity in our lives that enables us to experience feelings and sensibility. What do we mean by these terms? When we talk about our feelings, we are describing an experiential state that builds within us in response to sensations, sentiments, or desires we encounter. Sensibility refers to our responsiveness toward other things or persons, such as the feelings of another person or changes in the environment.

If we were to collect all the words in the English language that express our emotions, they would probably number in the hundreds. The paradox, however, is that with all those words, we still have great difficulty describing our emotional experiences to others. Why is that? Perhaps it stems from the view of emotions throughout the history of Western civilization. Emotions have, for the most part, been seen as a disruption to rational thinking and a hindrance to making good decisions. But now that view is changing.

John Mayer, a psychologist at the University of New Hampshire, and Peter Salovey, a psychologist at Yale University (currently Dean of Yale College), proposed the concept of emotional intelligence, defining it as "the ability to monitor one's own and others' feelings and emotions, to discriminate among them, and to use this information to guide one's thinking and action" (Mayer & Salovey, 1993. p. 433). Mayer and Salovey have been joined by another psychologist, David Caruso, in systematizing the study of emotional intelligence and developing a tool for measuring it (*Mayer-Salovey-Caruso Emotional Intelligence Test*, or *MS-CEIT*, 2002). Daniel Goleman (1995), a journalist specializing in the area of the brain and psychology, worked from the writings of Mayer and Salovey to popularize the concept of emotional intelligence in his international bestseller, *Emotional Intelligence*.

Rather than seeing emotions as some sort of a primitive aberration in people that leads them to make mistakes and experience regrets, the findings show "that emotion is not just important but absolutely necessary for us to make good decisions, take optimal action to solve problems, cope with change, and succeed" (Caruso & Salovey, 2004, p. ix). It is not hard to see, then, that emotional strengths play an important part in the discovery of a Life Calling. The basis for emotional intelligence is made up of four skills or strengths:

1.   **Identify and Express Emotions.** This is the fundamental ability to recognize feelings and emotions by (a) being aware of emotional clues in yourself and in people around you, (b) being able to discern between different types of emotion, (c) being able to identify the level of intensity to which the emotion is present, and (d) being able to identify what these emotional clues mean.

     This ability makes us better pilots of our lives because we have a surer sense of how we really feel about personal decisions from whom to marry to what job to take. We are also tuned in to the emotions of others and as a result have healthier and stronger relationships.

2. **Use or Generate Emotions.** This is the ability to know which emotions or moods are best for different situations and to get us into the "right mood."

    This ability enables us to employ our feelings to enhance our thinking and endeavors. We realize that emotions, when rightly used, can help us solve problems, make better decisions, reason out situations, and be more creative. We will be more self-motivated and will prioritize our thinking process based on emotional input.

3. **Understand Emotions.** This is the ability to recognize and grasp emotional information. This starts by gaining an emotional vocabulary—knowledge of simple and complex emotional terms. It then adds emotional comprehension—understanding how emotions combine to form another emotion, progress or intensify, or transition from one emotion to another. Finally, emotional analysis occurs—being able to understand possible causes of emotions and predict what kinds of emotions people will have in different situations.

    This ability gives us a solid grasp of emotional intelligence. We will tend to be more accurate in our interpretation of moods and emotional situations, and as a result will be more likely to deal correctly with such situations.

4. **Manage Emotions.** This is the ability to regulate emotions within us and in other people. This involves monitoring, observing and distinguishing differences, and accurately labeling emotions as they are encountered. This ability is based on the belief that feelings and moods can be improved or modified, with strategies being developed to accomplish this. This does not mean, however, the denial or suppression of our emotions or the emotions of others.

    This ability gives us the capacity to bounce back quickly from life's setbacks and upsets. We will be able to assess the effectiveness of how we recognize and handle emotions in various situations.

If it is true that emotions are not just important but absolutely necessary for us to make good decisions, then emotional strength is clearly necessary for discovering our Life Calling. That being the case, everyone needs to develop some competency in this domain. Figure 7.2 illustrates a blueprint that can guide development in emotional intelligence.

The progression of these emotional abilities from 1 to 4 move from what are relatively less complex to those that are more developmentally complex (Mayer, Salovey, & Caruso, 2008).

A Blueprint for Emotions

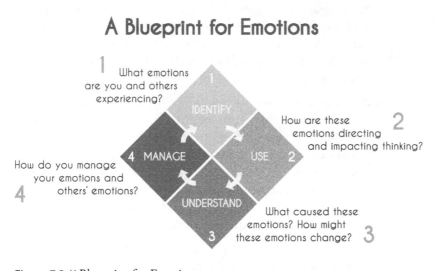

Figure 7.2 // Blueprint for Emotions
© Copyright 2006, EI Skills Group. Used by permission.

So from a strengths perspective, it is likely that some will have greater strength in more complex abilities than others. This can be valuable insight in discerning our Life Calling, just as much as is discovering that we are more adept at musical strengths than brute force in the domain of physical strengths. However, the elements of emotional strengths are not as easily separated as in some of the other strengths domains. As a result, if we return to the car illustration in Chapter 5, this is an area of strengths where it is vital to drive the car at least to the middle zone and eliminate the weaknesses that can lead to decline. While we may not excel at the most complex levels of understanding emotions, we need to be able to function at a fundamental level that will allow us to effectively relate to others and carry out our Life Calling.

SCRIPTURAL INSIGHT

When the Bible addresses emotions, it most often uses the heart to identify the source of these emotions. Scriptures associated with the role of emotions provide valuable insight related to how these can affect our pursuit of a Life Calling.

Insight 1 // Who Do You See When You Look in the Mirror?

If any of you think you are something when you are nothing, you deceive yourselves. Each of you should test your own actions. Then you can take pride in yourself, without comparing yourself to somebody else, for each of you should carry your own load. GALATIANS 6:3-5

Have you ever been around people who have a very unrealistic view of themselves? Sometimes it is seen in a very negative self-image, but many times it manifests itself in an image that is something quite a bit better than is warranted.

Consider the giant Goliath as an example. He had convinced himself that he was invincible. He failed to realize that adeptness was as important as size in combat. When he saw David (who, if you remember, was rather physically fit himself) come out to meet him, he ridiculed him. "'Am I a dog, that you come at me with sticks?' And the Philistine cursed David by his gods. 'Come here,' he said, 'and I'll give your flesh to the birds and the wild animals!'" (1 Samuel 17:43-44). Of course, you know the end of this story. David defeated Goliath.

Such a distorted view of self can hinder the discovery of a Life Calling. That's why the Apostle Paul was constantly exhorting those whom he taught to strive toward a more effective Christian life. He had a keen insight into the human condition, and that's why he cautioned in the passage in Galatians 6 that we need to have a realistic view of ourselves.

We need to take caution that we don't misread what Paul counseled in this passage. He is not saying that we should think of ourselves as nothing, in the sense of being worthless. Instead, he is concerned about people who do not have good self-awareness. They either see themselves in a manner no one else does, or they fail to see themselves in a manner in which nearly everyone else does. In either case they lack self-awareness. The emotional strength Paul encourages is for each of us to look inside of ourselves and test ourselves so that we know who we are. He cautions not to try to be somebody else, but to know ourselves and to be ourselves. That is what he means by carrying our own load.

In the search for a Life Calling, those who have this emotional strength will find the search easier. They will avoid the confusion caused by copying someone else's self-identity rather than living their own identity.

> **PERSONAL REFLECTION**
>
> Who do you see when you look in the mirror? Have you learned to see yourself with a healthy reality and praise God for who you are? What can help you have better self-image?

Insight 2 // Learn To Know in Your Spirit as Well as Your Mind

Immediately Jesus knew in his spirit that this was what they were thinking in their hearts... MARK 2:8

For most of his years of ministry, Jesus lived in the town of Capernaum. One day when he was at the home where he stayed, some men brought a friend of theirs who was paralyzed to Jesus so that he could heal the man. There was such a crowd around Jesus that they could not get to him. Just a few months prior to writing this section of the book, I stood in the ruins of that house. It was not very big, so if a crowd was around Jesus, it would have been impossible to get a man on a stretcher through to Jesus. The friends were not deterred, however. They climbed to the roof, likely made of palm branches and mud, and made an opening through which they lowered their friend. We pick up the story in Mark 2:5-12.

When Jesus saw their faith, he said to the paralyzed man, "Son, your sins are forgiven."

Now some teachers of the law were sitting there, thinking to themselves, "Why does this fellow talk like that? He's blaspheming! Who can forgive sins but God alone?"

Immediately Jesus knew in his spirit that this was what they were thinking in their hearts, and he said to them, "Why are you thinking these things? Which is easier: to say to this paralyzed man, 'Your sins are forgiven,' or to say, 'Get up, take your mat and walk'? But I want you to know that the Son of Man has authority on earth to forgive sins." So he said to the man, "I tell you, get up, take your mat and go home." He got up, took his mat and walked out in full view of them all. This amazed everyone and they praised God, saying, "We have never seen anything like this!"

In our study of emotional strengths, the key phrase in this story is, "Immediately Jesus knew in his spirit that this was what they were thinking in their hearts." The mistake on our part would be to think that only Jesus could know this. As we learn to listen to the emotions of others more closely, we will find that we can develop the ability to recognize them even without any words being spoken.

Consider the example of King Artaxerxes and Nehemiah. Nehemiah was troubled about his fellow Jews in Jerusalem, and when he came before the king, Artaxerxes could recognize this. He asked Nehemiah, "Why does your face look so sad when you are not ill? This can be nothing but sadness of heart" (Nehemiah 2:2). This emotional sensitivity by the king led to a great initiative for the Jews leading to the rebuilding of Jerusalem.

Because of how each person is "wired" internally, this is an emotional strength that is easier for some and more difficult for others. However, it is something all of us can learn to do at some level. Because our Life Calling is directly tied to service to others, we can be far more effective at discovering our purpose and carrying it out when we can recognize the emotions of others.

PERSONAL REFLECTION

Do you take time to read the emotions of others, or do you just plunge on ahead in your life regardless of what is happening with others? What can you do to strengthen your ability to identify the emotions of others and to value them?

PRODUCING THE POWER OF PURPOSE

How do emotional strengths help produce the power of purpose in our lives? Once again, the answer to this question is very similar to the one given in Chapter 5 in relationship to strengths in general. God created us with an intricate design in a fearful and wonderful manner that was part of his intent before we ever came into being. Applying this specifically to our emotional attributes, we will discover that this intentional, intricate design includes the emotional dynamics of our lives. As we develop our emotional strengths, we will unleash an important element of our Life Calling, and we will enhance the power of purpose in our lives. Thus, discovering these emotional strengths is a critically important step in determining what our purpose and calling are.

CHAPTER SUMMARY

Fundamental to the concept of a Life Calling is the ability to recognize our strengths and employ them to make good decisions in response to our calling. Emotions are an absolutely necessary element in helping us to make good decisions. That being the case, everyone needs to develop some competency in this domain.

Ironically, emotional strengths may be confused in our modern society with weakness, and society responds by not placing as great a value on this strengths domain. As a result, we end up with a culture where relationships are confused and people try to hide from each other. This inner turmoil often leads to feelings of inferiority and self-doubt and causes confusion in the search for a Life Calling.

Four abilities form the core of emotional strength: 1) the ability to identify and express emotions, 2) the ability to use or generate emotions, 3) the ability to understand emotions, and 4) the ability to manage emotions. Effectiveness in pursuing our Life Calling requires a base level in all four abilities. Greater ability and development in the more complex levels (3 and 4) may begin to differentiate the level of strength this domain has in our overall uniqueness.

Emotional strengths are harder to detect than physical strengths. Once again, one of the most effective ways is listening to what others who know us well say about us. Another way is to complete exercises and assessments of our emotional strengths. We will look more closely at some examples of how to do this in the activities associated with this chapter.

Remember, all of the strengths domains provide synergism among the other dimensions. Emotional strengths provide the dynamic of *feelings* among the other strengths. What do we mean by this? It is through our emotions that we actually sense and feel what is going on with the other strengths. This adds color and vitality to our lives, as well as provides valuable information that will help us understand what is going on in the other four domains.

INTERACTING WITH YOUR LIFE CALLING ——————

This is your opportunity to interact with the Life Calling concepts introduced in this chapter and develop habits that will help you implement the concepts into your life.

The list below outlines the activities related to this chapter you will find in the *Life Calling Activities Supplement*. Access the supplement and find these activities listed. Then follow the instructions that will be given there.

1. **Activity 7.1** *Exploring Your Own Emotional Intelligence.* In this activity you will explore the eight categories of spiritual strength and assess each of these in your own life.

2. **Activity 7.2** *Expanding Your Understanding of Your Emotional Abilities Using the Emotional Assessment 360.* This activity will enable you to engage people all around you who know you well and have them give input into your understanding of your unique emotional strengths.

3. **Activity 7.3** *Emotional Strengths and Your Life Map.* Over these chapters you will have the opportunity to reflect on the various elements that help make you the unique person you are. In this activity you will focus on what you have learned about your emotional strengths. You will collect these observations to use in constructing your life map in chapter 12.

As always, make sure you save all of these activities in a safe place that is easily accessed as you continue through the rest of this book, because you will want to revisit them as you look at other concepts and activities.

REFERENCES

The following resources have been used in this chapter.

Caruso, D., Kornacki, S., & Brackett, M. (2006). *Teaching emotional intelligence skills*. Stamford, CT: EI Skills Group.

Caruso, D., & Salovey, P. (2004). *The emotionally intelligent manager*. San Francisco, CA: Jossey-Bass.

Mayer, J. D., Salovey, P., & Caruso, D. (2008). *Emotional intelligence: New ability or eclectic traits*. American Psychologist, *63*(6), 503–517.

Mayer, J. D., & Salovey, P. (1993). *The intelligence of emotional intelligence*. Intelligence, *17*, 433–442.

Salovey, P., & Mayer, J. D. (1990). E*motional intelligence*. Imagination, Cognition, and Personality, *9*, 185–211.

The following resources may be useful to you in your continuing exploration of Life Calling as you look at your *Unique Design* and your emotional strengths.

Goleman, D. (1995). *Emotional intelligence: Why it can matter more than IQ*. New York: Bantam Books.

Livermore, D. (2009). *Leading with cultural intelligence: The new secret to success*. New York, NY: AMACOM.

Saccone, S. (2009). *Relational intelligence: How leaders can expand their influence through a new way of being smart*. San Francisco, CA: Jossey-Bass Publishers.

Schwen, M. R., & Bass, D. C. (Eds.). (2006). *Leading lives that matter: What we should do and who we should be*. Grand Rapids, Michigan: Erdmans Publishing Co.

STRENGTHS
INTELLECTUAL

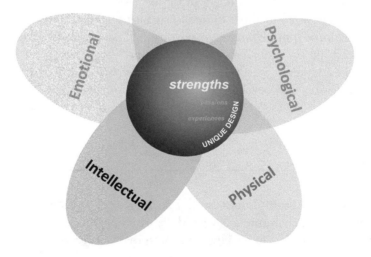

Figure 8.1 // Intellectual Domain of the Strengths

In looking at strengths, we will consider five domains. In this chapter
we will explore **intellectual strengths**.

CHAPTER 8

INTELLECTUAL STRENGTHS: EXPLORING THE ASSETS OF YOUR MIND

> *Intellectual growth should commence at birth and cease only at death.*
>
> Albert Einstein

Intellectual strengths are those assets in our lives that give us the capacity to acquire, process, and understand information. We often take too rigid of a view when it comes to intellectual capacity and development. Our educational systems tend to operate as if all people learn, or at least should learn, in the same manner. The contrary is actually the case; we learn and exercise our intellectual capacities in a broad variety of ways. Recognizing this and developing our unique approaches will lead to a much greater ability to not only acquire knowledge, but to understand it.

WORDLIST

Words often have multiple meanings. Effective communication requires that we know which meaning of a word we are employing when we use it in our discussion. The following words need that clarification.

Apply   to make use of as relevant and important to a situation or action

Discovery	observing and learning about something for the first time in one's experience
Domain	an area or range of personal distinctness characterized by specific qualities
Ever-expanding	ongoing process that is constantly making progress in a positive manner
Understand	perceive the meaning of something learned; grasp the idea of its significance; comprehend
Intellectual Strengths	the capacity of our lives that enables us to acquire knowledge and develop an ever-expanding understanding of this knowledge in a manner that produces wisdom
Intelligence	capacity for learning, reasoning, understanding, and similar forms of mental activity
Strengths	qualities or features that bring power, force, vigor, or sustenance
Wisdom	the power to discern and judge properly what is true or right or of moral value

DESCRIPTION

Probably everyone has asked themselves, "How smart am I?" In our primary and secondary school experiences, state-mandated standardized testing may have given us one answer. At the end of high school, SAT or ACT scores may have given us another answer. GPA from high school and college has given us another answer. We may have even taken IQ tests to find the answer to that question. The fact that we get different answers from these various sources might mean that they may not be the most reliable sources for answering that question. The problem is that we might be asking the wrong question. Maybe we need to focus less on "if" we are smart and more on "how" we are smart. What do we mean by that? We defined the *intellectual strengths* domain as the capacity in our lives that enables us to acquire knowledge and develop an ever-expanding understanding of this knowledge in a manner that produces wisdom. Let's examine how this takes place.

Intellectual Capacity

Throughout recent history, intellectual capacity has been correlated to what has been termed the "intelligence quotient," better known as IQ. This is determined by measuring an individual's ability to respond to visual imagery, to respond to verbal input, and to apply skills in both areas to the solution of problems. This ability is related to many different capacities. Ten of the more commonly recognized capacities are listed below:

- Verbal Capacity = the ability to read and write, remember, and think with words

- Quantitative Capacity = the ability to recognize, manipulate, comprehend, remember and think with quantitative concepts and relationships represented by numerical symbols

- Image Capacity = the ability to perceive, analyze, synthesize, re-member, and think with visual patterns

- Auditory Capacity = the ability to detect, analyze, synthesize, and discriminate auditory stimuli, especially those related to speech

- Short-term Memory = the ability to store and recall information within a few minutes

- Long-term Memory = the ability to store information and to ef-ficiently retrieve it later in the process of thinking

- Reasoning Capacity = the ability to form concepts and solve problems

- Processing Capacity = the speed with which an individual can perform automatic cognitive tasks

- Reaction Capacity = the immediacy with which an individual can react to stimuli or a task

- Informational Capacity = the amount of specific information acquired and retained by an individual

More recent studies have shown that equating intellectual strengths sole-ly to intellectual capacity is too narrow a focus. Howard Gardner (1983), who we referred to earlier in Chapter 4, has proposed the idea of multiple intelligences. In other words, people might be "intelligent" or "smart" in different ways.

A significant problem arises from these multiple intelligences. They all impact the way we perform on standardized tests, but these tests, for the most part, have been designed with a narrow focus on intellectual capacity. As a result, if a person is not wired with an intellectual capacity that closely matches that of the standardized test, the test results may characterize the person as below normal when in reality the "normal" identified in the test only exists in that test. Let's look at two areas that can have such an impact on intellectual performance.

Learning Styles

One of the primary reasons that the intellect needs to be looked at with a broader perspective is that people learn in different ways or styles. One

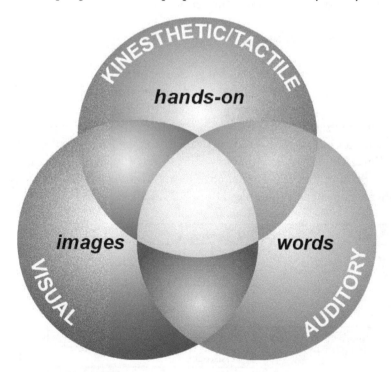

Figure 8.2 // Learning Styles

simplified approach to learning styles divides people into three primary groups of visual, auditory, or kinesthetic/tactile learners as illustrated in Figure 8.2.

- Visual learning occurs primarily through looking at images, such as pictures, diagrams, demonstrations, and body language.

- Auditory learning occurs primarily through hearing words—both spoken and written.

- Kinesthetic/Tactile learning occurs through hands-on doing and interacting.

Notice that the spheres in Figure 8.2 overlap each other. This represents the true nature of learning styles. People rarely, if ever, learn only in one style. The reality is much more a preference in learning styles. However, it is important to understand what style we prefer. This can help us approach learning and studying in a more effective manner. Later in the Activities section of this chapter we will have the opportunity to explore this more in depth and apply it to our own situation.

Learning Atmosphere

A second approach to learning that gives us distinctiveness as individuals and impacts our intellectual capacity develops around our preferred atmosphere or setting for learning. This concept suggests that each person has unique strengths and preferences across a full spectrum of physiological, sociological, psychological, emotional, and environmental elements. The interaction of these elements occurs differently in everyone and will affect the way they concentrate on, process, absorb, and retain new and difficult information (Dunn & Dunn, 1992, 1998, 1999).

Stimuli	Elements
Environmental	Sound
	Light
	Temperature
	Design
Emotional	Motivation
	Persistence
	Responsibility
	Structure

Sociological	Self, Pair, or Team
	Feedback from Authority
	Variety vs. Routine
Physical	Perceptual
	Intake
	Time
	Mobility
Psychological	Global/Analytic
	Right/Left Hemisphere
	Impulsive/Reflective

Table 8.1 // Learning Atmosphere

Knowing our own strengths and preferences in this learning atmosphere can be important to success in formal education and in life after that formal education is completed. Later in the Activities section of this chapter, we will have the opportunity to explore this more in depth and apply it to our own situation.

Intellectual Disciplines

One other area that needs to be considered in understanding intellectual strengths centers on the disciplines of the mind that help us build the ability to discover, understand, and apply truth in an ever-expanding manner. Jay Wood (1998), a philosophy professor at Wheaton College, refers to these as intellectual virtues. James Sire (2000), a professor at the University of Missouri, considers these to be habits of the mind. Assessing our strengths in these disciplines and developing them will greatly help us as we move beyond mere knowledge acquisition to the development of true wisdom.

Our definition of intellectual strengths identifies three categories of intellectual disciplines: (1) those we use to discover knowledge; (2) those we use to process the knowledge into an understanding of truth; and (3) those we use to apply the truth after we understand it. Figure 8.3 illustrates the various disciplines that lead to intellectual strengths in each of these three categories.

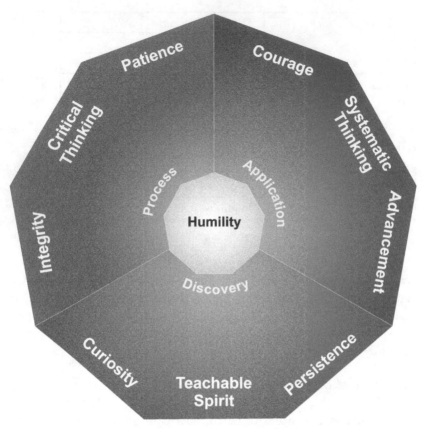

Figure 8.3 // Intellectual Disciplines

Discovery Disciplines

- Curiosity. A strong desire to learn more about something. People who are curious have an excitement for knowledge and eagerness to search for truth. They openly inquire about why things are the way they are. They truly are explorers in the galaxy of information and comprehension.

- Teachable Spirit. A willingness and eagerness to learn. People who are teachable are characterized by an absence of a "know-it-all" attitude. They are not indifferent to knowledge. They are open to diverse views and forms of knowledge.

- Persistence. A firm and steadfast, continual search for knowledge and truth. People who are persistent keep on pursuing truth despite obstacles, warnings, or setbacks. They do not give up their quest even when data is inconsistent, obscure, or seemingly nonexistent.

- Humility. Discovery humility is a modest view of one's own importance pertaining to the possession of knowledge. People who have intellectual humility always see themselves as a learner and are always willing to be taught by others.

Process Disciplines

- Integrity. The quality or condition of interpreting information collected with honesty. People who have intellectual integrity do not make data fit their preconceived ideas. Instead they collect data with an open mind and then allow this data to inform the conclusions they make.

- Critical Thinking. The mental process of actively and skillfully conceptualizing, applying, analyzing, synthesizing, and evaluating information to reach an answer or conclusion. People who think critically ask "why" questions constantly. They rarely accept things at face value.

- Patience. The capability of calmly awaiting an outcome or result even in the face of obstacles or challenges. People who are intellectually patient do not come to hasty conclusions and are not impulsive in their interpretations.

- Humility. Process humility is a modest view of one's own importance pertaining to the possession of understanding. People who have intellectual humility do not see themselves as omniscient and hold very few "truths" as absolute. To them, the search for meaning and understanding is a lifelong adventure.

Application Disciplines

- Courage. The quality of spirit that enables a person to face the unknown or new ideas without fear of implications or repercussions. People who are intellectually courageous avoid being dogmatic. They are willing to take risks in proposing new ideas or relinquishing old ideas that no longer appear to be valid.

- Systematic Thinking. The mental process of formulating concepts into an organized set of interrelated ideas or principles that can be applied to life. People who think systematically realize that knowledge and understanding are useful only if others can see how to interact with and use them.

- Advancement. The application of an understanding of knowledge to improve on what was already known. People who advance intellectually take forward steps in acquiring and understanding knowledge. Their desire is to see intellectual activity as a developmental process that leads to progress. They are not satisfied with the status quo.

- Humility. Application humility is a modest view of one's own importance pertaining to thrusting one's own understanding on others. People who have intellectual humility do not see themselves as a dogmatist whose duty it is to tell others how they should live. People with intellectual humility instead see their role as inspiring others to join the journey of discovering, understanding, and applying truth.

SCRIPTURAL INSIGHT

The Bible promises that we can have perfect peace in our lives if we have minds that are steadfast and that this steadfastness comes from trust in God (see Isaiah 26:3). Scripture also provides insight on how we can develop the strength of mind.

Insight 1 // Strong Minds Are a Gift from God

To these four young men God gave knowledge and understanding of all kinds of literature and learning. And Daniel could understand visions and dreams of all kinds. DANIEL 1:17

Do you ever look at other people and wonder how they can know so much? They always seem to have the right answers. A few years ago on the television game show *Jeopardy*, a show that in part tests a person's accumulation of information, there was a contestant named Ken Jennings who won seventy-four games in a row—by far, a record. Everyone wondered how he could have so much information in his mind.

Intellectual strength, of course, is more than the accumulation of information. It is the capacity of our lives that enables us to discover, understand and apply truth in an ever-expanding manner. Daniel and his three companions were a good example of this. When Babylon's King Nebuchadnezzar put these four to the test, Daniel 1:20 records that, "in every matter of wisdom and understanding about which the king questioned them, he found them ten times better than all the magicians and enchanters in his whole kingdom." I think we can all admit—that's pretty good. We'd all be happy with half that level. Notice, though, in the original verse at the beginning of this devotion that at least some element of this was a gift from God.

There is a gift factor to strengths and this applies to intellectual strengths, as well as the others. There is a component in our intellects that comes as a gift from God in the unique design of our lives. We can describe it as heredity or whatever else we want to call it, but it is in us because of the overall design of the human race. We can complain that we were not given enough, but that really takes us back to the Parable of the Talents in Chapter 5. God gives us gifts each according to our capacity. And then it's a matter of what we do with what we have been given.

An interesting observation in life is that people who have the greatest mental capacity based on their gifts do not always end up with the greatest level of wisdom or practical understanding. In speaking of spiritual wisdom, Jesus said, "I praise you, Father, Lord of heaven and earth, because you have hidden these things from the wise and learned, and revealed them to little children" (Matthew 11:25).

PERSONAL REFLECTION

Are you using the intellectual strength that God has given you to its fullest potential? How are you using your mind to pursue your Life Calling?

Insight 2 // Intellectual Strength Begins with Trust

Trust in the LORD with all your heart and lean not on your own understanding; in all your ways acknowledge him, and he will make your paths straight. Do not be wise in your own eyes; fear the LORD and shun evil. This will bring health to your body and nourishment to your bones.
PROVERBS 3:5-8

Proverbs 3:13-14 informs us of the value that occurs when we go beyond knowledge to understanding: "Blessed are those who find wisdom, those who gain understanding, for she is more profitable than silver and yields better returns than gold." Fortunately scripture also helps us to find out how to get the proper understanding to go along with the knowledge we collect. Proverbs 1:7 says, "The fear of the LORD is the beginning of knowledge, but fools despise wisdom and discipline." When we add to this the passage for today's devotions from Proverbs 3:5-8, we can begin to see the proper context for building intellectual strengths.

First of all, this does not mean that we should not try to understand things on our own. It does not mean that we should turn off our minds. It means that we should begin our search for knowledge with the fear of the Lord. This means that we acknowledge God as the source of all knowledge and wisdom and look to him to inspire our understanding.

Second of all, when we acknowledge the Lord in all our ways, he will make our paths straight. This goes back to that foundational value of faith we looked at earlier in our study. If we hope to find that straight path which is our Life Calling, we need to start by acknowledging that it comes from God, not our own cleverness.

Third of all, intellectual strength built upon our own estimate of ourselves is no real strength at all. True intellectual strength is built upon a rightful estimate of God and the role he plays in our minds.

Last of all, intellectual strength based on a relationship of trust in God builds physical strength as well. The body and the mind are connected.

> **PERSONAL REFLECTION**
> Does your knowledge begin with trust in God or trust in yourself? How can you increase your trust in God as the starting point for building your intellectual strength?

PRODUCING THE POWER OF PURPOSE ————

How do intellectual strengths help produce the power of purpose in our lives? We continue to emphasize that the answer to this question is very similar to the one given in Chapter 5 in relationship to strengths in general. God created us with an intricate design in a fearful and wonderful manner that was part of his intent before we ever came into being. Applying this specifically to our intellectual makeup, we will discover that this intentional intricate design includes the intellectual dynamics of our lives. Of course we apply intellectual disciplines to develop our unique intellectual design. As we do this, we will open up a much greater understanding of our Life Calling, and we will enhance the power of purpose in our lives. Thus, discovering our intellectual strengths is a critically important step in determining what our purpose and calling are.

CHAPTER SUMMARY ————————————

For the most part, when people talk about intellectual strengths, they are referring primarily to IQ. As a result of this, we end up with a culture where people may think they are smart when they really aren't. This confusion often leads to feelings of inferiority and self-doubt related to IQ and causes uncertainty in the search for a Life Calling.

From our discussion we see that true intellectual strengths are affected by our learning style and our preferred learning atmosphere. Further, we found that if we want to grow our intellectual strengths to a level of wisdom, we need to develop disciplines that encompass a far greater spectrum than just IQ. The confused view of society, in regard to intellect and the complexity of our intellect, makes it a challenge to our strengths makeup in this domain. Again, one of the most effective ways is listening to what others who know us well say about us. We will also look at another way to explore intellectual strengths in the Activities section.

Remember, each of the strengths dimensions provides a synergism among the other dimensions. Intellectual strengths provide the dynamic of wisdom among the other strengths. What do we mean by this? It is through our intellect that we learn about what is going on with the other strengths and seek to understand them. Our intellectual strengths add the knowledge and understanding required to live our lives.

INTERACTING WITH YOUR LIFE CALLING ———

This is your opportunity to interact with the Life Calling concepts introduced in this chapter and develop habits that will help you implement the concepts into your life.

The list below outlines the activities related to this chapter you will find in the *Life Calling Activities Supplement*. Access the supplement and find these activities listed. Then follow the instructions that will be given there.

1. **Activity 8.1** *Learning Styles Inventory.* In this activity you will explore three basic styles of learning and assess how strong each of these is in your own life.

2. **Activity 8.2** *Expanding Your Understanding of Your Learning Styles Using the Learning Styles 360.* This activity will enable you to engage people all around you who know you well and have them give input into your understanding of your unique intellectual strengths.

3. **Activity 8.3** *Intellectual Strengths and Your Life Map.* Over these chapters you will have the opportunity to reflect on the various elements that help make you the unique person you are. In this activity you will focus on what you have learned about your intellectual strengths. You will collect these observations to use in constructing your life map in chapter 12.

As always, make sure you save all of these activities in a safe place that is easily accessed as you continue through the rest of this book, because you will want to revisit them as you look at other concepts and activities.

REFERENCES ——————————————————————

The following resources have been used in this chapter.

Millard, B. (2006). *Explorer's guide to life calling*. Marion, Indiana: Center for Life Calling and Leadership.

Sire, J. W. (2000). *Habits of the mind*. Downers Grove, Illinois: InterVarsityPress.

Wood, J. W. (1998). *Epistemology: Becoming intellectually virtuous*. Downers Grove, Illinois: InterVarsityPress.

———————————————————————————————

The following resources may be useful to you in your continuing exploration of Life Calling as you look at your *Unique Design* and your intellectual strengths.

Schwen, M. R., & Bass, D. C. (Eds.). (2006). *Leading lives that matter: What we should do and who we should be*. Grand Rapids, Michigan: Erdmans Publishing Co.

STRENGTHS
PSYCHOLOGICAL

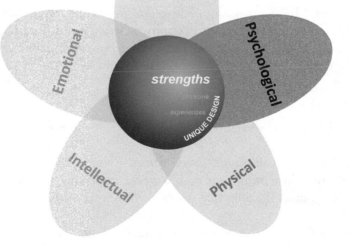

Figure 9.1 // Psychological Domain of the Strengths

In looking at strengths, we will consider five domains. In this chapter we will explore **psychological strengths**.

CHAPTER 9

PSYCHOLOGICAL STRENGTHS: EXPLORING THE ASSETS OF YOUR WILL

> *The meeting of two personalities is like the contact of two chemical substances; if there is any reaction, both are transformed.*
>
> Carl Jung

Psychological strengths are those assets in our lives that relate more to our personalities. These personality traits often impact the way we exercise the other four strengths domains in our lives. Recognizing our personality preferences enables us to be more effective in how we exercise our wills in making choices and coming to decisions for our lives.

WORDLIST

Words often have multiple meanings. Effective communication requires that we know which meaning of a word we are employing when we use it in our discussion. The following words need that clarification.

Decision	the act of or need for making up one's mind
Domain	an area or range of personal distinctness characterized by specific qualities
Information	important or useful knowledge or facts obtained in some manner as input from some source

Preference	feel more comfortable with, select, give priority to, or hold above other choices or things in estimation
Process	a continuous, systematic series of actions taking place in a definite manner directed to some end
Psychological Strengths	the capacity of our lives that enables us to exercise our will in deciding on courses of action
Psychology	the science of the mind or of mental states and processes
Strengths	qualities or features that bring power, force, vigor, or sustenance
Will	higher nature in human beings that enables them to reason critically and make moral judgments

DESCRIPTION

From the time we were old enough to think (which is pretty early), our entire life experience has been a constant process of making choices. In childhood these choices include what toys to play with, in high school it may be who to hang out with or date, and in college it includes what classes to take, when to take them, and whether or not to go to class or buy the books for the class. After college it includes what job to pursue, whether or not to get married, where to live, when and what to eat, whether to go to church and where, and the list goes on and on. This can often produce a great deal of anxiety and concern for people who ask themselves, "How can I make the best decisions when confronted by these choices?" Understanding *psychological strengths* can help us begin to answer this question because this can help us see how we make decisions.

The general study of psychology examines the science that deals with all mental processes and behavior. Often emotional behavior is included in this. However, in our study of strengths, we have chosen to consider emotional strengths as a separate category. As a result of this, in looking at psychological strengths, we have chosen to define a narrower spectrum of mental processes and behavior and have defined the psychological strengths domain for this study as the capacity in our lives that enables us to exercise our will in deciding on courses of action. What does "exercise our will" mean? The term *will* used here refers to the higher nature in human beings that enables them to reason critically and make moral judgments—that is, deciding what is right and wrong based on our value system.

Psychologists are behavioral scientists who study our mental processes and behavior trying to figure out how they work. One of these psychologists, Carl Jung (1971), outlined a simplified theory. He proposed that this psychological process, as we have narrowly defined it, functions primarily with two activities: first, we take in information, and second, we evaluate the information and come to conclusions. Observations of this psychological process indicate that when our minds are active, we are involved with one or the other of these activities (Figure 9.2).

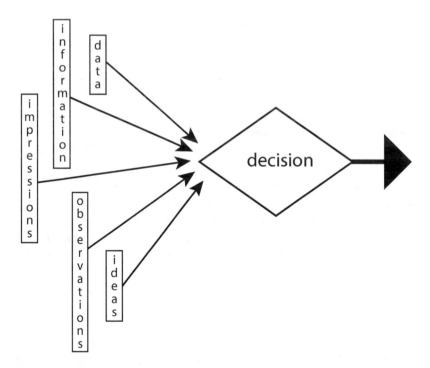

Figure 9.2 // Psychological Process

When we approach these activities, we tend to come at them in different ways. Observations show that these differences can be determined along a scale measuring preference toward two end values. It is important to note, however, that both ways of taking in information are used by everyone, but one is usually preferred, and as a result, we feel more comfortable in activities associated with that preference and will develop it in our own lives more effectively. This can be an important concept to understand for students in any school setting because it has a definite impact on how they learn and how they will make judgments concerning what they learn.

Gathering Information

The first of the two scales measures our preferences in how we take in information in the process of deciding on courses of action. This intake of information is a process called "perceiving." Figure 9.3 illustrates that we have a preference in how we perceive. Some people have a perceiving preference that relies primarily on the process of observing facts or events through one or more of the five senses. Not surprisingly, this preference is referred to as *sensing*. Other people have a perceiving preference that relies primarily on the less obvious process of observing meanings, relationships, and possibilities in an instinctive manner that operates beyond the normal mechanics of the conscious mind. This preference is referred to as *intuition*.

The first of the two scales measures our preferences in how we take in information in the process of deciding on courses of action. This intake of information is a process called "perceiving." Figure 9.3 illustrates that we have a preference in how we perceive. Some people have a perceiving preference that relies primarily on a process of observing discrete facts or events through one or more of the five senses. Not surprisingly, this preference is referred to as *sensing*. Other people have a perceiving prefer-

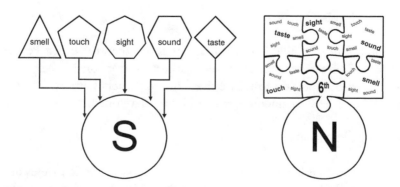

Figure 9.3 // How Do We Prefer to Take In Information?

ence that relies primarily on a less obvious process of observing meanings, relationships, and possibilities that instinctively combines sensory information in an interactive, puzzle-like manner that operates beyond the normal mechanics of the conscious mind. This is sometimes referred to as a sixth sense. This preference is referred to as *intuition*.

Our distinct preferences in the way we handle information operate quite differently for sensing or intuition. Table 9.1 outlines some of these distinctions.

Sensing	Intuition
See information in specific parts and pieces	See information in patterns and relationships
Concentrate on information related to the present, enjoying what is there	Concentrate on information related to the future, anticipating what might be
Prefer working with practical information that solves immediate issues	Prefer imaginative information that leads to possibilities
Like information that is definite and measurable	Like information related to opportunities for being inventive
Start at the beginning, and evaluate information one step at a time	Jump in anywhere in looking at information, and may leap over steps
Work hands-on with parts to understand overall design	Study overall design to see how parts fit together
Enjoy using and refining information that is known and familiar	Enjoy experimenting with information that is new and different

Table 9.1 // Sensing-Intuition Contrast

It is important to note that one way is not better than the other. People with either preference will effectively gather information in their own way. It is also important to realize that both approaches are used by everyone, but one is usually preferred and better developed.

Making Decisions

Once we gather information by whichever process we prefer, we evaluate the information and come to conclusions. The second scale of the two scales mentioned earlier measures people's preferences in how they come to conclusions and make decisions (Figure 9.4). Some people have a preference toward coming to conclusions and making their decisions by relying primarily on an impersonal basis of rational consequences. This preference is referred to as *thinking* and relies heavily on a logical approach. Other people have a preference toward coming to conclusions and making their decisions by relying primarily on a personal basis of social values. This preference is referred to as *feeling* and relies heavily on a relational approach.

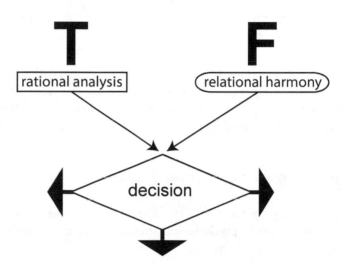

Figure 9.4 // Preferred Basis for Making Decisions

Our distinct preferences in the way we come to conclusions and make decisions also operate quite differently based on our preference for a logical-oriented *thinking* approach or relational-oriented *feeling* approach. Table 9.2 outlines some of these distinctions.

Thinking	Feeling
Come to conclusions primarily with the head	Come to conclusions primarily with the heart
Rely on logic to make decisions	Rely on personal convictions to make decisions

Give priority to principles such as truth and justice	Give priority to values such as relationships and harmony
Evaluate information as an onlooker from an outside a situation	Evaluate information as a participant from within a situation
Start with a critique that afterward may lead to appreciation	Start with appreciation that afterward may lead to a critique
More comfortable at analyzing plans	More comfortable at understanding people
May seem distant or condescending to others in the decision-making process	May seem too involved or emotional to others in the decision-making process

Table 9.2 // Thinking-Feeling Contrast

Remember, one way is not better than the other. People with either preference will effectively come to conclusions in their own way. And as we observed with the sensing-intuition difference, both the *thinking* and *feeling* approaches are used by everyone, but one is usually preferred and better developed.

Further Factors Impacting the Two Scales

While understanding the two scales discussed previously provides the primary explanation of psychological strengths, two other factors affect how these operate in our lives.

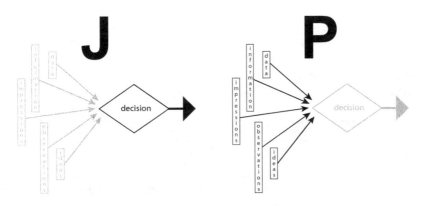

Figure 9.5 // Preferred Activity

First Impacting Factor: Which Activity We Prefer

The first of these influencing factors arises from the observation that we tend to operate in one of the psychological activities—*judging* or *perceiving*—more than the other one (Figure 9.5). It is important to understand what is meant by *judging*. It simply refers to the process of coming to a conclusion and making a decision. It does not refer to the negative connotation often associated with this term that suggests the formation of a critical or negative opinion.

Table 9.3 outlines distinctions between people who prefer operating primarily in the judging psychological process and people who prefer operating primarily in the perceiving psychological process.

Judging	Perceiving
Characterized by others as an organized person	Characterized by others as a flexible person
Appear to need definite order and structure	Appear to be able to go with the flow
Prefer to have life under control	Prefer to experience life as it happens
Seem to find fulfillment in being decisive	Seem to find fulfillment in being curious, discovering surprises
Like clear limits and categories	Like freedom to explore without limits
Feel need to establish closure	Feel the need to maintain openness
Meet deadlines by planning in advance	Meet deadlines by last-minute pressure

Table 9.3 // Judging-Perceiving Contrast

As we have stated before, it is important to remember, one way is not better than the other. People with either preference will effectively reach their objectives in life by following their own preferred way. And as we observed with the other two differences we have already looked at, both the *judging* and *perceiving* approaches are used by everyone, but one is usually preferred and better developed.

Second Impacting Factor: Where We Gain Energy From in the Process

The other factor that affects the two main psychological processes emerges from the observation that our mental process is greatly influenced by where we get our energy in life for these processes (Figure 9.6). Some of us find that when we are taking in information and making decisions about it, we gain the greatest energy by interacting with the external world of people, experiences, and activities. We call this preference *extraversion*. Others find that we gain more energy by interacting with the internal world of ideas, memories, and emotions when we are taking in information and making decisions about it. We call this preference *introversion*. When we use that term, it is important to understand that this is not the typical use of that word that refers to a shy person who has some sort of social phobia and avoids other people. Instead, we are referring to

Figure 9.6 // Preferred Environment

a person who prefers to process and make decisions internally.

Table 9.4 outlines distinctions between people who prefer taking in information and making decisions primarily in an environment of *extraversion* and people who prefer taking in information and making decisions primarily in an environment of *introversion*.

Extraversion	Introversion
Act, then (maybe) reflect	Reflect, then (maybe) act
Talk thoughts out while formulating them	Formulate thoughts out before speaking them
Inclined to talk often regardless of whether or not it is necessary, usually using many words	Inclined to talk only when necessary, usually using few words
Animated and exuberant	Quiet and reserved
Take the lead in initiating relationships	Wait for others to initiate a relationship
Energized by a high level of social interaction	Drained by a high level of social interaction
Seek relationships with many people at the same time	Seek very private, closely personal relationships with a few people

Table 9.4 // Extraversion-Introversion Contrast

We will repeat one last time: it is important to remember, one way is not better than the other. People with either preference will effectively be energized as they take in information and make decisions in their own preferred way. And as we observed with the other three differences we have already looked at, both the *extraversion* and *introversion* approaches are used by everyone, but one is usually preferred and better developed.

SCRIPTURAL INSIGHT ————————————————

The Bible presents quite a few choices for individuals to make as they pursue a Life Calling. For instance, at the end of his life as leader of Israel, Moses challenged the Israelites with these words:

> This day I call heaven and earth as witnesses against you that I have set before you life and death, blessings and curses. Now choose life, so that you and your children may live and that you may love the LORD your God, listen to his voice, and hold fast to him. (Deuteronomy 30:19-20)

The need for each of us to use our wills to make right choices is a constant theme of the Bible. This need lies at the very heart of the existence of our souls.

Insight 1 // You Have to Make the Choice Yourself

Now fear the LORD and serve him with all faithfulness. Throw away the gods your forefathers worshiped beyond the River and in Egypt, and serve the LORD. But if serving the LORD seems undesirable to you, then choose for yourselves this day whom you will serve, whether the gods your forefathers served beyond the River, or the gods of the Amorites, in whose land you are living. But as for me and my household, we will serve the LORD.
JOSHUA 24:14-15

Do you ever look at other people and wonder how they can know so much? They always seem to have the right answers. A few years ago on the television game show *Jeopardy*, a show that in part tests a person's accumulation of information, there was a contestant named Ken Jennings who won seventy-four games in a row—by far, a record. Everyone wondered how he could have so much information in his mind.

Joshua not only followed Moses as the leader of Israel, but also followed Moses' example in challenging the Israelites to make right choices. At the end of his tenure as their leader, Joshua was frustrated by the increasing trend of some of the Israelites turning away from God and worshiping other gods. In Joshua 24:14-15, he calls on them to exercise their wills and decide upon a course of action.

In our study and characterization of strengths, we defined psychological strength as the dimension of our lives that enables us to exercise our will in deciding upon courses of action. When it comes to our search for a Life Calling, this is incredibly important because the pursuit of Life Calling will come down to an ability to decide upon courses of action.

Joshua had gathered his facts and was obviously convinced that the right choice was to serve the Lord. However, he tells the Israelites to gather their own facts concerning the desirability of serving the Lord. He also advises them to consider their options and then make their own choices.

You will need to follow that same advice as you consider your Life Calling. You cannot follow someone else's path. If you do, you will just be living that person's life. Instead, you are going to have to gather your own information and facts and then exercise your will and make decisions and choices.

It is clear that our strengths do not act independently of each other. Psychological strengths are greatly affected by the way we have used our intellectual strengths. If we have "correctly handled the word of truth," we will have better information with which to make decisions using our psychological strengths.

PERSONAL REFLECTION

Do you have a hard time making decisions? Are you tempted to just follow someone else's path? What could help you make better decisions in your own in life?

Insight 2 // You Need to Become a Person Who Sees the Promised Land Rather Than Giants

Then Caleb silenced the people before Moses and said, "We should go up and take possession of the land, for we can certainly do it." NUMBERS 13:30

Let's look at some examples in the Bible of this psychological decision-making process in action. We start with a story from the latter part of the Exodus era. The Israelites had been traveling through the desert on their way from Egypt to Canaan, the Promised Land. They arrived at an oasis known as Kadesh, a location about ninety miles south-southwest of Jerusalem. Moses decided to send spies up into Canaan to check out the land before taking the entire group. He chose twelve who went throughout the southern areas of what is now the nation of Israel. The twelve all saw the same sights; they collected the same data. But they processed the data quite differently.

Two of the spies, Joshua and Caleb, saw the fruitfulness of the land and combined this with data they had earlier collected related to God's miraculous actions in bringing the people of Israel out of Egypt, across the Red Sea, feeding them with manna, and giving them water from a rock. Based on this, they were convinced that God would deliver Canaan into the hands of the Israelites, and so they made this decision and advocated it to Moses and the people, as we read in our passage for today: "We should go up and take possession of the land, for we can certainly do it."

The other ten spies also saw the fruitfulness of the land. They, too, had seen the miraculous actions of God, but they did not give current credence to these acts. Instead, they were worried about the people of Anak who were reported to be descendants of the Nephilim. There are quite a few different speculative ideas about who these Nephilim were, but one thing seems to be common among all ideas—the Nephilim were giants among giants. So the ten were afraid and made their choice based on this fear. In Numbers 13:31-33, they strongly contended that no attempt be made to enter the land of Canaan.

But the men who had gone up with him said, "We can't attack those people; they are stronger than we are." And they spread among the Israelites a bad report about the land they had explored. They said, "The land we explored devours those living in it. All the people we saw there are of great size. We saw the Nephilim there (the descendants of Anak come from the Nephilim). We seemed like grasshoppers in our own eyes, and we looked the same to them."

The report of fear captivated the Israelites more than the message of optimism and faith delivered by Joshua and Caleb. The people complained bitterly against Moses, and in the end they did not go into Canaan, but instead wandered in the desert for forty years. The adults all died and it was their children who actually entered the Promised Land. Two adults did not die but did enter along with the children—Joshua and Caleb. They had psychological strengths that were much greater than the other Israelites. They were able to take in and process all the relevant data and then make a sounder choice.

If we are going to find and follow a Life Calling, we will need to be like Joshua and Caleb. Our decisions will need to be guided by relevant data leading to sound choices rather than by fear.

PERSONAL REFLECTION

Are you following a path of sound choices in your life or are you guided by your fears? What could help you find more relevant data in your life on which to base your decisions?

PRODUCING THE POWER OF PURPOSE ——————

How do psychological strengths help produce the power of purpose in our lives? We continue to emphasize that the answer to this question is very similar to the one given in Chapter 5 in relationship to strengths in general. God created us with an intricate design in a fearful and wonderful manner that was part of his intent before we ever came into being. Applying this specifically to our psychological makeup, we will discover that this intentional intricate design includes the psychological dynamics of our lives. Understanding the way we make decisions will enable us to make better decisions that will in turn free us to pursue our Life Calling more effectively. This will continue to enhance the power of purpose in our lives. Thus, discovering our psychological strengths is a critically important step in determining what our purpose and calling are.

CHAPTER SUMMARY ———————————————

While the general study of psychology examines the science that deals with all mental processes and behavior, in our study of strengths, we chose to consider a narrower spectrum of mental processes and behavior and focused specifically on the capacity in our lives that enables us to exercise our will in deciding on courses of action. We learned that in this exercise of our will, when our minds are active, we are involved with one or the other two activities: 1) taking in information, or 2) evaluating the information and coming to conclusions. We also learned that we have preferences in the way we approach these activities.

Why is it important to understand this psychological process and its centrality to psychological strengths? The importance is obvious when we realize that this affects the way we will come to conclusions about our Life Calling and make ultimate decisions concerning our calling. Psychological strengths, like emotional strengths, are harder to detect than physical strengths. Once again, one of the most effective ways is listening to what others who know us well say about us. Another way is to complete exercises and assessments of our psychological strengths. We will look at some examples of how to do this in the *Activities* section of this chapter.

Unfortunately, our modern society tends to value certain preferences in the psychological process more than others. Consequently, we end up with a culture where people are often trying to be someone they are not. This often leads to frustration and self-doubt and causes confusion in the search for a Life Calling.

Remember, each of the strengths dimensions provides a synergism among the other dimensions. Psychological strengths provide the dynamic of reason among the other strengths. What do we mean by this? It is through the psychological process of taking in information, organizing it, and then coming to conclusions about this information that we provide a rational approach to what is going on with the other strengths. This helps to establish a moral framework for our lives.

INTERACTING WITH YOUR LIFE CALLING ————

This is your opportunity to interact with the Life Calling concepts introduced in this chapter and develop habits that will help you implement the concepts into your life.

The list below outlines the activities related to this chapter you will find in the *Life Calling Activities Supplement*. Access the supplement and find these activities listed. Then follow the instructions that will be given there.

1. **Activity 9.1** *Understanding Your Psychological Strengths Through MBTI.* The best assessment related to psychological strengths is called the *Myers-Briggs Type Indicator (MBTI)*. This psychometric questionnaire measures psychological preferences in how people perceive the world around them and and then make decisions about those perceptions. If you are able to engage in this activity through an institution or life coach, you will have the opportunity to discover your preferences on four scales with mutually exclusive end points and assess how strong each of these preferences is in your own life. From this information you will identify a four-letter type out of sixteen possibilities.

2. **Activity 9.2** *How Do You Make Decisions?* If you are unable to complete the *MBTI*, Activity 9.2 can serve as an alternative introduction to understanding your psychological strengths and how you use these strengths in making decisions. While not the rigorous tool that *MBTI* is, this activity is based on the same concepts and scales.

3. **Activity 9.3** *Your Psychological Type and School.* This activity is designed specifically for people who are in a formal learning situation. It will help you apply what you have learned about your psychological type in creating strategies to make you more effective in school or other learning situations.

4. **Activity 9.4** *Expanding Your Understanding of Your Psychological Type Using the Psychological-Type 360.* This activity will enable you to engage people all around you who know you well and have them give input into your understanding of your unique psychological strengths.

5. **Activity 9.5** *Psychological Strengths and Your Life Map.* Over these chapters you will have the opportunity to reflect on the various elements that help make you the unique person you are. In this activity you will focus on what you have learned about your psychological strengths. You will collect these observations to use in constructing your life map in chapter 12.

As always, make sure you save all of these activities in a safe place that is easily accessed as you continue through the rest of this book, because you will want to revisit them as you look at other concepts and activities.

REFERENCES

The following resources have been used in this chapter.

Briggs-Myers, I., McCalulley, M. H., Quenk, N. L., & Hammer, A. L. (1998). *MBTI manual: A guide to the development and use of the Myers-Briggs type indicator* (3rd ed.). Palo Alto, CA: Consulting Psychologists Press, Inc.

Jung, C. G. (1971). *Psychological types. Collected Works of C. G. Jung* (Vol. 6). Princeton, N.J.: Princeton University Press.

Millard, B. (2006). *Explorer's guide to life calling.* Marion, Indiana: Center for Life Calling and Leadership.

The following resources may be useful to you in your continuing exploration of Life Calling as you look at your *Unique Design* and your psychological strengths.

Harbaugh, G. L. (1990). *God's gifted people: Discovering your personality as a gift.* Minneapolis, Minnesota: Augsburg Fortress.

Kise, J. A. G., Stark, D., & Hirsh, S. K. (2005). *Lifekeys: Discover who you are.* Bloomington, Minnesota: Bethany House Publishers.

Schwen, M. R., & Bass, D. C. (Eds.). (2006). *Leading lives that matter: What we should do and who we should be.* Grand Rapids, Michigan: Erdmans Publishing Co.

Smith, G. T. (2011). *Courage and calling: Embracing your God-given potential.* Downers Grove, Illinois: Intervarsity Press.

STRENGTHS
SPIRITUAL

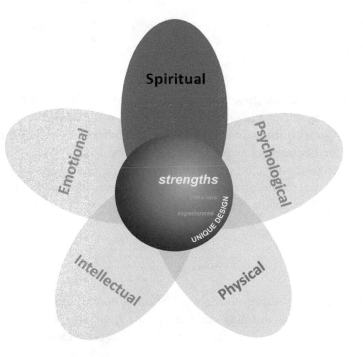

Figure 10.1 // Spiritual Domain of the Strengths

In looking at strengths, we will consider five domains. In this chapter
we will explore **spiritual strengths**.

CHAPTER 10

SPIRITUAL STRENGTHS: EXPLORING THE ASSETS OF YOUR SPIRIT

> *No one can enter the kingdom of God unless they are born of water and the Spirit. Flesh gives birth to flesh, but the Spirit gives birth to spirit.*
>
> Jesus

Spiritual strengths are those assets in our lives that enable us to comprehend and respond to a higher Source of power and guidance. Spiritual strengths gives us the desire and capacity to serve others—the primary context for our existence and Life Calling. Because of this, spiritual strengths transcend the other domains by guiding our premises, setting the context and providing supernatural guidance for how we will use the other strengths domains in discovering and carrying out our Life Calling.

WORDLIST

Words often have multiple meanings. Effective communication requires that we know which meaning of a word we are employing when we use it in our discussion. The following words need that clarification.

Divine   of or pertaining to a Supreme Being/Power in the universe

Habit	an acquired behavior pattern, practice, or custom regularly followed until it has become almost involuntary
Intrinsic	permanent and inseparable element, quality, characteristic, or attribute that exists within a person, usually from birth
Motivation	force that arouses a person to action toward a desired goal; the reason for the action; that which gives purpose and direction to behavior
Spiritual	of or pertaining to the aspect of human existence that is apart and distinguished from the physical nature
Spiritual Strengths	the capacity of our lives that enables us to discern and respond in service to the mysterious inner leading of God
Transcendental	beyond ordinary or common experience, thought, or belief; existing above and independent of the ordinary range of perception in the material universe and the space-time continuum
Well-being	thriving state or condition of existence characterized by health, happiness, prosperity, and contentment

DESCRIPTION

You could study and examine physical, emotional, intellectual, and psychological strengths from a purely human point of view. If you did, however, you would overlook the greatest domain of the strengths, *spiritual strengths*. You can assess yourself, study theory, engage in personal development, and all the other valuable activities available to you, but in the long run, if you truly have a Life Calling, then you need to recognize that there is a power outside yourself greater than you who is calling you. It is no mistake that one of the twelve steps learned by persons working to overcome addictions is "recognizing a greater power that can give strength." This power comes from a dimension that transcends those connected to the other four strengths. To a great extent, this brings us back to the discussion in Chapter 1 regarding intentional existence in the universe. In most cultures this spirituality is attributed to a divine source or God.

We defined the *spiritual strengths* domain as the capacity of our lives that enables us to discern and respond in service to the mysterious inner leading of God. What does that mean? There is level of interaction that occurs in our lives that cannot be explained by the processes we observe in the natural world. This can be referred to as God's inner leading, yet it would be incorrect to define this as if it was the only strength in which God leads. God works in all five of the strengths domains and, consequently, leads us through all of these domains. However, because the spiritual domain functions outside the natural realm, it often makes it easier to allow God's influence to occur in this domain.

The definition of spiritual strengths identifies two primary areas of spiritual interaction—discerning and responding. Discernment focuses more on the receptive interaction where we listen and gain direction for our lives. Responding focuses more on the active part of the spiritual domain where we carry out the directions we have gained through discernment.

It is important for us to understand that spiritual strength is something that each one of us needs to have in our lives if we are truly going to live a life directed by the sense of calling. So there are areas within the spiritual domain that we all need to develop. There are also spiritual gifts that we receive that will vary from one person to another. These will be what give us distinctive spiritual strengths. To start with, however, let's explore areas within the spiritual domain that we all need to develop.

Spiritual Discernment

In all people there is an almost universal desire for meaning, significance, and hope. Yet many times the fast pace of life can leave us feeling that none of these exist in our life. One of the most important things we can do to address this problem is to take time in our life to develop spiritual well-being. This can lead us to discern the spiritual influences at work in our life.

It is easy to get caught up in the physical, intellectual and emotional challenges of life and forget that there is an abstract level of interaction that occurs in our life that cannot be explained by the processes we observe in the natural world. It is a dimension that exists apart from concrete existence. In fact it transcends dynamics associated with the other physical, emotional, intellectual, or psychological strengths.

When we neglect our spiritual wellness, often all other areas of our life begin to encounter problems, and we feel like we have no spiritual direction. This makes it very difficult to discover a Life Calling. So what spiritual habits can we develop that can help keep this spiritual neglect from happening and help promote spiritual well-being? Figure 10.2 shows eight important spiritual disciplines we can develop that will increase our spiritual strength and help us gain clearer spiritual discernment.

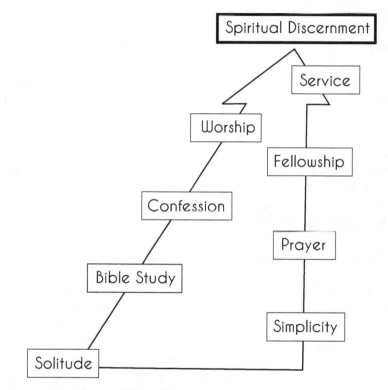

Figure 10.2 // Spiritual Disciplines

Meditational Solitude. Spend time by yourself so that you can listen to God's voice in your spirit.

Simplicity. Reduce the distractions in your life that keep you from hearing God.

Bible Study. Read passages in the Bible and seek to understand them and then apply the principles learned to your life.

Prayer. Dialogue with God about both God's concerns and yours.

Confession. Admit it to other people and to God when you have done something wrong to them and seek forgiveness.

Fellowship. Join with other people in small groups and in large gatherings to pursue spiritual growth.

Worship. Offer reverent honor and homage to God.

Service. Develop a decided pattern of engaging with others to solve problems or needs encountered by these others.

If we are going to hear the inner voice of God in our lives, we need to develop these spiritual disciplines. Failure to do so will make it almost impossible to hear God's voice calling us. A good place to start in assessing where we are at in our spiritual wellness is to assess our current spiritual well-being. In the *Activities* section of this chapter, we will have the opportunity to complete such an assessment.

Spiritual Development

As we pursue the development of spiritual strengths in our lives, we will progress through a spiritual path that will lead us to a mind-set of love, the true foundation of servanthood. This will be the source of power that can lead us to flourish.

In the writings of Peter, a leader of the early Christian church, Peter outlined a progression of eight spiritual qualities that will produce character development and maximize our spiritual strengths. "Make every effort to add to your faith goodness; and to goodness, knowledge; and to knowledge, self-control; and to self-control, perseverance; and to perseverance, godliness; and to godliness, brotherly kindness; and to brotherly kindness, love" (2 Peter 1:5-7).

This is a progression and, as such, requires that we add each of these spiritual efforts to achieve the character development that produces spiritual strength. In other words, we don't receive a few of these qualities and forget about the others. To the contrary, Peter presents these qualities in a sequence (illustrated in Figure 10.3), and that full spiritual strength of character is not achieved until all the qualities are present.

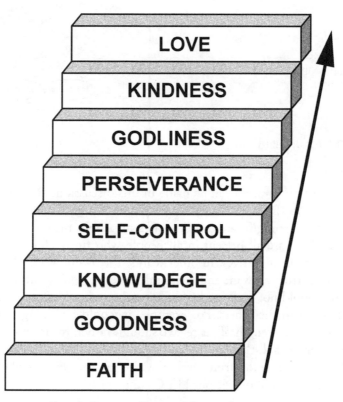

Figure 10.3 // Peter's Steps to Spiritual Strength

Spiritual Fruit

How do we know when spiritual dynamics are working in our lives at a level that produces spiritual strength? The key is in what Paul identified in a letter to the Galatians as *fruit of the Spirit*. When explored in the context of other writings by Paul, it becomes clear that this fruit comes in response to a process of a growing presence of God's Spirit within us (Figure 10.4). We are first of all drawn to God by the Spirit. We then invite God into our lives, and his Spirit takes up actual residence within us. With the Spirit's guidance imparting direction from within, we live by the Spirit. We then respond to this guidance by walking in step with the Spirit. When this happens, our lives produce spiritual fruit. Paul provides a list of these virtues: *love, joy, peace, patience, kindness, goodness, faithfulness, gentleness,* and *self-control.*

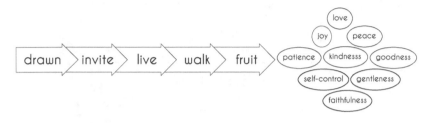

Figure 10.4 // Spiritual Fruit

An important observation can be made in this discussion. The singular "fruit" is used in the title rather than the plural "fruits." Unlike spiritual gifts, where different gifts are given to different people, the nine elements of spiritual fruit are all present in all people who freely allow spiritual power to work in their lives. In other words, this is not a list where we choose which fruit we want and disregard those we don't want. Because of this, we should not focus on highlighting the strength of one element in relationship to the others. For example, it would be wrong to say I have the spiritual strength of peace. We should, rather, focus on measuring the presence of all elements of fruit in assessing the spiritual strength in our lives. The more this fruit develops within us, the greater will be our ability to discover and pursue our Life Calling.

Spiritual Response

As we begin to develop the ability to discern spiritual influences in our life, we need to realize that these supernatural interactions take place on at least three different levels in our life. Most dramatic, of course, would be the *phenomenal* level. This level would involve miraculous events that guide or enable our path with no rational explanation. Second is the *informational* level. Here we receive thoughts and impressions that clearly do not come from our own mind, but provide us with crucial guidance. Third would be the *giftedness* level. At this level unique spiritual forces are placed in our lives as part of God's calling.

These inner forces are placed in our life to compel and guide how we serve others. This is the virtue of *servanthood*, a concept that was introduced in Chapter 3, as the context of our existence.

Spiritual Gifts

The concept of spiritual gifts has existed within Christianity from its earliest days. In general these spiritual gifts have been thought to be capacities that are freely given by God to individuals, and because of this, they cannot be earned or merited. The gifts are distributed, with no individual possessing all of the gifts. The primary purpose of these gifts is to build up God's work among his followers.

It is important to note that there is no comprehensive, all-inclusive list of spiritual gifts in the Bible, so any inventory is at best a compilation from various sources. Because of this it is also likely that no inventory is complete. That is to say, new gifts may arise with contemporary needs that may not have been listed in the Bible because in that context they were not needed. So any list of spiritual gifts should be explored as an open list of possibilities rather than a closed list of restrictions.

One of the clearest and most useful discussions of spiritual gifts comes from the first-century writings of Paul, a keen observer of human nature, a leading theologian of that time, and an early leader of Christianity. Table 10.1 outlines four widely acknowledged first century letters of Paul.

Romans 12:3-8	1 Corinthians 12:7-11	1 Corinthians 12:28	Ephesians 4:11-13
Prophesying	Wisdom	Apostles	Apostles
Serving	Knowledge	Prophets	Prophets
Teaching	Faith	Teachers	Evangelists
Exhorting	Healing	Miracles	Pastors
Giving	Miracles	Healers	Teachers
Governing	Prophecy	Helpers	
Mercy	Discernment	Administrators	
	Tongues	Tongues	
	Interpretations		

Table 10.1 // Spiritual Gifts

Paul starts his discussion in the Corinthians letter with the exhortation, "Now about spiritual gifts . . . I do not want you to be uninformed." He goes on to say that "there are different kinds of gifts, but the same Spirit distributes them. There are different kinds of service, but the same Lord. There are different kinds of working, but in all of them and in everyone it is the same God at work."

In trying to understand spiritual gifts, here is what we can extract from Paul. First, these operate in the spiritual domain of our lives as gifts brought into that domain by God. Second, the primary (and possibly only) context of spiritual gifts in our lives is service to others. Third, the power that operates spiritual gifts is directly from God. Finally, spiritual gifts occur in all people at some level of God's empowerment. With that understanding, let's look at Paul's four lists.

The Romans letter lists seven gifts that are tied to the Greek word that means "gift of grace." This implies that these different gifts come into our lives according to the grace given to us by God, not by our own doing. The context also suggests that these gifts should be allowed to motivate us from within to serve others in a particular way.

The Corinthians letter contains two lists. The first list outlines nine gifts as manifestations, or expressions, of God's Spirit in our lives. These are given to us for the common good, in other words, to benefit all of us in service to each other, not just for a person to use in isolation from other people. God gives these gifts to each person, just as God determines, not as the person seeks or chooses.

The second Corinthians list identifies eight gifts as appointments by God of service to the church.

In the Ephesians letter, Paul again speaks of spiritual gifts, specifically mentioning five as given to some that they might prepare God's people for service. Three of these five match similar appointments in the second Corinthians list.

What can we learn from spiritual gifts that we can apply to our search for a Life Calling? First of all, they are very important elements in the dimension of our spiritual strengths that help to prepare us to carry out a distinct Life Calling. Second, because of this distinctiveness, we will each find particular roles in our Life Calling that better suit us than other roles. Finally, our Life Calling will best be discovered in the larger context of service to others rather than a career search. In fact, even our career searches should be conducted in a larger context of how we can best serve others—the concept of servanthood discussed in more detail in Chapter 3.

In Chapter 3, servanthood was described as love acting in life's relationships. However, servanthood will express itself in a variety of ways as we will serve each other differently based on the differing spiritual gifts that have been placed within us. These gifts will strongly influence the way we respond to people, situations, and problems in the world. The patterns of our gifts also help determine the roles we will adopt as a result of these spiritual strengths. Because of this, they also form good guidelines for our Life Calling. As such, it will be beneficial to explore all possibilities related to spiritual gifts as we seek to discover all aspects of our Life Calling.

A good way to start is to examine a segment of spiritual gifts with a specific focus. Those listed by Paul in Romans 12 provide a good choice. The implication in Paul's discussion is that these gifts are intrinsic motivators. The concept of intrinsic motivation can be traced back as far as classical Greek philosophy. However, looking at intrinsic motivation in a spiritual context, and more specifically the context of spiritual gifts, one of the more effective classifications of intrinsic motivations can be patterned after the seven identified in Romans 12 by Paul.

Based on historical context, plus assessing how they occur in thousands of individuals, the seven intrinsic motivations can best be labeled and defined as follows (Millard, 2012):

1. **Proclaiming.** The inward motivation and capacity to:
   - discern what is morally right and wrong in situations
   - respond in service by publicly speaking out from internal convictions concerning what has been discerned

2. **Helping.** The inward motivation and capacity to:
   - discern legitimate needs or tasks others have
   - respond in service by finding practical ways to provide physical assistance to help them fulfill these needs and tasks

3. **Teaching.** The inward motivation and capacity to:

- discern truth through careful research
- respond in service by clearly presenting this truth to others in such a way that it will be easy to learn

4. **Exhorting.** The inward motivation and capacity to:
    - discern encouragement and practical solutions needed for life problems
    - respond in service by outlining practical steps of actions others should take to overcome problems

5. **Giving.** The inward motivation and capacity to:
    - discern financial needs others have in their lives or efforts
    - respond in service by financially investing in and supporting other worthwhile people and projects

6. **Managing.** The inward motivation and capacity to:
    - discern the organizational needs others have when working collectively together
    - respond in service by organizing, coordinating and guiding their activities and setting goals for their endeavors

7. **Comforting.** The inward motivation and capacity to:
    - discern the emotions of others
    - respond in service by providing mercy to those who are in emotional distress

The pattern of these seven motivations in our lives will strongly influence the way we respond to people, situations, and problems in the world. The patterns will also help determine the roles we tend to adopt as a result of these spiritual strengths. Because of this, they also form good guidelines for our Life Calling. Similar to the earlier discussion of spiritual gifts in general, it is important to note that there is no statement by Paul indicating that this is an all-inclusive list of intrinsic spiritual motivations, so there may be more than seven. However, the seven in Romans 12 do provide useful possibilities to examine in our lives as a valuable source of direction. We will explore this more in the *Activities* section at the end of this chapter.

SCRIPTURAL INSIGHT

Jesus taught us that there is a spiritual dynamic that operates within the human nature that is separate from all the other strengths. In speaking with the Jewish leader Nicodemus, Jesus referred to the other strengths as "flesh." "Jesus answered, 'Very truly I tell you, no one can enter the kingdom of God without being born of water and the Spirit. Flesh gives birth to flesh, but the Spirit gives birth to spirit'" (John 3:5-6). The Bible has much to say about this area of strength in our lives.

Insight 1 // Seeing Should Not Always Be Believing

There is a way that appears to be right, but in the end it leads to death.
PROVERBS 14:12

Earlier in the *Description* section, we discussed that God works in all five of the strengths domains; consequently he leads us through all of these domains. However, because the spiritual domain functions outside of the natural realm, it often makes it easier to allow God's influence to occur in this domain. Why is this? Proverb 14 helps us understand the answer to this question. When we rely only on the other four strengths domains (physical, emotional, intellectual, and psychological), we will end up seeing things in our life path that appear to be "right." But when we travel down that path, we may end up encountering destruction. There are many aspects of our Life Calling that can only be "seen" with spiritual eyes.

At the beginning of the story of Paul's second great missionary journey recorded in Acts 16, he was traveling with Silas and Timothy. Paul wanted to travel into the region of Bithynia. It appeared to him to be the right thing to do. But verse 7 states, "...the Spirit of Jesus would not allow them to." In fact, a few nights later, Paul received a vision of a man in Macedonia begging him to come and help them. So that is where Paul and his companions went. Some very dramatic events took place because of this and a great work was accomplished.

Can you imagine Paul trying to explain his decision to others? They probably shook their heads and rolled their eyes. God expects us to use our physical, emotional, intellectual, and psychological strengths in making decisions about life. For the most part, that's where we should begin—just like Paul did in this story. And in most cases that will be the best path to follow. However, we should always be open and ready for God to block our path and take us in a different direction that makes little or no sense to us. When that happens, we will need to rely on that first foundational value of faith, knowing that God has a bigger plan that we can't see.

> **PERSONAL REFLECTION**
>
> Do you follow only those ways that seem right to you, or are you open to God's leading in a direction that might not make sense to you? Do you take time to listen in your spirit to hear God's Spirit speaking to you?

Insight 2 // Start First by Seeking the Right Things

But seek first his kingdom and his righteousness, and all these things will be given to you as well.   MATTHEW 6:33

The mistake that many people make when it comes to the domain of spiritual strengths and input in their lives is to believe that they should just sit back and wait for visions like Paul had, or a burning bush like Moses encountered, or a talking donkey like Balaam heard. They may even try to set up such miraculous events like Gideon did with his two fleece experiments. But Matthew 6:33 helps us to see that this is the wrong place to start in the area of the spiritual and supernatural domain. Instead, we should begin with God's kingdom and his righteousness. And there is nothing hidden or secret about these two. Ninety-nine percent of what you need to know about God's kingdom and righteousness is revealed in the Bible. So when we are confronted about decisions to make in life, that is the best place to start.

The problem that many of us have is that we wait until a decision is upon us before we start seeking God's kingdom and his righteousness. I have heard all sorts of interesting stories about people frantically searching for information in times like this. Some just let the Bible fall open and whatever page appears, they believe they will find the guidance they need on that page. This seems closer to a magical approach than a spiritual approach to seeking God's will. I have heard that others start reading the Bible from Genesis 1:1 every time they need some guidance. While this may result in many good opportunities to read the Bible, it is not an efficient way to work with God. A far more efficient and effective approach to God's kingdom and his righteousness is to be constantly studying the Bible. That's what Matthew 6:33 means when it says to seek first. When we have made that effort earlier in our lives, we will be prepared to hear and discern God's Spirit when critical times arise in our lives demanding decisions. Paul had studied God's Word thoroughly prior to his vision of the Macedonian man. Hence, he was not thrown off guard when the vision came.

In Matthew 7:7-8, not too far removed from the verse we are looking at, Jesus reiterates the need to take action in seeking God's will with these words: "Ask and it will be given to you; seek and you will find; knock and the door will be opened to you. For everyone who asks receives; those who seek find; and to those who knock, the door will be opened."

When we are not willing to put forth the effort of seeking, we will find it difficult to find God, his kingdom and righteousness, or our Life Calling.

> **PERSONAL REFLECTION**
>
> Are you regularly seeking God's kingdom and righteousness for your life and by doing this, preparing ahead of time for crucial decisions? How can you make this a higher priority in your life?

Insight 3 // Turn On the Lights

Your word is a lamp to my feet and a light for my path.   PSALM 119:105

Psalm 119 is the longest of the Psalms and also the longest chapter in the Bible. The basic theme of Psalm 119 is centered on what it refers to as God's word. At the time this psalm was written, this word consisted of the five books of Moses (Genesis through Deuteronomy). Later, of course, sixty-one other books were added to create the present-day Bible. However, the counsel contained in Psalm 119 still seems to apply and is useful for our study three thousand years later. Psalm 119:105 is a useful continuation of the discussion concerning Matthew 6:33 and seeking first God's kingdom and righteousness. In that discussion we found that the Bible was the place to start that seeking, and Psalm 119:105 lets us know why. God's word provides both a lamp to our feet and a light for our path. At first we might be tempted to think those are just two different ways to say the same thing, but when we look deeper, we find that two separate ideas are contained in this statement that are very valuable to our search for a Life Calling and in knowing God's will.

First, God's word is a lamp for our feet. This means that as we take each step of our lives, we can and should look to the Bible for enlightenment related to that individual step. In other words, we can seek first God's kingdom and righteousness as found in his word for each and every decision we make. Hopefully we have stored up his word in our memory so that we will have it immediately when we need it rather than having to start from Genesis 1 every time we make a decision!

Second, God's word is a light for our path. This means that as we make longer-term plans for our lives, we can and should again look to the Bible for guidance. That's why regular Bible study is so important to the process of discovering a Life Calling. It greatly illuminates the plans we should form and becomes the guiding principle for our lives.

The pursuit of our Life Calling is a balance between taking individual steps and making plans for those steps. Psalm 119:105 lets us know that the Bible plays a crucial part in both actions.

PERSONAL REFLECTION

Are you using God's Word to guide your individual steps in your life? Are you using God's Word to make the long-range plans for your life?

PRODUCING THE POWER OF PURPOSE

How do spiritual strengths help produce the power of purpose in our lives? We continue to emphasize that the answer to this question is very similar to the one given in Chapter 5 in relationship to strengths in general. God created us with an intricate design in a fearful and wonderful manner that was part of his intent before we ever came into being. Applying this specifically to our spiritual makeup, we will discover that this intentional intricate design includes both universal spiritual dynamics and specific unique gifts in our lives. The general and the individual spiritual strengths combine to help us comprehend and respond to God's higher source of power and guidance within a context of service. Understanding this context enables us to see the path of our Life Calling more clearly, and this increases the power of purpose in our lives. Thus, discovering our spiritual strengths is a step that transcends all others in determining what our purpose and calling are.

CHAPTER SUMMARY

Spiritual strengths enable us to comprehend and respond to God's power and guidance. This often occurs through a mysterious inner leading that transcends the other strengths domains. Spiritual strengths give us the desire and capacity to serve others—the primary context for our existence and Life Calling. If we are unwilling to serve others, we will likely never discover our true calling. Spiritual strengths encompass general areas for all, such as spiritual discernment, development, and fruit. Spiritual strengths also include gifts that uniquely vary from one person to another. The synergistic interaction of the general with the individual will help us discover and carry out our Life Calling.

INTERACTING WITH YOUR LIFE CALLING ————

This is your opportunity to interact with the Life Calling concepts introduced in this chapter and develop habits that will help you implement the concepts into your life.

The list below outlines the activities related to this chapter you will find in the *Life Calling Activities Supplement*. Access the supplement and find these activities listed. Then follow the instructions that will be given there.

1. **Activity 10.1** *Understanding Your Intrinsic Spiritual Motivations through IMAGE.* IMAGE is an very effective tool for assessing intrinsic spiritual motivation within the spiritual strengths domain. This questionnaire explores to situations of service as you respond to the needs of people, locations, problems, and opportunities. If you are able to engage in this activity through an institution or life coach, you will have the opportunity to discover your pattern of seven motivations and assess how strong each of these is in your own life. From this information you will identify a pilot motivation and two other proactive motivations.

2. **Activity 10.2** *What Motivates You to Serve?* If you are unable to complete *IMAGE*, Activity 10.2 can serve as an alternative introduction to understanding intrinsic spiritual motivation. While not the rigorous tool that *IMAGE* is, this activity is based on the same concepts and patterns.

3. **Activity 10.3** *Expanding Your Understanding of Your Intrinsic Motivations by Using the IMAGE 360.* This activity will enable you to engage people all around you who know you well and have them give input into your understanding of your unique spiritual strengths related to intrinsic motivation.

4. **Activity 10.4** *Assessing Your Spiritual Wellness.* This activity helps you explore a very important part of your spiritual strengths—your spiritual well-being.

5. **Activity 10.5** *Spiritual Strengths and Your Life Map.* Over these chapters you will have the opportunity to reflect on the various elements that help make you the unique person you are. In

this activity you will focus on what you have learned about your spiritual strengths. You will collect these observations to use in constructing your life map in chapter 12.

As always, make sure you save all of these activities in a safe place that is easily accessed as you continue through the rest of this book, because you will want to revisit them as you look at other concepts and activities.

REFERENCES

The following resources have been used in this chapter.

Drury, K. W. (2005). *With unveiled faces.* Indianapolis, Indiana: Wesleyan Publishing House.

Fortune, D., & Fortune, K. (1987). *Discover your God-given gifts.* Old Tappan, New Jersey: F. H. Revell Co.

Foster, R. J. (1998). *Celebration of discipline.* (20th Anniversary ed.). San Francisco: HarperSanFrancisco.

Millard, B. (1996). *When the Spirit comes.* Ventura, CA: Life Discovery Publications.

Millard, B. (1992–2008). *Intrinsic motivation assessment guide & evaluation.* Marion, Indiana: Life Discovery Publications.

Millard, B. (1992–2008). *IMAGE QuickLook.* Marion, Indiana: Life Discovery Publications.

Millard, B. (2012). *Discover your uniqueness and value!* (2nd ed.). Marion, Indiana: Life Discovery Publications.

The following resources may be useful to you in your continuing exploration of Life Calling as you look at your *Unique Design* and your spiritual strengths.

Geen, R. G. (1995). *Human motivation: A social psychological approach.* Pacific Grove, CA: Brooks/Kole Publishing Company.

Kise, J. A. G., Stark, D., & Hirsh, S. K. (2005). *Lifekeys: Discover who you are.* Bloomington, Minnesota: Bethany House Publishers.

Oglilvie, L. J. (1984). *Freedom in the Spirit.* Eugene, OR: Harvest House Publishers.

Schwen, M. R., & Bass, D. C. (Eds.). (2006). *Leading lives that matter: What we should do and who we should be.* Grand Rapids, Michigan: Erdmans Publishing Co.

Smith, C. S., & Denton, M. L. (2005). *Soul searching: The religious and spiritual lives of American teenagers.* New York: Oxford University Press.

Smith, C. S., & Snell, P. (2009). *Soul in transition: The religious and spiritual lives of emerging adults.* New York: Oxford University Press.

Smith, G. T. (2011). *Courage and calling: Embracing your God-given potential.* Downers Grove, Illinois: Intervarsity Press.

Wagner, C. P. (2005). *Discover your spiritual gifts: The easy-to-use, self-guided questionnaire that helps you identify and understand your various God-given spiritual gifts.* Ventura, CA: Regal Books.

Yancey, P., & Brand, P. W. (2004). *In the likeness of God.* Grand Rapids, Michigan: Zondervan.

Yohn, R. (1987). *Discover your spiritual gift and use it.* Wheaton, IL: Tyndale House Publishers.

PASSIONS

Figure 11.1 // Life Calling Model Focusing on Passions

The second main component of the Life Calling Model is Unique Design. The second element of this design is focused on our **passions**.

CHAPTER 11

PASSIONS: THE INNER CATALYSTS THAT DRIVE US

> *If you have men who will only come if they know there is a good road, I don't want them. I want men who will come if there is no road at all.*
>
> David Livingston

Passions we have for life form the second element in our *Unique Design*. Passions are those things we desire intensely. They burn within our hearts and often drive the actions or paths we take. These passions emerge on three levels in our lives: interests, desires, Life Calling.

WORDLIST

Words often have multiple meanings. Effective communication requires that we know which meaning of a word we are employing when we use it in our discussion. The following words need that clarification.

Catalyst	something that precipitates or accelerates an event or change
Compel	steer you toward a course of action
Desire	wish, crave, or long for as for something that brings satisfaction or enjoyment
Force	energy or power to influence, affect, or control

Impel	cause you to actually start moving in the right direction
Inner	the intrinsic or inherent realm of our existence
Interest	attraction to or curiosity about something; fascination with something captivating
Passions	deep forces in our lives that burn within our hearts and often drive the actions or paths we take
Propel	keep you moving forward or onward in the right direction
Risk	exposure to hazard and the chance of injury or loss
Sacrifice	to surrender or give up, or permit injury or disadvantage to, for the sake of something else

DESCRIPTION

A sad thing happens to people on the road from childhood into their teen and college years and then life beyond. Somewhere along that road, they lose their ability to dream. When they were young, they would imagine all sorts of things and pretend they were great people. Then somewhere or sometime they were told that such dreams were foolish and that they could never achieve anything like that. But that's not the saddest part to this story. The saddest part is that they began to believe what they were told and gave up dreaming and turned their backs on the passions they once had. They started following paths somebody else outlined for them and entered careers somebody else recommended. In those careers they performed tasks somebody else gave them and were evaluated by some-body else's opinion. And at the end of their lives, they look back with some level of remorse because they realize they gave up on their dreams and abandoned their passion and instead lived somebody else's life. In other words they ended up only impersonating themselves rather than living out their own true lives.

Such a life has no passion because passion begins with dreams. Do you still have any dreams as you continue to move through your life experi-ence? What do you care about more than anything else in life? Do you have any idea what that is? The clearer you are about the answer to that question, the more likely you are to have the potential for passion in your life that also can bring greater focus to your pursuit of direction. One of the real challenges we face in our search for a Life Calling relates to whether or not we have passions in our lives that can help guide us to that purpose.

I am a cyclist. I have what others might consider a pretty advanced Trek bicycle that I can easily carry around with one hand. I can ride it at pretty high speeds. Yet I am not now, nor have I ever been, a threat to the riders in the Tour de France or any other professional bike race. What makes the difference between a professional athlete and an avid enthusiast like me? One of the most critical factors is passion. There is a certain drive that leads accomplished athletes, musicians, artists, and others to set everything else aside and endure the grueling schedule of practice and workouts needed to reach that high level of performance in their area. And to be honest, I don't have that level of drive as a cyclist, so I have to be satisfied with my average level of performance.

Passions Defined

In this section of the book, we are looking at the second major component of the Life Calling Model, *Unique Design*. We saw that it has three main elements—*strengths*, *passions*, and *experiences*. The second of these elements is made up of our *passions*, exactly what we have been talking about in the previous paragraphs. We define *passions* as deep forces in our lives that burn within our hearts and often drive the actions or paths we take. A good way to think of these is inner catalysts. A catalyst is something that precipitates or accelerates action, movement, or change in us. In chemistry catalysts speed up chemical reactions. It takes on a small amount of the catalyst to produce a dramatic increase in the rate of the reaction. This is because the reaction proceeds by a different pathway with the catalyst than it would if the catalyst was not present.

Our passions work the same way in our lives. They cause us to move forward more quickly than we would if we had no passion. This level of passion has to be more than a passing interest. Passions that become catalysts for athletes, musicians, or artists to succeed are more than just interests. Passions that can become catalysts for our discovery of a Life Calling are more than just interests as well. Catalytic passions are deep forces that *compel*, *impel*, and *propel*. To be a catalytic passion that inspires and directs a Life Calling, the deep force must be *compelling*, which means it needs to produce an overwhelming pressure that stirs us to take action. To be a catalytic passion that inspires and directs a Life Calling, the deep force must be *impelling*, which means it needs to exert a moral pressure that leads us to act because it is the right thing to do. Finally, to be a catalytic passion that inspires and directs a Life Calling, the deep force must be propelling, which means it causes action that moves us forward or onward.

Passions Developed

How does such a deep force form in our lives? Figure 11.2 illustrates three tiers or levels that build to create passion at the Life Calling intensity.

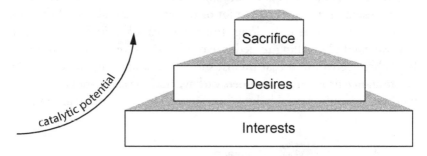

Figure 11.2 // Three Levels of Passion

Level 1—Interest. The initial stage of passion development starts with our interests. These are options in life that attract our curiosity. The key word is *curiosity*, a condition in which the novelty of something makes you want to learn more about it. Although we may find our fascination aroused at this level, we certainly do not know enough about it to make major moves in our lives. Ironically, many career counselors rely heavily on assessments of interests as a source to guide clients in selecting career paths. It is not surprising that such advice has limited success in helping people find an overriding purpose for their lives.

Level 2—Desire. The second stage of passion development occurs as we identify interests we would definitely pursue if we had no limitations. At the level of desire, there is more than just curiosity involved. Now wishes and longings enter the picture. We find that certain interests bring us pleasure and enjoyment, and we find ourselves pursuing them with greater intensity. Still, we have not yet achieved true passion. There is a big difference between wanting and enjoying something and being convinced that we need to pursue it no matter the cost. That requires the next level.

Level 3—Sacrifice. The final stage of passion development comes when our desires reach an intensity where we care enough about them that we would be willing to set aside other interests or desires and dedicate (in some cases even risk) our life for these passions. That qualifier of setting aside or risking truly sets this level apart from the other two. To reach this intensity, the desire must bring a deep satisfaction to our lives, something that gives us a sense of meaning, significance, and hope, as discussed on a spiritual level in Chapter 9. Something this intense is rare. It is easy to be interested or curious about a lot of things. We can also find that our list of desires can be quite long. But when we ask ourselves what it is that we would be willing to dedicate our lives to—or even risk our lives for—then we will find that the list shortens dramatically. If we were to create an inventory of the numbers we have in these categories during our lifetime, it would probably look like Figure 11.3. The dramatic impres-

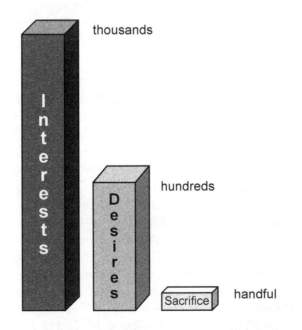

Figure 11.3 // Comparison of Interest, Desire and Sacrifice in our Life

sion left by that illustration clearly helps us to see why sacrificial passions are the ones that can truly help us discover our Life Calling. These are the ones that really matter in our lives.

Problems with Identifying Passions

One of the real problems with discovering our passions starts at the interest level. In our society today it is often hard to distinguish what are really our own interests and what are the interests of others that have been thrust on us. This can come from peer pressure or the aspirations of parents hoping to bring success into our lives. It can also come from media and advertising seeking to move us in a direction favorable to their financial or social interests. So it is important for us to take time to think carefully about our interests, desires, and passions to know that they are really ours.

On the other hand, peers, parents, and other mentors do play a valuable role in the exploration of interests that may become passions. They introduce us to areas we might not otherwise explore. They also model to us their own excitement about areas of interest, and we become intrigued to explore them.

SCRIPTURAL INSIGHT

In Proverbs 4:23 this good advice can be found: "Above all else, guard your heart, for it is the wellspring of life." The *Description* section of this chapter helped us see that the passions of our heart form an important component that can be a "wellspring" calling us to our Life Calling. Other scriptures provide additional insight concerning our passions.

Insight 1 // What Shapes the Desires of Your Heart?

Trust in the Lord and do good; dwell in the land and enjoy safe pasture. Take delight in the Lord and he will give you the desires of your heart. Commit your way to the Lord; trust in him and he will do this: He will make your righteous reward shine like the dawn, your vindication like the noonday sun.
PSALM 37:3-6

The second level on our climb toward Life Calling passions is our desires. Psalm 37:4 speaks of our getting the desires of our heart and is often misinterpreted to mean that whatever we want we will get if we trust enough in the Lord to give it to us. Let's look at this passage in its fuller context of verses 3-6.

Three important conditions set up qualifications for receiving the desires of our heart—trusting in the Lord, taking delight in the Lord, and committing our ways to the Lord.

First, when we trust in the Lord's ways as being good, our desires will be for those good ways. David put it this way in Psalm 20:7-8, "Some trust in chariots and some in horses, but we trust in the name of the Lord our God. They are brought to their knees and fall, but we rise up and stand firm."

Second, when we delight in the Lord, our desires will be for that in which we delight—the Lord and his ways. In Paul's thorough discussion of love in 1 Corinthians 13, he makes this observation in verse 6, "Love does not delight in evil but rejoices with the truth." When this happens, our desires will be consistent with what God wants.

Third, when we commit our ways to the Lord, we will restrict our desires to only those ways that are of the Lord. Paul discusses this in Romans 8:5 by describing two different types of people. "Those who live according to the sinful nature have their minds set on what that nature desires; but those who live in accordance with the Spirit have their minds set on what the Spirit desires."

The passage in Psalm 37 closes out by giving us an accountability assessment for our desires to make sure they are in this context. The desires must lead to righteousness and justice. When we experience desires of our heart at a level that matches this context, then we have reached a level of passion that is part of our Life Calling. When this happens we can experience another promise found in the Psalms: "May he give you the desire of your heart and make all your plans succeed" (Psalm 20:4).

> **PERSONAL REFLECTION**
>
> Are the desires of your life based on trust and delight in the Lord and a commitment to his ways? Do your desires lead to righteousness and justice? How can you increase this in your life?

Insight 2 // Develop Interests that are Based on Values

Each of you should look not only to your own interests, but also to the interests of others. PHILIPPIANS 2:4

At one time or another as I grew up, I had interests in being a trash collector, pilot, baseball player, astronaut, military officer, lawyer, journalist, world explorer, park ranger, actor, billionaire, ship captain, spy, even the President of the United States. I ended up in careers where I have worked as a teacher, geologist, business owner, pastor, life coach, and leader— none of which were on my original list. So what happened? The answer is found in the relationship of interests to passions.

As we ascend toward passions at a Life Calling level of sacrifice, interests are at the first and lowest level. Interests form a fascinating window into who we are. They say a lot about our makeup and wiring. But they are not the foundation on which a Life Calling will be discovered because they are usually caught up in an attitude of self-centeredness and self-interest.

This is what led the Apostle Paul to advise us in Philippians 2:3-4, "Do nothing out of selfish ambition or vain conceit, but in humility consider others better than yourselves. Each of you should look not only to your own interests, but also to the interests of others." Paul goes on in verses 5-11 to tell us that our attitude should be the same as the attitude that Jesus had which led him to sacrifice his life on the cross. This remarkable passage in scripture certainly lets us know that our passions must go far beyond just self-interests if they are to guide our search for a Life Calling. Unfortunately, the interest surveys used so often in career exploration rarely go beyond the self-interest level and end up causing confusion in our search for a Life Calling.

Later in Philippians 2:20-21 Paul commends Timothy to the people of Philippi. "I have no one else like him, who takes a genuine interest in your welfare. For everyone looks out their own interests, not those of Jesus Christ."

There is nothing wrong with us having interests. Curiosity is a good thing. It helps us consider many options in life, just like all those interests I had growing up. However, the problem with a life guided only by our interests is that it may not look out for the interest of Jesus. It rather tends to focus on our own interests, and a self-centered life will never lead to discovery of a true Life Calling. It is when we move into the two higher levels of passion we will look at in the next two devotions that we begin to move more in a direction of looking outside our own self-centered concerns and into the realm of purpose.

PERSONAL REFLECTION

What are your interests in life right now? Are your interests guided by self-interests, or by higher values?

Insight 3 // The Highest Level of Passion Comes from an Undivided Heart

Teach me your way, Lord, that I may rely on your faithfulness; give me an undivided heart, that I may fear your name. PSALM 86:11

What are you fervent about? What would you really like to do in life? We have defined passion as a deep force in our lives that burns within our hearts that compels, impels and propels the actions or paths we take in life. This occurs when these driving forces are singular. Psalm 86:11 describes an "undivided heart." This is the kind of passion that leads to a Life Calling.

The word passion is used in a rather widespread context of meanings. On the shallow end, it is used to describe sexual feelings. On the deepest end, it is used to describe the sufferings of Jesus during the period following the Last Supper through his crucifixion. In the Life Calling Model, we have chosen to define passion at the deeper level, which is not achieved until we are ready to sacrifice our lives for our passion. Sacrifice does not mean we have to die for our passion, but it does mean we are ready to dedicate our lives for our passion.

When passions rise to this level of sacrifice in our lives, they compel us by steering us toward right courses of action. They are like that voice described in Isaiah 30:21, "Whether you turn to the right or to the left, your ears will hear a voice behind you, saying, 'This is the way; walk in it.'"

Secondly, when passions rise to a level of sacrifice in our lives, they will also impel us by causing us to actually start moving in the right direction. This is the kind of drawing force described in Isaiah 2:3. "Many peoples will come and say, 'Come, let us go up to the mountain of the Lord, to the house of the God of Jacob. He will teach us his ways, so that we may walk in his paths.'"

When passions rise to a level of sacrifice in our lives, they will also propel us to keep moving forward or onward in the right direction. Again we can turn to Isaiah (Isaiah 40:29-30) for a description of this:

He [the Lord] gives strength to the weary and increases the power of the weak. Even youths grow tired and weary, and young men stumble and fall; but those who hope in the Lord will renew their strength. They will soar on wings like eagles; they will run and not grow weary, they will walk and not be faint.

If you are struggling with focus in your search for a Life Calling, you might want to ask yourself if you have a confused or divided heart. If that is the case, you may need to return to the prayer of Psalm 86:11 and ask the Lord to give you an undivided heart that can become the compelling, impelling, and propelling passion leading to a Life Calling.

PERSONAL REFLECTION

Do you hear a lot of voices in your heart or is it undivided? Why not ask God to give you an undivided heart that can produce true passion in your life?

PRODUCING THE POWER OF PURPOSE

How do passions help produce the power of purpose in our lives? If we accept the words of Psalm 37, then we need to acknowledge that it is God who gives us the desires of our heart—including having the desires to begin with. Spiritual power is required for a desire to achieve the highest sacrificial level in the passions continuum. This leads us back to faith that God created us with an intentionally unique design that includes our passions. It make sense, then, that we should pay careful attention to those passions he instills in us in order to fully understand the Life Calling God gives us. When we do this the catalytic impact of passions can greatly increase the power of purpose in our lives. This will continue to enhance the power of purpose in our lives. Thus, discovering our passions is a critically important step in determining what our purpose and calling are.

CHAPTER SUMMARY

Passions are deep forces in our lives that often drive the actions or paths we take, acting as inner catalysts. Passions develop through a continuum that starts with curious interest, moves through more intense desire, and finally reaches a sacrificial level that involves setting aside other interests and even possibly risk. We will likely have many interests, but few sacrificial passions.

When looking at the various strengths, we consistently emphasized that one of the most effective ways to discover them was to listen to what others who know us well say about us. This is not the case with passions. Although others might help us explore interests, it is almost impossible for another person, even those very close to us, to know what passions reside in our hearts at the sacrificial level. So how can we determine if something is our passion? A combination of contemplation and reflection provides the best source of information. When we take time to quietly do this and ask ourselves those deep questions related to meaning, significance, and hope, we will begin to distinguish the true passions from those that are nothing more than interests or desires.

INTERACTING WITH YOUR LIFE CALLING ———

This is your opportunity to interact with the Life Calling concepts introduced in this chapter and develop habits that will help you implement the concepts into your life.

The list below outlines the activities related to this chapter you will find in the *Life Calling Activities Supplement*. Access the supplement and find these activities listed. Then follow the instructions that will be given there.

1. **Activity 11.1** *Exploring Your Interests.* Passions often start at the interest level. In this activity you will have the opportunity to explore your interests and their application to careers by working with the Holland Codes/Holland Occupational Themes, a widely-used assessment of interests.

2. **Activity 11.2** *Passions and Your Life Map.* This is the last chapter in which you will have the opportunity to reflect on the various elements that help make you the unique person you are. In this activity you will focus on what you have learned about your passions. You will collect these observations to use in constructing your life map in chapter 12.

As always, make sure you save all of these activities in a safe place that is easily accessed as you continue through the rest of this book, because you will want to revisit them as you look at other concepts and activities.

REFERENCES

The following resources have been used in this chapter.

Millard, B. (1996). *LifeQuest: Planning your life strategically*. Ventura, CA: Life Discovery Publications.

The following resources may be useful to you in your continuing exploration of Life Calling as you look at your *Unique Design* and your passions.

Holland, J. L., & Gottfredson, G. D. (1996). *Dictionary of Holland occupational codes* (3rd ed.). Odessa, Florida: Psychological Assessment Resources Inc.

Schwen, M. R., & Bass, D. C. (Eds.). (2006). *Leading lives that matter: What we should do and who we should be*. Grand Rapids, Michigan: Erdmans Publishing Co.

Smith, G. T. (2011). *Courage and calling: Embracing your God-given potential*. Downers Grove, Illinois: Intervarsity Press.

EXPERIENCES

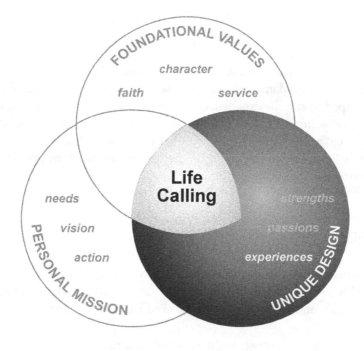

Figure 12.1 // Life Calling Model Focusing on Experiences

The second main component of the Life Calling Model is Unique Design. The third element of this design is focused on our **experiences**.

CHAPTER 12

EXPERIENCES: THE FORCES THAT SHAPE OUR LIVES

> *Two roads diverged in a wood and I—I took the one less traveled by, and that has made all the difference.*
> Robert Frost

Experiences form the third element in our *Unique Design*. Our strengths and passions are fundamental to our *Unique Design*, but these are molded and reshaped by our life experiences. Life experiences have a great impact on shaping us into the persons we are. Each of us has these experiences that have changed our lives—whether they are good or bad, dramatic or seemingly insignificant. Reflecting on these is important to the process of discovering our Life Calling.

WORDLIST

Words often have multiple meanings. Effective communication requires that we know which meaning of a word we are employing when we use it in our discussion. The following words need that clarification.

Circumstances	existing conditions or surroundings
Critical	of essential and decisive importance with respect to an outcome
Experience	process or fact of personally observing, encountering, or undergoing something

| **Intensity** | the degree or extent of strength or severity |
| **Phobia** | persistent, abnormal, and irrational fear of a specific thing or situation that compels one to avoid it |

DESCRIPTION

As you go through life, you don't leave one stage and get to the next stage with a blank slate. You carry along with you a great deal of personal history. You may be the only child in a happy family where your parents paid a great deal of attention to you and made you feel special. Or you may be one of four kids in a family where your parents divorced when you were very young, and you have had to fight to get any attention. You may have lost a good friend to a car accident. You may have struggled with physical or mental illness. You may be the top student in your high school and have a great deal of optimism about how you will do in college. Or you may struggle in high school and be worried about whether or not you are up to the challenge ahead. You may be the most popular student in your college, or the one nobody else seems to pay attention to. You may be the person who always gets the raise at work, or you may have been fired from your last job. And the list could go on. Whether your history was good or bad, it has had a definite impact on who you are today.

A few years ago I led a group of students enrolled in a leadership class on an expedition to a series of indigenous villages deep in the jungles of Costa Rica. The hike to one of the villages required us to make several river crossings through deep, rapid-flowing water. I was swept away in one crossing, pulled down by the current under the water, and nearly drowned. An overwhelming feeling of terror gripped me as I fought to get back to the surface so I could breathe. But just when I thought there was no hope and that I would die, spiritual strength from God and a strong emotional commitment to my family gave me energy I did not think I had, and I was able to finally find a rock underwater that I used as a platform to push myself up to the surface, where I was able to breathe again. Others from the team came and helped me get from the rock out of the river and back onto dry land. As you read this, you no doubt could even begin to feel a little of the terror just by hearing the story. You can imagine the impact it has had on my life. In fact, I had to get help dealing with the posttraumatic stress on my return home because I would relive the event every night in my dreams.

It is amazing, however, to begin uncovering lessons that this experience has taught me about my life. For instance, I learned that when you are down to your last breath, it is relationships that matter, not money, jobs, positions, titles, or accomplishments. I also learned that the relationships that matter most are those to whom you are the closest. There are enough of these lessons that I am collecting them into a short inspirational book entitled *Lessons from the Bottom of the River*.

But as I reflect back on my life, I realize that it is not just the dramatic experiences that have shaped me. When I was a small child, my mother used to take me with her when she was shopping for a new dress. My mother had a very hard time making decisions in life, and these shopping trips would run into multiple hours. Even now I can remember the feeling of sitting on the floor under all the dresses on the rack thinking that it would never end! Well it is not surprising that these many years later, I do not like shopping, and when I do have to shop, I go in with a decisive manner and get it done as quickly as possible—a pattern not necessarily understood or appreciated by my wife. A small, undramatic experience in my life still continues to impact me. I guess I should also think about writing a book entitled *Lessons from the Bottom of the Dress Rack*.

Life experience has a great impact on shaping us into the persons we are. Each of us has these experiences that have changed our lives—some dramatic and some seemingly insignificant. Reflecting on these is important to the process of discovering our Life Calling.

Strengths, *passions*, and *experiences* comprise the three main elements of our *Unique Design*, the second major component of the Life Calling Model. Defining the third of these elements, *experiences*, is rather simple. Our strengths and passions are developed and shaped in a distinct pattern based on the unique events, situations, and influences we encounter throughout our lives. These can be full of blessings, triumphs, and achievements, or they can be burdened by misfortunes, ordeals, and trials. Either way, these experiences will shape us and will help determine the *Unique Design* we take into our Life Calling.

Why is this important when considering our *Unique Design*? Two individuals could have similar strengths. It is also possible, though less likely, that these two individuals could have the same passions. But even if this was the case, their experiences in life would be different, and this would result in the two individuals ending up quite different from each other, even though they shared so many similarities.

Critical Forces

How do we begin to understand these life-changing experiences? An effective way to evaluate our life experiences is to analyze the three critical forces that influence them (Figure 12.2).

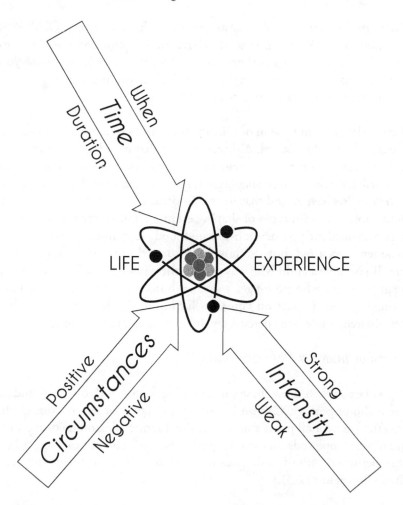

Figure 12.2 // Critical Forces Impacting a Life Experience

Circumstances. The quality of the elements that affect an experience in our life. Positive experiences tend to shape us in a reinforcing manner. Negative experiences tend to shape in a reactionary manner. If you grew up in a family where you and your siblings did a lot of things together and got along well, you will likely be a person who expects to have good relationships and who enjoys social interaction. If, on the other hand, you grew up in a family where you felt your siblings always picked on you, you might have become the kind of person who is always approaching relationships in a combative manner, and you might find that close relationships are difficult for you to establish or maintain.

Intensity. The level of influence an experience has on our life. Obviously, experiences of high intensity tend to have more of an impact on our lives than those of low intensity. For example, breaking up with someone you were seriously dating for several years will affect you more than having a casual friend move to another town.

Time. The point of time in our life in which an experience occurred, and the length of time it lasted. Although things that have happened recently in our lives will be more present in our memories, that does not mean they will have the greatest shaping influence on our lives. Developmental psychologists have found that in certain periods in our lives we are more vulnerable to certain types of shaping events. Phobias, for instance, have a greater tendency to develop in childhood. It is not just when some experience occurred, but also how long it lasted. It is easy to understand that if you were a child who was permanently placed in a foster home by a single parent who no longer was able to take care of you, it will have a much greater impact on you than having to live for one year with a grandparent while your parents regained some financial stability.

Example from the Physical Earth

A good example of how these three shaping forces work can be found in the realm of geology. Carbon is a very important element on this earth. It is the basis for all plant and animal life. Elemental carbon compounds are those compounds on earth formed of nothing else but carbon. When this elemental carbon undergoes varying experiences, it forms different minerals (Figure 12.3).

The experiences vary by the heat and pressure involved. This is similar

Carbon
C
6

Figure 12.3 // Carbon Products

to the life experiences we encounter. Coal is formed from carbon that has gone through minimal heat and pressure. When carbon experiences a greater amount of heat and pressure, it may well form graphite. When tremendous amounts of heat and pressure are put to bear on carbon, diamonds may be formed.

An important thing to notice in this illustration is that based on the experience, different forms of carbon occurred. Each of these forms has different valuable uses. Coal is the best source of fuel among the three. Graphite is the best lubricant, and when it is placed in a pencil, it also serves as the best writing material. Diamonds, on the other hand, have great value in the industrial world because of their hardness. Because of their beauty, they also form the best candidate of the three to be incorporated into jewelry. Can you imagine the reaction of a woman who would be offered an engagement ring containing a one-carat piece of coal or graphite?

Collecting Our Experiences

How do we start exploring our life experiences in a way that will give us insight into our Life Calling? One of the best ways is by writing a simple autobiography—our personal life story. A good way to get started in this process is by creating "biologs." These are historical journals we generate by reflecting back on our lives and listing the experiences that may have had an impact on making us who we are. We can create these from our own memories, but it is also very valuable to interview others who have been close to our lives. Once these experiences have been identified, we then reflect on the impact they had on us. What attitudes have they caused in us? What values have they cultivated in us? What habits have we developed because of them? Have they created any phobias in us? Have they been a source of inspiration? What have we learned about God through these experiences? The answers to these questions, and others we might ask, can be combined with the experiences we identified to form our autobiography.

Learning from the Experiences of Others

So far we have been looking primarily at our own personal experiences, and these have the greatest impact in shaping who we are. However, we also have been affected by the experiences of others. This can be as close as parents or other family members to classic history of others who lived thousands of years ago. One of the reasons most schools require students to study some history is because of the value that understanding these experiences of others can have in helping us understand ourselves.

SCRIPTURAL INSIGHT

The words of David in the twenty-third Psalm provide a picture of what our life experiences can be like.

> The Lord is my shepherd, I lack nothing. He makes me lie down in green pastures, he leads me beside quiet waters, he refreshes my soul. He guides me along the right paths for his name's sake.
>
> Even though I walk through the darkest valley, I will fear no evil, for you are with me; your rod and your staff, they comfort me.
>
> You prepare a table before me in the presence of my enemies. You anoint my head with oil; my cup overflows.
>
> Surely your goodness and love will follow me all the days of my life, and I will dwell in the house of the LORD forever.

A common theme throughout the Bible is that God uses the events of our lives to shape who we are and who we will become.

Insight 1 // All Things Can Work Together for Good

And we know that all things work together for good to them that love God, to them who are the called according to his purpose. ROMANS 8:28 (KJV)

Without a doubt, this is the most important scripture that applies to experiences we face in life. We first quote it here from the classic King James Version. *Experiences* are the third element in our *Unique Design*. We define *experiences* as the unique situations, influences and occurrences we encounter throughout our life. These can be blessings, triumphs or achievements, or they can be misfortunes, ordeals or trials. No matter what quality they have, these experiences shape us and definitely impact our Life Calling.

At the end of my junior year in high school, my dad decided to move from California to Massachusetts. I had gone through elementary, middle school, and nearly all of high school with my friends. I was really upset with my father for making this move. Six months later I found out that I was very sick and that if I had not been taken to a world-renowned health center in Massachusetts that specialized with my problem, I would have died. God used what seemed to me like a terrible life experience to accomplish something remarkably good in my life.

When we love God and respond to his call to follow him, all of our experiences will work together in a good way to develop our Life Calling. Now let's look at the passage as quoted with a slight difference in Today's New International Version, the version we have been using consistently in this book. "And we know that in all things God works for the good of those who love him, who have been called according to his purpose."

The thought that is added from this interpretation is that when we are in relationship with him, God actively works through our experiences to bring about good in our lives that will guide our Life Calling.

What we can learn from Romans 8:28 is that our life experiences form one of the best places to explore when searching for our Life Calling. The passage also encourages us to start moving forward in life as part of our search. As we experience life, whatever takes place will be woven into our Life Calling—in other words, it will continue to evolve as we encounter these events. In the next four devotions we will look at four remarkable stories from the Bible that illustrate this.

PERSONAL REFLECTION

Are you harboring bitterness for things that have happened in your life that you really feel should not have been? How can you learn to entrust these to God to work with and accomplish good in your life?

Insight 2 // What Others Intended for Evil God Can Redirect for Good

Then Joseph said to his brothers, "Come close to me." When they had done so, he said, "I am your brother Joseph, the one you sold into Egypt! And now, do not be distressed and do not be angry with yourselves for selling me here, because it was to save lives that God sent me ahead of you. GENESIS 45:4-5

The first example we will look at from the Bible comes from the story of Joseph. Joseph's brothers sell him into slavery. He is purchased by Potifar. Potifar recognizes Joseph's trustworthiness and puts him in charge of Potifar's household. Joseph develops good management skills. Some time later Potifar's wife falsely accuses Joseph of adultery. He is put in prison.

Joseph's management skills learned in Potifar's home are recognized by the warden, and Joseph is put in charge of all the other prisoners. He works in this position for several years. In this position, Joseph comes in contact with the Pharaoh's cupbearer and baker who had been thrown into prison. Joseph interprets their dreams. The butler is restored to service and promises to put in a good word for Joseph.

The butler forgets until two years later when Pharaoh needs a dream interpreted. The butler mentions Joseph. Joseph interprets the dream. Pharaoh elevates him to second in command over all of Egypt. In that position, Joseph is able to take care of Jacob, his father, and all his family during a terrible famine, no doubt sparing them from extinction were they to face the famine on their own.

From the time Joseph was sold into slavery until the time he became second in command over Egypt, twenty years had passed. For a good share of those years, things seemed to be going against Joseph. If anyone had a right to be bitter about life experiences, he certainly did. But he did not harbor such bitterness. When he talked to his brothers, he told them that the plans they had for evil were used by God to accomplish great good.

During all those years that seemed to be problematic, God continued to work for Joseph's good, weaving together a Life Calling that would accomplish great service to God's plan.

> **PERSONAL REFLECTION**
>
> Have you learned to trust God with your life experiences? How can you start to view the things you see as hardships in your life as building blocks God can use to accomplish great things through you?

Insight 3 // By the Grace of God I Am What I Am

For I am the least of the apostles and do not even deserve to be called an apostle, because I persecuted the church of God. But by the grace of God I am what I am, and his grace to me was not without effect.
1 CORINTHIANS 15:9-10

The last example we will look at is the Apostle Paul in the New Testament. He was a highly respected Jew of the tribe of Benjamin. He was considered a Hebrew of Hebrews—the top of the line. He was a highly educated Pharisee who knew every aspect of the law. He had been trained by Gamaliel—a leading authority in the Jewish Sanhedrin and celebrated scholar of the Mosaic Law. Paul had no tolerance for people who did not fully support the Jewish religion. He was faultless when it came to legalistic righteousness. On top of all of this, he was a Roman citizen—no small fete for a Jew in those days. Paul was on the fast-track to Jewish leadership.

Paul thought he knew his purpose in life included getting rid of the followers of Jesus. He collaborated in the stoning of the Christian martyr Stephen. He then obtained documents authorizing him to go to Damascus and take prisoner anyone who was a follower of Jesus. He was determined to wipe out this hated sect.

What a terrible life! Most of us would have no use for such a person. But God saw all of this as useful material for taking a man and using him to shape the Christian religion rather than wiping it out. All Paul lacked was a willingness to be this man, so God took care of that with a bright light on the road to Damascus.

After Paul's conversion to Christianity, everything did not suddenly turn into a bed of roses. His life was marked by one hardship after another. But look at Paul's words from the passage at the beginning of this devotion: "By the grace of God, I am what I am." God used Paul's life experiences—good and bad alike—to develop a person who had more impact on the development of Christianity than any other person except Jesus himself. What a Life Calling!

As we look back at the examples of both Joseph and Paul in this chapter, at face value, almost everything that happened to them in the first part of their lives seemed to be leading them away from what we might have chosen in outlining their Life Callings. Yet God used every event in their lives to craft the calling he wanted for them. God will do the same for us if we allow him to do so.

PERSONAL REFLECTION

Are you letting your life move forward with events that you turn over to God? Are you allowing God to work them together for good in your life and in his plan for using you in service? How can you learn to let your experiences become the God-mastered building blocks of your Life Calling?

PRODUCING THE POWER OF PURPOSE ————

How do experiences help produce the power of purpose in our lives?
If there is one constancy in our existence, it can be characterized in the saying, "life happens." We really do not have any choice about this. Every hour of every day we are alive, something will take place. Sometimes it will be intense and sometimes it will be dull. Sometimes it will seem wonderful, and sometimes it will seem terrible. Sometimes it will last just a moment, and sometimes it will seem to last forever. No matter which it is, this "happening life" will mold us and shape us into unique individuals. The lesson we can learn from this is that as our experiences shape us into unique individuals, we will find that our compatibility with various callings in life correlates to the persons we have become. If we can adopt the attitude of David in Psalm 23 or accept the premise of Paul in Romans 8, we can begin to see that our life experiences are a guide to our Life Calling and provide significant energy to the power of purpose in our lives.

CHAPTER SUMMARY ————————

Life experiences have a great impact in shaping us into unique individuals. They range from highly dramatic to very mundane, but no matter their nature, they have an effect on us. These experiences vary in their impact on us based on their circumstances, intensity and time. Even when these critical forces produce experiences that seem bad in our lives, God can work them together to produce goodness when we live a life that follows his calling. With all this in mind, we need to understand that a valuable source of information about our Life Calling can be gleaned from collecting and reflecting on our life experiences.

INTERACTING WITH YOUR LIFE CALLING ———

This is your opportunity to interact with the Life Calling concepts introduced in this chapter and develop habits that will help you implement the concepts into your life.

The activity below related to this chapter you will find in the *Life Calling Activities Supplement*. Access the supplement and find this activity. Then follow the instructions that will be given there.

1. **Activity 12.1** *Completing Your Life Map*. A Life Map is a way of looking at your past experiences as a collective influence on your life. This influence has had a great impact on shaping who you are and what Life Calling you have to fulfill. Over the preceding several chapters, you have had the opportunity to explore and collect information about yourself to use in your Life Map. This activity will help you complete your Life Map.

Make sure you save all of these activities in a safe place that is easily accessed as you continue through the rest of this book, because you will want to revisit them as you look at other concepts and activities.

REFERENCES

The following resources have been used in this chapter.

Trent, J. T. (1998). *Life mapping*. Colorado Springs, CO: Waterbook Press.

The following resources may be useful to you in your continuing exploration of Life Calling as you look at your *Unique Design* and your life experiences.

Bennet, W. J. (Ed.). (2008). *The moral compass: Stories for a life's journey*. New York: Touchstone.

Palmer, P. J. (2000). *Let your life speak*. San Francisco: Jossey-Bass.

Schwen, M. R., & Bass, D. C. (Eds.). (2006). *Leading lives that matter: What we should do and who we should be*. Grand Rapids, Michigan: Erdmans Publishing Co.

Smith, G. T. (2011). *Courage and calling: Embracing your God-given potential*. Downers Grove, Illinois: Intervarsity Press.

SECTION II

UNIQUE DESIGN: SUMMARY INTEGRATION

Element Integration

The elements of our *Unique Design* do not operate independently in isolation from each other. Rather they are synergistically connected, each having an enhancing influence on the others (Figure SIIS.1).

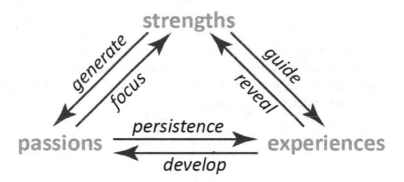

Figure SIIS.1 // Unique Design Integration

Strengths generate *passions*; we usually begin to care about areas in which we have some degree of effectiveness. *Strengths* also initiate many of our life *experiences*. We tend to do what we are good at. *Strengths* also guide the path of these experiences. Within an experience we tend to migrate in directions where we are effective and move away from areas of failure.

Passions influence our attitudes about *strengths* and we often focus on developing the strengths we care about the most. Similar to *strengths*, *passions* also initiate many of our life *experiences*. We tend to do what we care about the most. Passions also keep us going within a life experience when we come up against challenges or barriers.

Experiences are often where both our *strengths* and *passions* develop the most. *Experiences* will also influence our attitude about our *strengths* based on the outcome of what happens when we employ a strength. *Experiences* will have a similar impact on our *passions*. We will tend to grow in passion for an area based on the level of satisfaction or effectiveness we encounter within an experience.

Component Integration

The *Unique Design* component does not operate totally distinct from the *Foundational Values* and *Personal Mission* components. As we search to discover our Life Calling, the deeper we explore and further analyze all of the elements that make up our unique design, the greater will be our insight into our Life Calling and we will begin to express our uniqueness in the foundational values we hold. This really is where the search for a Life Calling begins to separate one person from another. Our *Unique Design* also provides the focus for concentrating our search and keeps us from saying "yes" to everything. When we don't follow this focus, we end up finding ourselves in many situations where we really are a misfit, and we are not truly carrying out our Life Calling.

SECTION III
PERSONAL MISSION

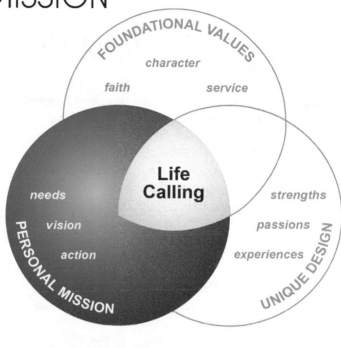

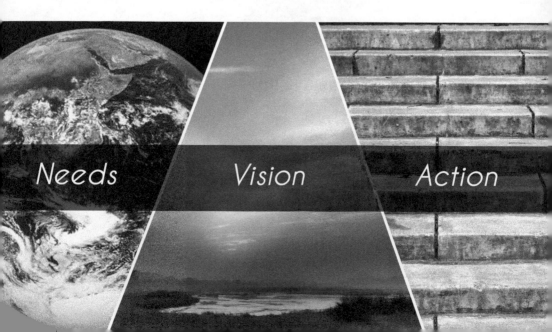

PERSONAL MISSION

Section III deals with the third main component of the Life Calling Model—*Personal Mission*.

Our *Foundational Values* and *Unique Design* motivate and focus us to discover how to carry out our Life Calling through a *Personal Mission*. If we do not go beyond reflecting on our values or becoming engrossed with our design, we will end up being little more than a statue immobilized on a pedestal. Somewhere in our search for a Life Calling we have to begin taking action. That is where a *Personal Mission* comes into play.

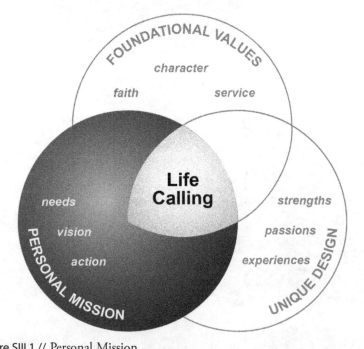

Figure SIII.1 // Personal Mission

Where does that strong sense of mission in our lives come from? A sense of mission emerges from an inwardly-developed conviction that there is some good that needs to be brought to the world in which we live. This conviction in part grows out of the passions we studied in Chapter 11. As this passion-born conviction evolves, it begins to define the reason for our existence and embody our philosophies, ambitions, virtues and values. As our conviction becomes more clearly articulated, it provides us a sense of direction and guides the decisions we make and the actions we take. At that point it becomes our *Personal Mission* in life—a key component of our Life Calling.

How does all of this happen in our lives? Let's look at where you are right now. As you think about your life, have you asked yourself where in the world you want to go and who you want to be working with when you get there? Many times if you can start with the end in mind, you can have a better idea of how to start. Think about your family vacations as an example. Would you start planning what to take on a vacation or which car to drive before you knew where you were going? That wouldn't make any sense. Instead, you start by talking about where you would like to go. Then you plan the vacation around that destination. That's what we mean by having the end in mind.

In Section I, we concluded that there is an intentional place for each one of us in the universe. In Section II we discovered that not only is our place in the universe intentional, but it is also unique and each of us is designed specifically to fill our place. In other words, we were both meant to be and designed to be! Now the question arises, what do we do about this? The answer to this question will emerge as a *Personal Mission*. We discover three important stages we must travel through on the way to begin actively pursuing our Life Calling. The first stage is to develop a sense of a mission formed in response to the *needs* of the world. In the second stage, this becomes clearer as we begin to form a *vision* by visualizing how things could be better if the mission is accomplished. Finally, in the third stage we outline and put into *action* a strategy to bring about the positive change we feel called to bring to the world.

As explained in the introductions to Sections I and II, the Life Calling Model in Figure SIII.1 is a Venn diagram depicting the three circles of the model overlapping rather than being totally separate from each other. This signifies that the three main components, rather than operating totally distinct from each other, instead interact. Each component (and the elements that make up the component) has a significant influence on the other two components, while at the same time it is influenced itself strongly by the other two.

When we have completed this section, we will see how this interactive model works in relationship to our *Personal Mission*.

We will learn that one of the greatest mistakes we can make in trying to discover our Life Calling is failing to narrow our focus. We cannot be everything to everybody in every situation. When we identify our mission in life, we can avoid this dilemma. As we carry out our *Personal Mission*, the efforts we encounter will provide evidence for our *Unique Design* and the focus it gives us in living out our Life Calling. As we respond in action to the drawing forces we sense calling us to our *Personal Mission* and the vision that inspires our mission, we will end up fulfilling the *Foundational Values* we hold at the core of our being. When we don't act to carry out our *Personal Mission*, we end up living a life unfulfilled and our Life Calling is never realized.

When we do develop a sense of *Personal Mission* and act to carry it out, we find that sense of hope that is part of the universal need experienced by all humans.

NEEDS

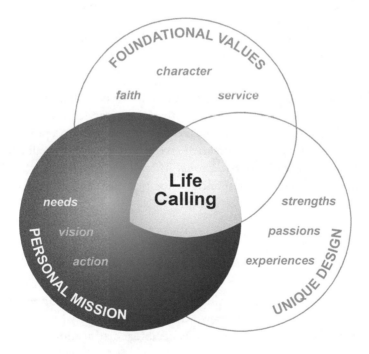

Figure 13.1 // Life Calling Model Focusing on Needs

The third main component of the Life Calling Model is Personal Mission. There are three important stages that must be addressed. In this chapter we will explore **needs** as the first of these stages.

CHAPTER 13

NEEDS: RESPONDING TO THE WORLD'S DEEP HUNGER

> *The kind of work God usually calls you to is the kind of work that you need most to do and that the world most needs to have done… The place God calls you to is the place where your deep gladness and the world's deep hunger meet.*
>
> Frederick Buechner

Personal Mission begins to emerge from our encounter with and response to the needs of the world around us—situations of service where we encounter different types of people, locations, opportunities and problems. It is impossible for any one individual to respond in service to all situations. To successfully discover a *Personal Mission* related to our Life Calling, we need the freedom to respond in a focused manner without feeling that we have to respond to everything.

WORDLIST

Words often have multiple meanings. Effective communication requires that we know which meaning of a word we are employing when we use it in our discussion. The following words need that clarification.

Ambition	a compelling desire for some type of achievement or distinction
Articulate	to make distinct and clear
Circumstances	existing conditions or surroundings

Draw   cause to move in a particular direction by or as if by a
                      pulling force

Location   place of settlement, activity, or residence

Need   lack of something deemed necessary

Opportunity   situation or condition in a good position, or with a
                      good chance or prospect for advancement or success

Philosophy   a system of principles used for guidance in practical
                      affairs

Problem   any question or matter involving danger, doubt,
                      uncertainty, or difficulty

Values   the things one believes have relative worth, merit, or
                      importance

Virtue   moral excellence

DESCRIPTION

As we start the process of putting together a *Personal Mission*, there are
four key questions to ask: 1) Who or what is the target of my mission? 2)
What is it that I will be doing? 3) What will it look like if my mission is
successful? 4) What do I need to do in order to get started? Right now
you might be tempted to think, *I wouldn't be reading this book if I had
those answers*, and you would probably be right! But be encouraged to
persist in your exploration, and answers will come. We will begin to find
answers to the first two questions in this chapter. Answers to the third
question will begin to emerge in the next chapter. And the chapter after
that will give us some guidance on how to get started.

In the preceding eight chapters in Section II, we focused on what makes
us unique individuals. We came to the conclusion that this uniqueness
provides strong guidance in what our Life Calling is and what we should
do with our lives. This constitutes to a great extent what Frederick
Buechner was referring to in his quote we encountered at the beginning
of this chapter. Our *Unique Design* indicates what we "need most to
do," and our *Unique Design* inspires our "deep gladness." But in finding a Life Calling, Buechner did not stop with just what we need to do
or what gives us deep gladness. He went on to say that it is where these
two personal dynamics within us intersect with the external dynamics of

what "the world most needs to have done" and where "the world's deep hunger" is that we will usually find God's call—our Life Calling.

In the game of tennis, one of the earliest lessons a serious player learns explains the concept of a "sweet spot" on the tennis racket. The sweet spot is the location on the racket where all of the strings are connected in just the right relationship to give the greatest power and control when a tennis ball is hit. A person can still make a shot when the ball is hit outside of the sweet spot, but it is just not as accurate or powerful. Buechner's idea is similar to this sweet spot. Sure, we can do things with our lives (and may have to at times to survive) that do not bring our uniqueness together with the needs of the world, but when we do this, we will not be as accurate or powerful—just like the tennis shot that is hit outside of that sweet spot.

Figure 13.2 // World Draw Hemispheres

In the eight chapters of Section II, we looked at all of the elements that make up the part of that sweet spot related to our uniqueness the gladness it produces. What remains for us to explore in completing our discovery of that sweet spot that leads to a Life Calling is the concept of world needs.

What is it that the world most needs to have done? What is its deep hunger? A rather long list could likely be created. In order to keep a manageable focus, let's restrict our look to four major categories of needs for the purpose of our study: people, location, problems and opportunities. Each of these categories has a capacity to draw us in its own unique way, independent of the other three. Looking at the categories from a different perspective, however, reveals that they have an interacting relationship as well. To help us comprehend this interacting relationship, let's use the analogy of *hemispheres* similar to what we might see on a world map (Figure 13.2).

People and locations form a northern and southern hemisphere. In Figure 13.3, individuals who are in the northern hemisphere (A) find that they are drawn more to the needs of specific people groups than they are by the needs of a location. Individuals who are in the southern hemisphere (B) are drawn more by needs related to locations than they are to the needs related to specific people groups.

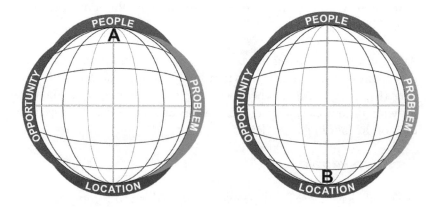

Figure 13.3 // People vs. Location Hemispheres

Opportunities and problems form an eastern and western hemisphere. In Figure 13.4, individuals who are in the eastern hemisphere (C) find they are drawn more by situations and conditions related to difficulty, struggles and peril in the world. Individuals who are in the western hemisphere (D) find that they are drawn more to situations and conditions favorable for innovation, progressive accomplishment and personal development.

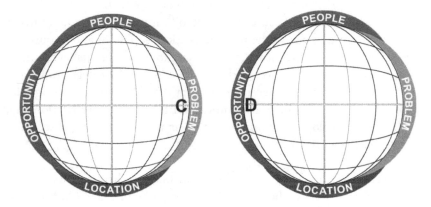

Figure 13.4 // Problem vs. Opportunity Hemispheres

The quadrants within these hemispheres illustrate that there can be more than one draw (Figure 13.5). The northwest quadrant would combine people and opportunities (E). The northeast quadrant combines people and problems (F). The southwest quadrant combines location with opportunities (G). The southeast quadrant combines location with problems (H).

At the center point along the axis lines, we would find individuals who are equally drawn by people with location (J) or opportunities with problems (K). And, based on where we locate it on the "map", we could end up with all four categories influencing us at some level. Let's examine each of the four in greater detail.

Drawn to People

We should have a love for all people and serve them with compassion and respect. That should be part of our *Foundational Values*, as we discovered in Chapter 3. However, for some the strongest draw in the world is to

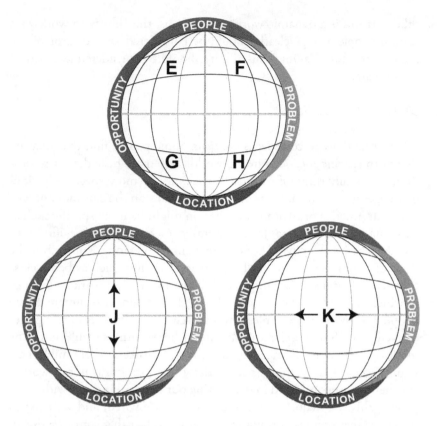

Figure 13.5 // Multiple Draws

work with specific groups of people. This attraction may form around age groups. Some might discover that they find greater enjoyment working with small children, while others may enjoy working with the elderly. Still others might prefer working with teenagers, or others might be drawn toward college students or young adults. Gender creates another drawing force. Some may feel more comfortable working with men, whereas others may be drawn to work with women. Ethnicity can be a drawing force for some people—a strong draw to work with certain groups of people who have a common racial, national, linguistic, or cultural heritage. Language may be a drawing factor with certain people. For instance, a person might be fluent in Spanish or Chinese and feel drawn to work with people who speak that language only or primarily.

We need to realize that although all of these groups are worthy, there is nothing wrong with the fact that we are drawn to certain ones and not to others. If this is a dynamic working within us, the affinity to work with certain people groups clearly should be considered an indicator of the focus of our Life Calling. This affinity should be considered as a part of who we are.

Drawn to Locations

The second draw to consider is *locations*. Some people find that they are drawn to specific locations in the world. When we hear the term location, we usually think of countries or regions, or more specifically cities or villages in the world. Some are drawn to work on the continent of Asia or South America or Africa. For others in might be more specific such as Armenia, China, Panama, Jordan, Zambia, or some other specific country. Maybe it's the city of London or Bankok or Hong Kong. But the draw of a location might also be an issue of vicinity such as being close to extended family, or we might feel drawn to live and work in the area in which we grew up. Location might also have to do with climate. Some people feel most comfortable in warmer climates, whereas others prefer cool climates. Some prefer arid climates, whereas others would rather be in a tropical climate. Some really like the four seasons. There might be a temptation at first to think that the draw of a location is not as worthy as other factors considered in discovering our Life Calling. Yet with some people, this is a major issue in the way they are wired, and we need to recognize that there is nothing wrong with the fact that some are drawn to certain locations and not to others. Again, if this is a dynamic working within us, the affinity to certain locations clearly should be considered in narrowing the focus of our mission. This affinity should be considered as a part of who we are.

Drawn to Problems

The third draw we will consider is problems. Some people find themselves drawn to challenge specific difficulties, struggles and perils in the world. For example, a person might feel drawn to work with the challenges of single-parent families or children with no parents. Another good example of this would be a person who responds to working with people in poverty. Issues related to national conflicts would be another good example of problems that might draw people in this third hemisphere. Spiritual confusion, disease, lack of education, and environmental pollution are other good examples. Political causes would fall within this category. The list is very long. Not one of us has the inclination or skill set to address every one of those areas of problems. Instead, we should accept that it is okay to be drawn to specific problems versus all problems. And we should accept that it is okay that some are drawn more to solve problems than others are.

Drawn to Opportunities

The final draw we will consider (realizing that there are likely others) is *opportunities*. For some people, opportunities exert the strongest draw. They might be drawn to take advantage of the right conditions if this gives them a good chance or prospect for advancement or success. They might be drawn to accept a good job position that they believe will help them pursue their Life Calling. These opportunities have a greater attraction than people, locale, or problems. Often people like this have an entrepreneurial spirit; they are drawn to use their strengths in an innovative endeavor. For instance, the drawing force for a person like this might be working with science, technology, medicine, education, business, economics, psychology or some other arena to come up with new ideas, products, solutions, etc. that others have not considered. Once again, we need to realize there is nothing wrong with the fact that we are drawn or respond to certain opportunities and not to others, or maybe these opportunities don't draw us at all. Discovering this can help us narrow the focus of our mission. Our preference for certain contexts and situations is a part of who we are.

What Are You Encountering Right Now?

If you are not sure about which needs in the world are drawing you, then examine what types of people, locations, opportunities, and problems within the world you find yourself most often encountering. Often the reason you have such encounters is because you are internally drawn there even though you may not be aware of the drawing force. The exploration of these drawing forces in the world forms a critical stage in our Life Calling discovery because what we find out will begin to point us in certain directions. As we enter this exploration, however, we will find that an interesting dynamic emerges, as illustrated in Figure 13.6.

For some, the draw of circumstances comes from just one of the components; for example, someone who is primarily attracted to working with

Figure 13.6 // Interaction of Drawing Forces

kids. For others it may involve two of the components. Still others might have three components drawing them. The majority of people, however, have some level of draw from all four of the components, as illustrated in Figure 13.6 by the larger light section in the middle. Exploring the four components is an important step in defining our Life Calling.

At the beginning of this chapter we identified four questions that can help us develop a sense of *Personal Mission* in our lives. The first two addressed who or what is the target of our mission and what is it that we will be doing. Our exploration of the drawing forces answer to a great extent who or what is the target of our mission. But if we think about it, what we are drawn to also starts to answer what it is that we will be doing. Even within the category of location that answer can be seen. We will either be drawn to a specific locale because it provides a location to do what we need to do (question answered) or we are drawn to a locale to simply be there and it doesn't matter what we do (again, question answered).

At the end of this discussion about drawing forces of the world, it is important to remind ourselves that if these drawing forces on our lives are going to be a guiding focus into our Life Calling, then they must draw us into Buechner's roles corresponding to "what the world most needs" and "the world's deep hunger." Furthermore, if our assertion in Chapter 4 is correct that service is the context of our existence, then these drawing forces must be understood and evaluated in that context. In other words, are we being drawn to people, locations, problems, or opportunities in order to serve the needs of the world, or are we being drawn merely to satisfy our own selfish desires? If the latter is the case, then little or no sense of purpose and calling will emerge.

SCRIPTURAL INSIGHT

Stewardship and service form the very core of a Life Calling. But these need to be guided and informed by our response to the needs of the world. The Bible has important insights that can direct us as we explore these circumstances.

Insight 1 // Our Call to Serve the World is Not Optional

Then Jesus came to them and said, "All authority in heaven and on earth has been given to me. Therefore go and make disciples of all nations, baptizing them in the name of the Father and of the Son and of the Holy Spirit, and teaching them to obey everything I have commanded you. And surely I am with you always, to the very end of the age." MATTHEW 28:18-20

As we develop a *Personal Mission* in our Life Calling, the first step is to examine what it is in the world that attracts us. These can be focused on people, locations, opportunities, or problems within the world. It is important to realize that we cannot be everything to everybody in every situation.

We start this insight with a scripture that contains the most universally accepted mandate for world service—what is often referred to as the Great Commission.

There are six important concepts in this passage that can guide the development of our *Personal Mission* and set the context for our overall Life Calling.

1. **Go.** Our *Personal Mission* and our Life Calling are implemented by moving outside of ourselves toward others. It is impossible to discover our Life Calling when we are unwilling to enter into service. Service is where Life Calling is carried out; it is also where we find out a lot about our *Unique Design*.

2. **Make Disciples.** At the beginning of this book we stated that Life Calling is something more than a college major, job, position, title, profession or life's work. In this scripture we find out what that "more" is. No matter what shape our Life Calling takes

or in what venue it takes place, it should be carried out with a prevailing intent to bring other people into a correct relationship with Jesus.

3. **Baptize.** Two actions help us "make disciples." The first action is restoration. Our Life Calling should always keep us aware of how we can help others discover how they can be reinstated into a relationship with Jesus no matter what path they have followed in becoming separated from him.

4. **Teach.** The second action is reformation. As we interact with others in our Life Calling, we need to find ways to instruct each other on how to redirect our lives so that they become more consistent with God's design for the universe and for our specific place in the universe.

5. **All Authority.** Two remarkable statements are made at the beginning of the passage and at the end of the passage that should give us tremendous hope and confidence in our Life Calling. At the beginning Jesus says the basis for the effectiveness of the Great Commission is the fact that all authority in heaven and earth has been given to him. When we bring our Life Calling into connection with Jesus' power, with that kind of backing, we will not fail.

6. **I Am With You.** At the close of the statement Jesus reassures us that he will be right there with us through it all. We can pursue our Life Calling knowing that we are never alone.

PERSONAL REFLECTION

How have you responded to the Great Commission? Do you see the Great Commission as part of your Life Calling?

Insight 2 // Recognize the People Who Need Your Response

On the contrary, they saw that I had been entrusted with the task of preaching the gospel to the Gentiles, just as Peter had been to the Jews.
GALATIANS 2:7

What did Buechner mean when he said we are called to the place where our deep gladness meets the world's deep hunger? There are deep emotions in our hearts that respond positively to certain circumstances in the world more than others. Sometimes these circumstances relate to certain groups of people. We may find ourselves most attracted to or most effective with certain groups of people. This does not mean that we don't care about other groups of people. In Matthew 22:37-40 Jesus responded to a question about what the greatest commandment is. "Love the Lord your God with all your heart and with all your soul and with all your mind. This is the first and greatest commandment. And the second is like it: Love your neighbor as yourself. All the Law and the Prophets hang on these two commandments." So we are expected to love everyone.

But that doesn't mean we will be equally drawn to or effective with all groups of people. Paul found he was more effective preaching to the Gentiles, while Peter was more effective preaching to the Jews. Certainly personal circumstances played a role in this. Because of his history, Paul was not very popular with Jews, especially Jews who were in any type of leadership. Part of this was because Paul's message was very radical. Many Jews felt that his disregard for circumcision and other Jewish laws was an affront to their religion. Peter seemed to weave his delivery of the gospel into a more subdued approach that, while not compromising the gospel, made it easier for Jews to listen to him.

God used these differences in approaches to spread the gospel in a remarkable way. Without the inclusion of the Gentiles, Christianity would have remained a small sect within Judaism. God can similarly use your affinity to certain people groups to accomplish his plans. Examining your draw to certain people groups is one good area to explore in searching for your Life Calling.

PERSONAL REFLECTION

What people groups in the world are drawing you? What do you think God is saying to you through these drawing forces?

Insight 3 // Recognize the Locations that Need Your Response

But you will receive power when the Holy Spirit comes on you; and you will be my witnesses in Jerusalem, and in all Judea and Samaria, and to the ends of the earth. ACTS 1:8

It would be easy to misinterpret the Great Commission in Matthew 28 as a call for each one of us to go into all the world. However, that is not practically possible today, and it certainly was not possible in the time Jesus gave this commission. The only way we can interpret this commission is to see it as a call for each of us to go to different areas. In the end, the sum of our travels will cover the entire world.

Just like we discovered with people groups, we will find that we will be drawn to specific locations in the world. The drawing forces may come from a variety of circumstances. That doesn't matter. God can use any of those circumstances to get the people he wants to the places he wants. After the crucifixion of Jesus, several of his disciples headed back to the Sea of Galilee. Why? Because it was where their families and friends lived and they felt comfortable there. That is often the draw of a location. On the other hand, Paul had a dream where a man from Macedonia was begging Paul to come and help him. Even though Paul was originally drawn to a different location, he changed his plan and went to Macedonia because he felt there was a real need.

The passage in Acts 1 proposes an orderly approach to locations for the preaching of the gospel. That could be the drawing force that directs our steps. The point is that different elements can be used to draw us to certain locations, and that is okay. There is one other key point, however, to be found in Acts 1. The receiving of power from the Holy Spirit was the indication of readiness to move toward the specific locations. An affinity to people groups or locations alone is not the complete indication of readiness or Life Calling. Spiritual power is much more important.

James gives a good perspective concerning how to consider our draw to different locations or circumstances. In James 4:13-15 he says,

> Now listen, you who say, "Today or tomorrow we will go to this or that city, spend a year there, carry on business and make money."

Why, you do not even know what will happen tomorrow. What is your life? You are a mist that appears for a little while and then vanishes. Instead, you ought to say, "If it is the Lord's will, we will live and do this or that."

As we consider the different factors in the world that draw us to them, we always need to evaluate them in the larger context of the Lord's will. When we place that as the highest priority, we will be more effective in finding our Life Calling.

PERSONAL REFLECTION

What locations in the world are drawing you? What do you think God is saying to you through these drawing forces?

PRODUCING THE POWER OF PURPOSE ———————

How do needs of the world help produce the power of purpose in our lives? It's pretty simple—they are the arena in which our purpose is carried out. As we begin to discern those needs that have the strongest draw on us, we will begin to see God's intention of where our Life Calling is leading us, and this will produce the power of purpose in our lives. Thus, discovering our needs is a critically important step in determining what our purpose and calling are.

CHAPTER SUMMARY ——————————————

Our Life Calling almost always will be found where our *Unique Design* intersects with the needs of the world. Exploring these needs within four broad categories can help us discover this intersection: people, locations, problems, and opportunities. It is important for us to conduct this exploration, however, within the context of service. When we do this, our particular response to specific needs in the world can become a guiding focus for our Life Calling.

It is easy to see that when all four components are drawing us, there may be a complex set of choices we will have to sort through in assessing this area of our Life Calling. We might be tempted at this point to complain that this is making life more complicated rather than helping us simplify the Life Calling discovery process. That is a valid observation. The problem many of us encounter, however, is that we do not have the patience to explore the complexity of what draws us into service in the world, and we end up making choices derived from pressure and guilt. When we do this, we rarely find satisfaction or fulfillment in what we do and often end up full of resentment and bitterness. Life Calling is complex, but learning where to look for answers and being willing to continue this search throughout our life makes the discovery a lot more successful.

INTERACTING WITH YOUR LIFE CALLING ───

This is your opportunity to interact with the Life Calling concepts introduced in this chapter and develop habits that will help you implement the concepts into your life.

The list below outlines the activities related to this chapter you will find in the *Life Calling Activities Supplement*. Access the supplement and find these activities listed. Then follow the instructions that will be given there.

1. **Activity 13.1** *Magnets of the World*. A sense of mission emerges from your encounter with and response to different types of people, locations, opportunities and problems in the world. As these encounters or responses take place, you will begin to experience a drawing toward these people, locations, problems and opportunities. This activity will help you start to identify those drawing forces in your life.

2. **Activity 13.2** *Personal Mission Statement*. This activity will help you take all of what you have learned so far and start crafting it into a single personal mission statement for you.

Make sure you save all of these activities in a safe place that is easily accessed as you continue through the rest of this book, because you will want to revisit them as you look at other concepts and activities.

REFERENCES

The following resources have been used in this chapter.

Buechner, F. (1993). *Wishful thinking: A seeker's ABC*. San Francisco: Harper SanFrancisco.

The following resources may be useful as you explore the role of needs in continuing your exploration of *Personal Mission* and Life Calling.

Millard, B. (2012). *LifeQuest: Planning your life strategically* (2nd ed.). Marion, IN: Education on Purpose®.

Schwen, M. R., & Bass, D. C. (Eds.). (2006). *Leading lives that matter: What we should do and who we should be*. Grand Rapids, Michigan: Erdmans Publishing Co.

VISION

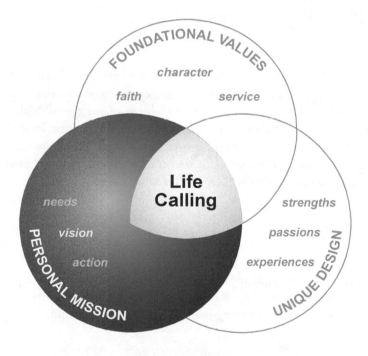

Figure 14.1 // Life Calling Model Focusing on Vision

The third main component of the Life Calling Model is Personal
Mission. There are three important stages that must be addressed. In
this chapter we will explore **vision** as the second of these stages.

CHAPTER 14

VISION: SEEING A BETTER PLACE TO BE

> *The only thing worse than being blind is having sight and no vision.*
>
> Helen Keller

The second element in our *Personal Mission* emerges as we begin to formulate a vision...a picture for a better future in response to the people, locations, opportunities and problems to which we are drawn. Vision is a picture, not a task or plan. What will that future we envision look like? This kind of vision arises from three qualities: imagination, inspiration, and independence. This vision can become the dream that will enable us to face the challenges we will encounter as we pursue our Life Calling.

WORDLIST

Words often have multiple meanings. Effective communication requires that we know which meaning of a word we are employing when we use it in our discussion. The following words need that clarification.

Aspire long for, aim at, or seek earnestly, with eager desire to achieve as something of high value

Courage the quality of mind or spirit that enables a person to bravely face challenge, difficulty, or pain in spite of the fear these forces might evoke

Dream	see in one's mind something of beauty, charm, value, or desirability
Embolden	to give a person courage and a daring spirit that will move him or her forward without hesitating or being controlled by fear in the face of actual or possible danger or rebuff
Imagination	ability to see in one's mind something that is not real in the immediate setting
Inspiration	ability to arouse an animating, quickening, or exalting influence
Picture	mental image representing something in a graphic sense
Task	job, assignment, chore, or act of work to be carried out
Vision	a vivid, imaginative conception or anticipation

DESCRIPTION

If you are working full time in a job, you have probably not given much thought to what will be said at your going-away party. If you are in high school or college, graduation is probably not at the forefront of your thoughts. But have you at least once allowed the picture to pass through your imagination of finishing a job well or marching across the stage and receiving your diploma? Imaginary pictures and dreams play an important role in our lives because they give us the inspiration to start or continue journeys.

In the last chapter, we identified four key questions to ask in putting together a *Personal Mission*. 1) Who or what is the target of my mission? 2) What is it that I will be doing? 3) What will it look like if my mission is successful? 4) What do I need to do in order to get started? We answered the first two; in this chapter we will address the third.

Have you ever wondered what it is that drives mountain climbers to risk their lives scaling dangerous peaks such as Mount Everest, K2, the Matterhorn, or the most deadly of mountains—Annapurna in Nepal? In talking with mountain climbers, I have discovered a common theme emerging. They all had a dream about being on top of the mountain and seeing the view before they ever started the climb. This dream was great enough to motivate them to overcome the fears they had about the many perils they would face on the journey up the mountain.

We can take this concept and apply it to all areas of our lives. The dream must be greater than the challenge! As we look ahead at where our lives might lead us, one thing is for certain—there will be challenges ahead. Some of these will seem so formidable that they will strike a great deal of apprehension and fear in us. Without a strong inspiring dream, those fears can easily overcome us, even to the point of stopping our journey. So it is very appropriate, indeed critical, to take time to paint a picture—a vision—that we can continually return to for encouragement during our journey.

That takes us to the second factor in the last of the major components that form the Life Calling Model—*vision*. In the *Wordlist* provided at the beginning of this chapter, vision is defined as a vivid, imaginative conception or anticipation. It is really a picture produced in our mind by our imagination. As simple as that may sound, it turns out to be one of the most difficult things for people to accomplish in our society. When people are asked to describe the vision they have for their lives, almost all of them respond by describing plans of actions or tasks they will accomplish. But if we return to our definition, we will clearly discover that vision is a picture, not a task.

VISION = PICTURE
VISION ≠ TASK

In the previous chapter we examined the concept of world needs as drawing forces that focus our efforts and attention. These provide the fertile soil for our vision. We now need to ask ourselves, "When I think about the needs within the world I identified and what I might be doing to serve these needs, what kind of picture of a better place do I envision in my mind that includes me playing some part in bringing this vision to fruition?"

This requires us to put our creative imagination to work. Anyone can do this. Dewitt Jones (2006), a well-known photographer for the *National Geographic*, stated, "We all have great creative potential within us. To begin to connect with it, we first have to define it. Let me offer a definition: creativity is the ability to see the ordinary as extraordinary" (emphasis added) (n.p.). That's what we need to do to set before us a vision in our lives—see the ordinary as extraordinary. Jones (2006) also believes creativity is "just falling in love with the world" (n.p.). He goes on to say,

> Think about it. First, when we're in love with something, it really is extraordinary. We see its uniqueness, feel its potential, celebrate its excellence, are open to its growth. Second, when we're in love with something we take care of it; we treat it with respect and compassion. Finally, when we're in love with something we find ourselves in touch with a source of incredible energy . . . we call it passion. (Jones, 2006, n.p.)

One of the best examples of this kind of passionate vision can be found in the *I Have a Dream* speech of Dr. Martin Luther King, Jr. Standing on the steps of the Lincoln Memorial in Washington, D.C., on August 28, 1963, Dr. King delivered one of the most memorable speeches in U.S. history. In the preceding chapter where we looked at needs of the world and the forces within these needs that draw us, we identified four—people, location, context, and problems. Dr. King was responding to all of these, including African Americans (people), the United States and specifically the South (location), racial bigotry (problem), and political change (opportunity). As his speech neared its end on that day in 1963, Dr. King wanted to paint a picture of his vision for responding to this world-drawing force. He painted that picture with words rather than outlining a plan or listing the tasks.

In one word picture Dr. King depicted descendants of former slaves and slave owners sitting at the same table. In another picture he dreamed of his own children living without being judged by their color. In still another picture, there were black children joining hands with white children and walking together. His last picture exploded with the vision of being free at last.

The full text, video and audio of this inspiring vision can be found by logging onto the Web site:
http://www.americanrhetoric.com/speeches/mlkihaveadream.htm

Dr. King went on to literally give his life to bring about this vision. It is important to note, however, he started with a vision. A *Personal Mission* that is not fueled by a vision will lack power and endurance.

Another good example of a vivid vision can be found in one of America's most beloved songs, America the Beautiful. In the various peaks that form the Rocky Mountains, few dominate the scenery like Pikes Peak. It towers over Colorado Springs, looming over the High Plains of eastern Colorado. It is the most visited mountain in North America and the second most visited mountain in the world besides Mount Fuji in Japan. The view at the top is amazing; it seems like you can see forever in all directions. It is at the top of this mountain where America the Beautiful got its inspiration. Today at the peak there is a bronze plaque that was placed in 1993 to commemorate the 100th anniversary of the writing of the song's lyrics. It contains the first two verses. Here are the words of the first verse on that plaque that are familiar to almost all Americans:

O beautiful for spacious skies,
For amber waves of grain,
For purple mountain majesties
Above the fruited plain!
America! America!
God shed his grace on thee
And crown thy good with brotherhood
From sea to shining sea!

Katherine Lee Bates painted a vivid picture with these words that read like a vision of America. When standing at the top of Pikes Peak, it's easy to see how she was inspired to write this verse. There is a vast and spacious sky around, no matter what direction one looks. Off to the east there are grasslands that gave inspiration to amber waves of grain. There are mountains all around that inspire the purple mountain majesties. This is how it is with the formation of a vision. Many times the things around us begin to inspire it. But something important happens as the words of the song progress. A fruited plain shows up which is not seen from the mountaintop. At the end of the verse, the seas on both coasts appear. Those certainly cannot be seen from Pikes Peak. That's where imagination takes a stronger role in the vision process. The unseen becomes seen. It's what DeWitt Jones (2006) referred to earlier in this chapter as *creativity*.

Scientists studying the human brain suggest that the creativity needed to see a vision takes place in a different part of our brains than the rational processes we are usually engaged in. This suggests that it is something we need to intentionally take time to do if we are going to create vivid vision-pictures to inspire our Life Calling. When we take this time, we need to intentionally allow three things to take place:

1. **Imagination.** When we think of the forces in the world that are drawing us, we need to begin seeing a picture in our mind of something we have never before wholly thought of in the reality or our present situation. Then we need to place ourselves in that future possibility.

2. **Inspiration.** As the imagination process takes place, we need to let the voices of our spirit, heart, and soul speak as loud as our mind and body. In other words, don't be too quick to rush toward critiquing the vision or quickly turning it into plans and tasks. How do we do this? We need to use three important brushstrokes. First, we need to paint with a brushstroke from our spirit—what will the future we envision look like? Second, we need to paint with a brushstroke from our heart—how will we, and others, be feeling in this future world? Finally, we need to paint with a brushstroke from our soul—how will people be relating to each other differently in this envisioned future?

3. **Independence.** As these inspiring dreams begin to emerge in our imagination, we need to guide them toward our own images rather than those of others. We need to move away from being bound by the past or the limits others have tried to place on us.

When we allow creativity to form this kind of vision in our lives, we enter the first phase in what I call the dream cycle (Figure 14.2). We are Dreamers.

In this first phase we create that vivid, imaginative picture of anticipation as a vision for our lives. But what do we do with that vision? Often we do nothing, and it dies. A good way to keep this from happening can be found in the second phase. Become a Dream Caster. What does this mean? It means we begin to share our dream with others around

Figure 14.2 // Dream Cycle

us, especially those whom we trust and who can speak wisdom into our lives. They will help assess and validate our dreams, and they will give us guidance on what to do with it. There will also be those we will share the dream with who will be important members of the community necessary for any of us to accomplish our dreams. Remember what we learned in Chapter 4? Life Calling is only found in the context of community and mutual influence. The final phase in the Dream Cycle is to become a Dream Maker. This is where our vision emboldens us to take actions and obtain resources that will actually move us toward our vision. What do we mean by embolden? Adapting the definitions in the *Wordlist*, we could say that a powerful and effective vision will give us the courage to bravely move forward without hesitating or being controlled by fear in the face of actual or possible danger, difficulties, rebuff or pain. In other words, our vision has become greater than our challenge. This is what we will need if we are going to take our Life Calling from a concept to action. We will look at that more closely in the next chapter.

SCRIPTURAL INSIGHT

When you hear the word "vision," especially when it is associated with the Bible, you probably think of some phenomenon that foretells the future. When the Bible speaks of visions, however, more times than not these were pictures of how a life well-lived should look. In fact, prophets throughout the Bible story spent far more time proclaiming messages of reform and issuing calls to holy living than they did predicting the future. So it is within this context of vision that we can look to the scriptures for insight about the role of vision in our own lives.

Insight 1 // Open Your Eyes

"Don't be afraid," the prophet answered. "Those who are with us are more than those who are with them." And Elisha prayed, "Open his eyes, Lord, so that he may see." Then the Lord opened the servant's eyes, and he looked and saw the hills full of horses and chariots of fire all around Elisha.
2 KINGS 6:16-17

The nation of Aram was at war with the nation of Israel. Every time the king of Aram led his army to attack, the army of Israel knew they were coming and would escape. The reason for this was that the prophet Elisha was informed of their plans by God and would tell the king of Israel before it happened. When the king of Aram found out about this, he was furious and sent a force of horses and chariots to surround the city where Elisha was in hopes of capturing him and doing away with this advantage Israel had. When Elisha's servant saw this, he was greatly afraid and cried out to Elisha in despair. And that's where our verses for today begin. Elisha offers a very remarkable response: "Don't be afraid. Those who are with us are more than those who are with them." At this point, Elisha's servant must be figuring that Elisha is either insane or really poor with numbers. But Elisha lifts up the request to God in our verse for today.

Elisha tells him not to worry because their side had more horses and chariots than Aram had. Now you have to realize that Israel didn't have any horses and chariots, so the servant was likely wondering what in the world Elisha was talking about. Then Elisha prayed that his servant would be given spiritual vision. When he was, he saw the hills full of horses and chariots of fire driven by spiritual forces from God—quite likely, angels.

Don't you think the servant's hopes greatly increased at that point? I think so! The vision now inspired him to see victory where without it he had only seen defeat. That is the key role of visions in our Life Calling. They help us to see possibilities where we formerly saw only challenges. They help us see victory where without them we only see defeat.

Let's go back to the story in 2 Kings 2. In the end Israel won a victory and Aram quit attacking Israel. The victory was spectacular as well, with the enemy smitten with blindness; Elisha then led them into a trap; the king of Israel wanted to kill the enemy; Elisha instead gave them a feast and sent them home! Crazy? But the raids against Israel ended. Why could Elisha do this? He saw a vision. There is a song that asks God to open our eyes because we want to see Jesus, even to reach out and touch him.

The song points out a problem in the Christian walk. We have never seen Jesus or God. The entire relationship exists outside of the reach of our physical senses. That's where vision can come into play. Visions take place in our thoughts and spirits rather than the retinas at the back of our eyeballs. In the *Description* section we learned that in our lives the dream must be greater than the challenges we face. Our Life Calling will be filled with many challenges, and in many cases what we want to accomplish will be something we have never seen in our lives. Our only hope at such times will be that same prayer Elisha offered: "O Lord, open my eyes so I may see."

PERSONAL REFLECTION

What is keeping your eyes closed right now and preventing you from seeing a vision for your life? What can help you open your spiritual eyes and see God's vision for you?

Insight 2 // Lift Up Your Eyes

Lift up your eyes and look about you: All assemble and come to you; your sons come from afar, and your daughters are carried on the hip.
ISAIAH 60:4

Isaiah served as a prophet to the Jews as their nation declined. In fact Israel had split into two nations—Israel and Judah. The nation of Israel went downhill quickly and was conquered by its enemies. Judah had a little more spiritual strength, but it too was headed downward morally and physically toward captivity. It was during this period that Isaiah prophesied. Many of his messages warned of the dire results that would befall the people of Judah if they did not change their ways. In chapter 60, however, God realized that the people needed a vision of what the future held for them when they finally returned to him. He gave Isaiah a vision of hope to share with the people of Judah. It was in this spirit that Isaiah said in verse 4, "Lift up your eyes and look about you." Listen to his words shared in the three verses that preceded verse 4:

> Arise, shine, for your light has come, and the glory of the Lord rises upon you. See, darkness covers the earth and thick darkness is over the peoples, but the LORD rises upon you and his glory appears over you. Nations will come to your light, and kings to the brightness of your dawn. (Isaiah 60:1-3)

What elements of this vision make it a source of hope and encouragement—even in a time of despair and discouragement? First, it calls for action. "Arise, shine, for your light has come." A good question we should ask ourselves as we consider our Life Calling is whether or not the light of God has come to our lives. Second, the vision gives the promise of something better ahead. "Nations will come to your light, and kings to the brightness of your dawn." We need to have a promise in our lives of something better coming ahead.

Just making up our own vision and giving ourselves false hope will do us no good. The hope of something better coming in the future needs to rest on God's promises. Once again, we are taken back to the *Foundational Values* we discussed at the beginning of our look at the Life Calling Model. Our faith is built around our assumptions about God and belief in his promises. These can become the fertile soil from which the seeds of vision can sprout and give us hope. These can become the dreams that will be greater than the challenges that we will face as we pursue our Life Calling. The first verse we looked at in this chapter said that without a vision, the people perish. At the end of this chapter, we can look at the positive side of this concept—with a vision we can flourish.

PERSONAL REFLECTION

Do you have a vision in your life that is a source of hope and encouragement—even in a time of despair and discouragement? What do you need to do to help you lift up your eyes rather than look downward?

PRODUCING THE POWER OF PURPOSE ——————

How do visions help produce the power of purpose in our lives? Visions are aspirational dreams, and it is that aspirational quality that fuels the power of purpose. Aspiration instills in us a longing to achieve as something of high value, causing us to aim at it and seek it earnestly. It gives us the courage to pursue our Life Calling in spite of risks. This produces a strong sense of purpose, and this purpose will form the core of our Life Calling. Thus, creating a vision for our lives is a critically important step in determining what our purpose and calling are.

CHAPTER SUMMARY ————————————

When we think about the needs within the world we find drawing us to them and what we might be doing to serve these needs, we need to envision a picture of a better place that results from us serving these needs. When we begin to dream such visions about the future, we will find that they emerge from the question, "What will I be like if the future I envision comes about?" But our dreams will also address the larger question, "What will the world be like if the future I envision comes about?" Some are daring enough to even ask what the universe will be like if the future they envision comes about. Few people are willing to dream at this level, but the ones who do are the people who bring about truly great changes. They are also the ones who steadfastly discover and pursue their Life Calling—no matter the cost.

Why is it so important to have a clear vision in our Life Calling? Every Life Calling takes a person along a path that will sooner or later encounter challenges. If we are to continue beyond the challenges, our vision must be greater than the challenges and provide us with the courage and willingness to take risks the challenges will present. If our vision is greater than the challenge, we will conquer the challenges and move on. If it is not, we will turn back and follow a path that has no real purpose or calling.

INTERACTING WITH YOUR LIFE CALLING ——————

This is your opportunity to interact with the Life Calling concepts introduced in this chapter and develop habits that will help you implement the concepts into your life.

The list below outlines the activities related to this chapter you will find in the *Life Calling Activities Supplement*. Access the supplement and find these activities listed. Then follow the instructions that will be given there.

1. **Activity 14.1** *Creative Visions.* This activity will help you start to practice creative dreaming by looking at something smaller and close to your present situation.

2. **Activity 14.2** *Life Dreaming.* In this activity, you will have the opportunity to engage in creative dreaming about some major aspects of your life.

Make sure you save all of these activities in a safe place that is easily accessed as you continue through the rest of this book, because you will want to revisit them as you look at other concepts and activities.

REFERENCES

The following resources have been used in this chapter.

Jones, D. (2006). *Seeing the ordinary as extraordinary: Techniques for unlocking your creative potential.* Retrieved October 19, 2006 from http://www.dewittjones.com/html/seeing_the_ordinary.shtml.

Millard, B. (2012). *LifeQuest: Planning your life strategically* (2nd ed.). Marion, IN: Life Discovery ePubs.

The following resources may be useful as you explore the role of vision in continuing your exploration of *Personal Mission* and Life Calling.

Schwen, M. R., & Bass, D. C. (Eds.). (2006). *Leading lives that matter: What we should do and who we should be.* Grand Rapids, Michigan: Erdmans Publishing Co.

ACTION

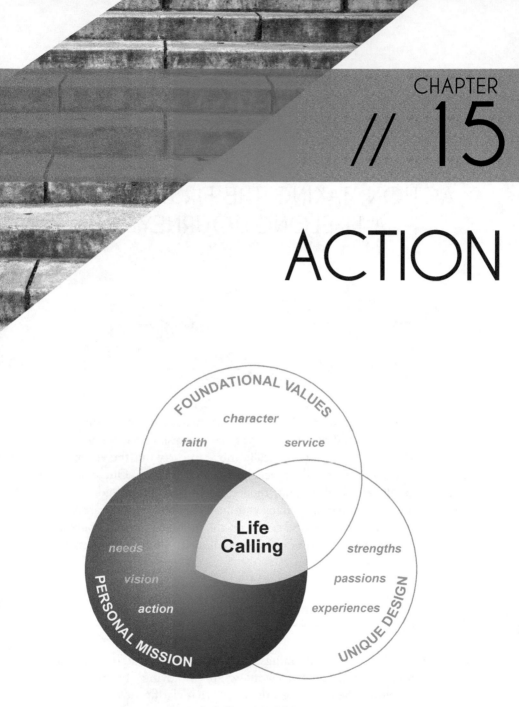

Figure 15.1 // Life Calling Model Focusing on Action

The third main component of the Life Calling Model is Personal Mission. There are three important stages that must be addressed. In this chapter we will explore **action** as the third of these stages.

CHAPTER 15

ACTION: TAKING THE FIRST STEP IN A LIFELONG JOURNEY

> *A journey of a thousand miles begins with a single step.*
>
> Confucius

Once we have begun to develop a sense of mission by responding to needs of the world, and as our vision of what our response will look like becomes clear, we begin to strategically move to carry out the vision in life-changing action that will impact the world around us. Our strategy will start by discerning directions, then creating goals, then finding the resources we need, and finally taking action. Whether or not we are able to truly act will depend to a great extent on the courage we have to pursue the strategy that emerges from our Life Calling and our willingness to take necessary risks.

WORDLIST

Words often have multiple meanings. Effective communication requires that we know which meaning of a word we are employing when we use it in our discussion. The following words need that clarification.

Action	doing or performing something, or something done or performed
Brave	possess courageous endurance

Courage	the quality of mind or spirit that enables a person to bravely face challenge, difficulty, or pain in spite of the fear these forces might evoke
Direction	a line of thought or action or a tendency or inclination leading from one point of reference to another
Goal	purpose toward which an endeavor is directed
Risk	to intentionally attempt something even when there is a chance of failure
Strategy	a plan, method, or series of actions for obtaining a specific goal or result

DESCRIPTION

As we think about the dream we have for life ahead of us, what will keep us right now from achieving that dream? The quote from Confucius at the beginning of this chapter exhorts us that any kind of long journey begins by taking a first step. But if we look at that concept in reverse, we will find another important concept. The thing that keeps most journeys from happening is fear to take that first step. One of the most common barriers that keeps us from realizing our dreams is fear of taking the first step. How can we change that in our life?

As we bring our study of the Life Calling Model to a close by looking at the final component of *Personal Mission*, we now consider the final factor that defines this mission—action. The reality is that we are only dreamers until we put our Life Calling into *action*. This really goes back to the concept of life congruence that we discussed in Chapter 2. When our Life Calling begins to unfold as we study all the other elements of the model, if we want congruence in our lives, we need to take actions consistent with what we have discovered. If we sense a drawing force to certain needs in the world yet do not respond to that draw, then no *Personal Mission* has taken place that carries out a Life Calling. If we paint the most vivid picture in our minds of a noble future, yet we do not allow that vision to embolden us to act, then we had nothing more than a daydream and again no *Personal Mission* takes place that carries out a Life Calling.

So how can we turn our dreams into action? Let's go back to the Dream Cycle introduced in Chapter 14 (Figure 15.2).

Figure 15.2 // Dream Cycle

In the first phase of the cycle we are *Dreamers* who create vivid, imaginative pictures for our lives. This is the element described in Chapter 14. In the second phase we become *Dream Casters* who share our vision with others and allow them to help us develop it.

Now we want to move forward to accomplish this vision. How do we take a vision and turn it into a reality in our lives? This is the point where many people fail to realize their Life Calling because they don't know how to put it into action. This is where the final phase in the Dream Cycle takes place. We become *Dream Makers*. We do this by taking action and obtaining resources that will actually move us toward our vision. But if we are going to do this effectively, two essential qualities will be required: *courage* and *risk*.

Courage. One of the greatest inhibitors that keeps people from pursuing or achieving their Life Calling is the lack of courage. What is courage? It's that inner force in our mind and spirit that enables us to bravely move forward even when it means facing challenge, difficulty, or pain in spite of the fear these forces might evoke. A lot of times people make the mistake of believing that courage is the absence of fear. That is definitely an erroneous view. Courage faces and overcomes the fear, it does not eliminate it. Too many people are fearful about their future and so they hunker down and attempt little or nothing supposing this will keep them safe. These are the people who will never move beyond surviving on the continuum of declining to surviving to thriving. If we are to find and achieve a Life Calling, it will take a great deal of courage.

Risk. Risk is the second quality that will be essential to effectively bring our visions into reality. Once again, we encounter a mistaken belief about risk. Many think this means careless disregard for the hazards or consequences of actions we might take. But that is not what we mean in regard to our Life Calling. The kind of risk that we will need is an inner force that will lead us to intentionally attempt something even when there is a chance of failure. What if a woman wanted to make sure she never saw a bad movie, so she made a rule for her life that she would never see a movie unless she had seen it one time before? We would think she was crazy because if she held firm to her rule, she would never see a movie. But that is exactly how many people are living out their lives in regard to Life Calling. They are so afraid of failure that they never attempt anything unless they are sure they will succeed. Just like the woman in our movie example, they end up attempting little or nothing and end up declining or at best surviving. They never reach the state of thriving—where Life Calling resides. We need to see failure not so much as something to avoid but as something to learn from. The greatest inventors have far more failures than success. The key was they learned something each time they attempted the unknown and were not successful. They applied what they learned to the next attempt, and in the end they finally succeeded.

When we have a courageous spirit and are willing to take the risks, we can be effective as *Dream Makers*. Four steps can help us cross the bridge from vision to action and avoid joining that group of people who never realize their Life Calling.

Step 1: Establish *directions* for life based on the vision. These directions will be general at this point in the journey from vision to action. They are like the direction "east." Have you ever noticed that there is no "East Pole" on the earth? When we travel north, we finally arrive at the North Pole. The same is true when we travel south. But when we travel east, we never get to a precise spot that identifies "east." This is the kind of direction we will set at this time—we may not be able to define a spot that tells us if or when we got there, but we can certainly tell if we are headed in the right direction. Here is an example related to work: I will work in the field of business even though I have not decided about a specific job in this field. Setting that direction gets us pointed toward the right path in carrying out this aspect of our Life Calling so that when we are ready for specifics, we will be moving in a compatible direction.

Step 2: Set *goals* for the journey to guide travel toward the direction that was established in Step 1. Now we begin to apply more detail to our plan of action. If these goals are going to be effective, we need to make sure they have certain qualities—these qualities are often identified by the acronym SMART.

Specific. Our goals should set definite targets we wish to reach. They should be stated as simply, concisely, and explicitly as possible. Let's look at an example. When completing Step 1, let's say we had identified the educational field as a direction for accomplishing our vision. A specific goal could be to start developing skills for the career of teaching elementary school by working as a classroom assistant.

Measurable. Our goals should be put together in a manner that allows us to determine if and when we accomplish them. In the example we are following, the measurement would be whether or not we had actually worked as a classroom assistant.

Achievable. Our goals should identify an outcome that is realistic in relationship to who we are and the resources we have available. This is a critical point in which we need to integrate our *Unique Design* into our *Personal Mission*. In our example of working as a classroom assistant, we would want to ask the question of whether or not we have the time and skill set to do this. At the same time we need to make sure there is a certain level of challenge in the goal, otherwise it will not keep us moving forward in our *Personal Mission*.

Relevant. Our goals should relate to and support the vision we have painted in response to the world-drawing forces. In other words, our goals should help us turn our vision into a reality. In our example, the goal we set to serve as a classroom assistant is relevant to our desire to explore becoming an elementary teacher. To help clarify this, we should look at a goal that would not be relevant. For example, if we had set a goal for ourselves to work six months as a junior accountant, that would not be relevant to exploring the educational field.

Timed. Our goals need to be set within a realistic time frame. Deadlines need to be set to provide accountability. Failure to do this is the death knell for many a vision and personal mission. In our example we could state our goal to explore the career of teaching elementary school by working as a classroom assistant during the following month. This provides the urgency necessary to take action based on the goal and allows us the criteria for evaluating whether or not we took action.

Step 3: Begin to *resource* the vision. Start with the three Ts of stewardship—talent, time, and treasure. First, as we explore how to turn our vision into a reality, it is a great opportunity to revisit our *Unique Design*. How do our strengths, passions, and experiences match up with this vision? How can we bring these to bear in the efforts it will take in accomplishing the vision? Second, visions will never become realities, callings will never turn into lives unless we make them a top priority and dedicate our time to their pursuit. How much time will it take? Where can we find that time in our schedule? What distractions do we need to eliminate from our time? Third, every vision we pursue requires some level of physical resources—money usually being at the top of the list. A vision-killer for many people is that they do not budget their resources for the vision. Similar to time, this requires choices. How much do we need? Where will we find it? What other expenses need to be eliminated in order for this to happen?

Let's continue to follow the example of working as a classroom assistant. Our resource strategy could include the following: consider which of our strengths will be our greatest assets in making us effective in this job, determine what hours we have available to do this work, and finally plan a personal budget that allows us to live on the financial impact working in a position of this income (probably pretty low) will have. Another important resource would be to identify an elementary teacher we know who might be willing to allow us to work as an assistant.

Step 4: *Act!* Remember what we said at the beginning of this chapter—one of the most common barriers that keeps us from realizing our dreams is fear of taking the first step. Our Life Calling is nothing more than a concept until we put it into action. Up until now we have been learning, reflecting, analyzing, assessing, and planning. Now we need to summon up courage and begin to actually act on our plans. We take the first step in spite of the risk we may encounter.

Using our example, we call the teacher we know and we let her know that we have a desire to work as a classroom assistant. This will help us explore elementary teaching as a possible career move. We ask her if she would be willing to let us work with her next month. If she answers "yes," then we can begin implementing our resource strategy to make this happen. If she says no, we can adjust our strategy to look for another teacher. At this point it is important to keep the process moving. We should not allow ourselves to become immobilized because we run into roadblocks. Our mind-set at this point should be to look for solutions, not excuses.

I took the two pictures in Figure 15.3 during winter in Indiana where I teach. The car on the left was parked on the street in front of a house halfway down my street. The car on the right is my car by my driveway.

Figure 15.3 // Inaction vs. Action

Both were nice cars in perfectly good running condition. The difference in the two pictures is that while I kept my car on the move, allowing the snowplow to keep my area clear, on the left, the owner never drove the car and the snowplow kept piling snow up around it until it could not move. That's what happens with Life Calling. If we do not keep acting and moving as we study and explore all the aspects of our Life Calling, life will begin to pile up all around us and we ultimately find ourselves immobilized and never truly experiencing our calling. Life Calling requires action!

SCRIPTURAL INSIGHT ———————————

In his letter to the early Christians, the Apostle James consistently exhorts that any life of faith needs to be accompanied by a life of action. If we had a purpose for our life and did nothing to accomplish it, then it was worthless. Our Life Calling will only experience fulfillment when we actually live it out. Scriptural insights can help us understand the need for this and the process that can make it possible.

Insight 1 // You Are Called to Action

After Paul had seen the vision, we got ready at once to leave for Macedonia, concluding that God had called us to preach the gospel to them.
ACTS 16:10

Earlier in Acts 16 Paul was forced to develop new goals and strategies based on a vision of a man in Macedonia begging him to "Come over to Macedonia and help us." The next verse in that story says, "After Paul had seen the vision, we got ready at once to leave for Macedonia, concluding that God had called us to preach the gospel to them." Once the goal was revised and the new strategy clear, action was taken.

In Chapter 2 we read where the Apostle James tells us, "Faith by itself, if it is not accompanied by action, is dead." We could also return to the parable of the talents in Matthew 25:26-27. The master rebuked the servant who did not take action.

> His master replied, "You wicked, lazy servant! So you knew that I harvest where I have not sown and gather where I have not scattered seed? Well then, you should have put my money on deposit with the bankers, so that when I returned I would have received it back with interest. (Matt. 25:26-27)

The Bible is not a purely philosophical discourse, though there is plenty of good philosophy in the Bible. To the contrary, the Bible is a call to action! Our Life Calling will be tested by our action.

This call to action starts early. Proverbs 20:11 says, "Even small children are known by their actions, so is their conduct really pure and upright?"

In a real sense, this takes us back to the *Foundational Values* at the beginning of the Life Calling Model and specifically to the element of character. What we believe should be carried out in consistent actions that match our beliefs. Character is faith carried out in action.

If we are to discover our Life Calling, it will ultimately be found in action. We may have to redirect our actions or change courses as we learn more about our Life Calling, but eventually we need to get moving—to take action.

> **PERSONAL REFLECTION**
>
> How are all other elements of the Life Calling Model being carried out in the actions of your life? What keeps you from moving forward in action?

Insight 2 // Fight the Good Fight

I have fought the good fight, I have finished the race, I have kept the faith.
2 TIMOTHY 4:7

Throughout our lives we will continue to explore our Life Calling and discover new aspects. As we do this, the more we move forward in action, the greater we will be able to make those discoveries about our Life Calling. This really is where Life Calling begins to become a reality and we sense fulfillment.

As Paul's life neared an end, he was able to look back at the same time he was looking forward, and his view in both directions was satisfying to him. He reflected on this in a letter to Timothy (2 Timothy 4:6-8):

> "For I am already being poured out like a drink offering, and the time for my departure is near. I have fought the good fight, I have finished the race, I have kept the faith. Now there is in store for me the crown of righteousness, which the Lord, the righteous Judge, will award to me on that day—and not only to me, but also to all who have longed for his appearing."

Years of observing and conversing with thousands of people have revealed that there is a universal need experienced by all humans for a sense of meaning, significance and hope in their lives. Even in situations that seem like there could not be possibility for these, the desire still remains. In his classic book *Man's Search for Meaning*, Victor Frankl shares his experiences as a prisoner in a Nazi concentration camp and what he did to find a reason to live. You might think that in such a situation, one would give up such a search. But that universal need still remained and was a driving force in Frankl's experience. The experience of Corrie ten Boom, another holocaust concentration camp survivor, reveals the same thing.

As an overriding purpose for our lives begins to develop, a sense of meaning develops from those *foundational values* we form. A sense of significance emerges out of the discovery of our *Unique Design*. But it is this final component of the Life Calling Model where we begin to develop a *Personal Mission* and a sense of hope arises. We see that there is something to do with our lives. We see, like Paul, that we can fight the good fight, we can run the right race, and we can keep the faith. Also, like Paul, we can look forward and see that our Life Calling does not end when this life ends. We see ahead the crown of righteousness that we will receive on the day of Jesus' appearing—the day on which we enter the next phase of our Life Calling and our *Personal Mission*!

PERSONAL REFLECTION

Do you have a sense of meaning, significance and hope in your life? If not, what is keeping your from having that sense? Are you looking forward toward the day of Jesus' appearing when the next phase or your Life Calling begins?

Insight 3 // Build Your Life Calling on a Solid Foundation

Therefore everyone who hears these words of mine and puts them into practice is like a wise man who built his house on the rock. The rain came down, the streams rose, and the winds blew and beat against that house; yet it did not fall, because it had its foundation on the rock. But everyone who hears these words of mine and does not put them into practice is like a foolish man who built his house on sand. The rain came down, the streams rose, and the winds blew and beat against that house, and it fell with a great crash. MATTHEW 7:24-27

There is no better scripture with which to end this chapter, and indeed this book, than Matthew 7. It gives us a good contrast between two groups of people. The first are those who discover a Life Calling from God and then live their lives with actions consistent with their faith. The second are those who don't. The first group of people have a Life Calling built on rock; the other group of people have a life guess built on sand. If we feel like we are stumbling along in life with no idea of where we are going, no sense of a Life Calling, no clear direction, no voice of God calling us, then one good place to begin looking for an answer is life congruence. Are we putting God's words into action? If we claim faith that God has a purpose for our life, yet we take no action as if that were true, then we are living on sand and we will not find a Life Calling guiding us.

One of the most dramatic illustrations of this can be found in the tragic story of Judas Iscariot. Here was a man who spent three years living very close to Jesus as one of the Twelve Disciples. He was a man of great talent and leadership, even among the other eleven disciples. Yet somewhere in this whole process he never made his actions subject to what he claimed was his faith. When confronted about this by Jesus, rather than changing his way he instead turned against Jesus and betrayed him. In the end Judas' life was one built on sand and he had no knowledge of where he was going, so he took his own life.

Peter denied Jesus publicly and Thomas doubted him after the resurrection. What was the difference between them and Judas? When they were confronted by the inconsistency of their proclaimed faith and their actions, they chose to change their actions and make them consistent with their faith. And in the end they were able to progress along a fruitful life path with a sense of Life Calling.

If we desire to have a clear understanding of our Life Calling and live a life built on a foundation of rock, matching our faith with our actions is a good place to start.

PERSONAL REFLECTION

Do you feel like your Life Calling is built on a solid foundation of rock, or do you feel like you have a life guess that is shaky and built on sand? If you feel like you are on sand, is there an area of your life where you are failing to put into action what you know to be consistent with God's calling? What would it take to get you to change that practice today?

PRODUCING THE POWER OF PURPOSE ——————

How does action help produce the power of purpose in our lives? The answer is quite obvious. The power of purpose is ultimately experienced in action. As we act and move ahead energized by a strong sense of purpose, this purpose will form the core of our Life Calling. Thus, taking action in pursuit of our Life Calling is an essential step in continuing to determine what our purpose and calling are.

CHAPTER SUMMARY ——————————————

We examined in detail how to develop a strategy for turning the visions of our Life Calling into reality. Why do we outline so much detail when looking at the action factor of our *Personal Mission*? If our Life Calling is ever going to materialize into *Personal Mission*, it will ultimately happen through action. As obvious as that seems, it is hard for many of us to implement this in our lives. In the middle of the twentieth century, there was a popular song about the future based on the Spanish phrase "que será será." The English translation of these words is "whatever will be, will be."

Many of us operate our lives with that same attitude. The future is something we can't see, and so we just move ahead with a fatalistic mind-set that whatever will happen, will happen. This really takes us full circle back to Chapter 1, where we looked at our *Foundational Values* and, more specifically, at our faith. We defined this as the value we hold about reality. If we believe that the universe is a closed system with all aspects, including its history, predetermined before any event ever takes place, then we should join in singing "que será, será." On the other hand, if we believe that the universe is an open and dynamic system where history is made, not imposed, then we will want to create visions and take actions that can make our history a productive one.

INTERACTING WITH YOUR LIFE CALLING ————

This is your opportunity to interact with the Life Calling concepts introduced in this chapter and develop habits that will help you implement the concepts into your life.

The list below outlines the activities related to this chapter you will find in the *Life Calling Activities Supplement*. Access the supplement and find these activities listed. Then follow the instructions that will be given there.

1. **Activity 15.1** *Next Steps*. In this activity you will use the example of climbing a mountain to actually start the process of taking action in your life that will move you toward your Life Calling.

2. **Activity 15.2** *Points of Entry*. This activity will help you discover that there are usually multiple paths you could take in moving toward your Life Calling.

Make sure you save all of these activities in a safe place that is easily accessed as you continue through the rest of this book, because you will want to revisit them as you look at other concepts and activities.

REFERENCES

The following resources have been used in this chapter.

Millard, B. (2012). *LifeQuest: Planning your life strategically* (2nd ed.).
   Marion, IN: Education on Purpose®.

The following resources may be useful as you explore the role of action in continuing your exploration of Personal Leadership and Life Calling.

Bolles, R. N. (2011). *What color is your parachute? 2011: A practical manual for job-hunters & career-changers*. Berkley, CA: Ten Speed Press.

Hakim, C. (1994). *We are all self-employed*. San Francisco, CA: Berrett Koehler Publishers.

Millard, B. (2003). *ChangeQuest: A process for modifying your organization*. Marion, IN: Life Discovery Publications.

Schwen, M. R., & Bass, D. C. (Eds.). (2006). *Leading lives that matter: What we should do and who we should be*. Grand Rapids, Michigan: Erdmans Publishing Co.

SECTION III

PERSONAL MISSION:
SUMMARY INTEGRATION

Element Integration

The elements of our *Personal Mission* do not operate independently in isolation from each other. Rather they are synergistically connected, each having an enhancing influence on the others (Figure IIIS.2).

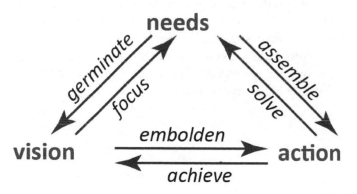

Figure SIIIS.1 // Personal Mission Integration

As we encounter the *needs* of the world, the intensity of this encounter provides the fertile soil for our *vision*. Those needs germinate the vision and then provide the nutrients for this vision to develop and grow. Our encounter with the needs of the world also is a driving force that begins to assemble the *actions* of our lives related to these needs and our Life Calling.

The *vision* we develop in response to the *needs* of the world will keep us focused on where we can have the most effective impact. The *vision* helps us know what to say yes to and what to say no to. And it is our *vision* that is the greatest inspiration for the *actions* that we actually take in our lives to live out our calling in response to the needs of the world. Without the vision, many times we would end up doing little or nothing.

Our *actions* form in response to the *needs* we encounter and are drawn to in the world as what we believe are the most effective solutions we can be a part of related to the needs. In a real sense, our *actions* are the achievement of the *vision* we developed in hopes of meeting the needs of the world to which we have been drawn.

Component Integration

The *Personal Mission* component does not operate totally distinct from the *Foundational Values* and *Unique Design* components. As we carry out our Personal Mission, the efforts we encounter provide evidence for our *Unique Design* and the focus it gives us in living out our Life Calling. As we respond in action to the drawing forces we sense calling us to our *Personal Mission* and the vision that inspires our mission, we end up fulfilling the *Foundational Values* we hold at the core of our being. When we don't act to carry out our *Personal Mission*, we end up living a life unfulfilled and our Life Calling is never realized.

CONCLUSION

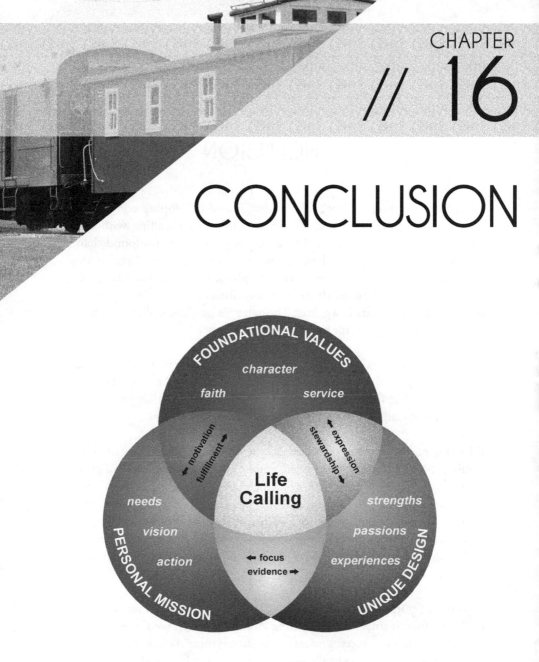

Figure 16.1 // Life Calling Model

CHAPTER 16

CONCLUSION

Everyone has a Life Calling. Discovering it and developing confidence in it is where problems arise. We often confuse Life Calling with our jobs, but Life Calling is larger than an occupation, more profound than a profession or life's work. These are worthy purposes in our lives, as are family relationships, community service, values, missions, and strengths. However, none of them by themselves constitutes our Life Calling. They are like individual stars in a galaxy. The galaxy is our Life Calling—where all the various purposes for our lives come together.

My pursuit of a Life Calling through relationships and circumstances was life-changing, for those around me and for me as well. As this occurred, I concluded that for purpose to be unleashed at a level that propels us toward a Life Calling, it must overcome four major barriers.

First, for purpose to be unleashed at a level great enough to gain Life Calling status, it must become strong enough to *overcome the selfishness of indifference*. Most of us search for our life's purpose in the context of "it's all about me." But when we invest time and resources into helping others discover their Life Calling, our own Life Calling is better developed and discovered through examination of who we help and how. There is an inward and outward focus that must be pursued to discover our Life Calling.

Second, for purpose to be unleashed at a level great enough to gain Life Calling status, it must become strong enough to *overcome the comfort of complacency*. It always seems easier not to do anything, but doing nothing leads to *nothing*. When we take action, we plant the first seed of achievement. The discovery of our Life Calling requires us to be active explorers, not passive bystanders.

Third, for purpose to be unleashed at a level great enough to gain Life

Calling status, it must become strong enough to *overcome the fear of failure*. Most of us fear failure, so we decide not to approach any significant challenges to avoid the opportunity for failure. The problem is that when we do this, we guarantee that we will never achieve anything significant. Most achievements occur as a result of many failures. Thomas Edison had far more failed inventions than he did successful ones, but he is remembered for his successful ones. If we hope to discover our Life Calling, we must be willing to take risks.

Fourth, for purpose to be unleashed at a level great enough to gain Life Calling status, it must become strong enough to *overcome the avoidance of pain*. Achievement always includes an element of change. Discomfort and pain are noticeable indicators of change and are nearly always encountered along the path to achievement. If pain is always avoided, then gain likely will be as well. In fact, it is when we face the painful circumstances of our lives that we often discover the clearest picture of our Life Calling. If we hope to discover our Life Calling, we must be willing to change.

When the various purposes in our lives combine into a Life Calling, an overriding and consistent context develops that motivates and guides a lifetime of endeavors and decisions. Until that happens, we will never overcome these four barriers.

As we have seen in this book, the discovery of our Life Calling emerges from exploration of three crucial life dimensions: *Foundational Values*, *Unique Design*, and *Personal Mission*. These three crucial components of Life Calling are not isolated from each other. Instead, they are interactive and integrated. Our *Foundational Values* inspire the inward search for *Unique Design* with a sense of stewardship, whereas the inward search for *Unique Design* manifests expression to the *Foundational Values* we hold. The *Foundational Values* we hold motivate our outward response through *Personal Mission*, whereas the *Personal Mission* fulfills the *Foundational Values* we hold. Finally, the *Unique Design* we possess gives focus to our *Personal Mission*, whereas our *Personal Mission* provides evidence of the *Unique Design* we possess as distinct individuals (see Figure 16.1 at the beginning of this chapter).

We encounter the dimensions of Life Calling in constantly reoccurring cycles. As each cycle takes place, we develop greater tools that help us explore more effectively each element of the Life Calling Model. The value of this is best illustrated when painful circumstances occur. At that point, we are faced with a choice: we can choose to allow these circumstances to become baggage that weighs us down into hopelessness, or we can choose to use Life Calling discovery tools to incorporate these circumstances into strengths for the future.

The absence of any component greatly diminishes the potential power of our Life Calling. If there are no *Foundational Values* as an anchor, there will be no deep meaning to guide our search for a Life Calling, and our search will be dominated by narcissism. If this is the case, we will find it hard to continue when life and circumstances get tough. If we ignore our *Unique Design*, there will be no clarity in our lives, our efforts will be misdirected, and we will fail to see the significance of our lives. If there is no outward response to the world through a *Personal Mission*, then our Life Calling will remain unfulfilled, and we will fail to experience the hope that comes from service.

The good news is that all three of these dimensions can be discovered and developed. When we make this discovery and bring all the components together, we can unleash meaning, significance and hope in our lives and truly live a life with the power of purpose!

INTERACTING WITH YOUR LIFE CALLING ————

This is your opportunity to interact with the Life Calling concepts discussed in this final concluding chapter and develop habits that will help you implement the concepts into your life.

The activity related to this final chapter you will find in the *Life Calling Activities Supplement*. Access the supplement and find this activity listed. Then follow the instructions that will be given there.

1. **Activity 16.1** *Integrating Your Life Calling.* This activity will lead you through a process of pulling together all the elements you have learned about Life Calling in this book.

Throughout this book, you have been advised to save all of your activities in a safe place so you could access them as you continued through the rest of the book. Now you are at the end. But the discovery of a Life Calling is not just a onetime process. It occurs over and over throughout a lifetime. Because of that, we recommend that you keep all of the work you have done in this book to revisit later when you enter into another cycle of discovery!